Music

.

Music:
Promoting Health and Creating Community in Healthcare Contexts

Edited by

Jane Edwards

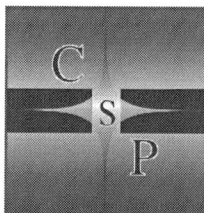

Cambridge Scholars Publishing

Music: Promoting Health and Creating Community in Healthcare Contexts, Edited by Jane Edwards

This book first published 2007 by

Cambridge Scholars Publishing

15 Angerton Gardens, Newcastle, NE5 2JA, UK

British Library Cataloguing in Publication Data
A catalogue record for this book is available from the British Library

ISBN (10): 1-84718-351-4, ISBN (13): 9781847183514

TABLE OF CONTENTS

FOREWORD

MUSIC AT THE HEART OF THINGS

I heard a story recently of a little boy who came home from school and told his mother excitedly that he had learned how to play 'a gold flute with a green top'. Further investigation revealed that this was a tin whistle! Perhaps it was the same little boy who went up to a musician after his performance and said 'that must be very hard to play because it's very hard to listen to'. At any rate, both stories have to stand in line with the one where an innocent but curious music follower asked a world famous classical music virtuoso: 'do you read music or are you gifted'? These stories carry something of the magic of music, of its mystery, of its humour, and of its unquestionable power – not least its power to heal.

This book resonates with the central themes of the Irish World Academy. Our Academy seems to be about many things – about transitions, mediations, flowings, voicings, birthings, and rebirthings. In these times of rapid change, a central concern is how we might contribute to the local-global dynamic. I call this dynamic 'lobal'. Lobality is a kind of listening. How can we resonate with this location in such a way as to strike a resonance in the whole earth? For us at the Academy, our listening to the traditional arts of music and dance in Ireland seems to empower us to mediate the duality of the ear and the eye – where the ear listens to the eye's power, and the eye observes the mystery of pure sound. These flows between orality and literacy are global flows. The integration of the one with the other is a global challenge. The invention and reinvention of the river banks of our structures and institutions is a call we all hear, a challenge we all see.

At the Irish World Academy of Music and Dance we equally enable gesture – from the foot-focus of close-to-the-ground traditional dance, through its various manifestations, and across contemporary and post-modern dance.

Another of our passions lies in the play between, transcendence and spirit – however you understand it. Our grounding is in chant and its ritual context. Again, we come quickly to a meeting of the motions and emotions of healing, with the deconstruction of our struggles and sufferings into a hope-filled remembering of our existence.

And in at the heart of that healing is Music Therapy. Our engagement with it began in 1996. Leslie Bunt and Tony Wigram were our early pivotal figures but carrier of the flame was Kaja Jennsen, at that time Head of Music Therapy at Southern Methodist University in Dallas. In February 1996 I was drawn down to Dallas to meet with her and to look at the program there. My initial impressions of the graciousness of her energy were quickly grounded when in her office I spotted a framed certificate on the wall declaring her to be the best teacher in SMU. I left after making her promise to come to Limerick to help us set up our program. Within months my colleague Helen Phelan and I had brought Leslie, Tony and Kaja together, and something unstoppable started its growth. Two years later, the first professional degree program in Music Therapy in Ireland commenced, and rapidly became a focal point for research, discussion, networking, learning, teaching, and clinical training; with a miraculous return of Kaja Jensen that saved the day when the helm was unmanned in the first semester of the program in 1998.

It was at this early point that the Australian ticket kicked in! Firstly there was Wendy Magee who became our first fulltime faculty member in Music Therapy in the first half of 1999. Rising star that she was, when Wendy moved on at the end of the first year of the course she seemed to create an Australian chorus in her wake – even if a brief Nordic presence warmed the chair for a while through the presence of Bent Jensen and Anne-Steen Møller in the Autumn of 2001; and of course, the arrival of Jane Edwards in October 1999 had copper fastened the process. Australian Angels flapped their wings most provocatively: Vicky Abad, Kat McFerran, and Jeanette Kennelly, all took a turn in the driving seat while the program steadied itself and came to ground.

Now it is Jane's vision that has drawn this book together. In many ways the *Music and Health* gathering at which the idea for this book was hatched was a rite-de-passage for Music Therapy in Ireland. It opened us out to a world of like-minded people. It connected our place with the places of the participants and the authors represented in this text, and in so doing it creates a new shared lobal space of human dialogue and heartfelt listening about music.

Let me end with a story and with a poem. The story is from ancient Ireland and tells how the Irish hero, Fionn Mac Cumhaill, was debating with his warriors as to what the finest music in the world might be. His son Oisin thought it might be the cuckoo calling from the highest tree. Another, Oscar, thought it was the ring of a spear on a shield. Others thought of the belling of a stag across water, the baying of dogs in the distance, the song of the lark, the laugh of friendship, or the whisper of a loved one.

'They are all good sounds' said Fionn. 'But tell us' they said, 'what do you think?'

'The music of what happens' said the great hero, 'that is the finest music in the word'.

Such a music of course is almost by definition a music that we never would have known to listen for. Seamus Heaney's first poem in his collection *Seeing Things* is entitled 'The Rain Stick', and this is the synesthetic sound we see in our imaginings. Indeed, it may also be one of the quintessential sounds of healing and as such is a fitting sound for the foreword of this book.

The Rain Stick

Upend the rain stick and what happens next
Is a music you never would have known
To listen for...

Who cares if all the music that transpires

Is the fall of grit or dry seeds through a cactus?
You are like a rich man entering heaven
Through the ear of a raindrop. Listen now again.

Professor Mícheál Ó Súilleabháin
Director, Irish World Academy of Music and Dance
University of Limerick

Based on the welcoming address to the ESF Music and Health symposium at the Irish World Academy, Limerick, September 19th, 2005

INTRODUCTION

Playing live music with people who are ill to promote optimal states of health and well being is as at least as enduring as the written historical record. Alongside burgeoning music therapy developments internationally there is an energetic movement to provide a broader range of arts practices in healthcare. In Ireland this has been progressed over recent years with funded projects developed in a range of hospital sites nationally, reflecting a similar movement in hospital arts in the UK. Potentially tensions could arise between aspirations held for the ongoing development and progress of the profession of music therapy and other arts health initiatives. An inquiring navigation of these potential tensions is undertaken here through presentation of some of the contemporary practices in the use of music to promote health and well being from authors in Australia, Denmark, Germany, Ireland, the UK, and the USA.

The idea for this book was developed following a symposium held in September 2005. Sixteen colleagues from 8 countries met at the University of Limerick on the theme *Music and Health* in an exploratory research workshop funded from the European Science Foundation. While ESF workshops encourage discussion rather than paper presentations as the basis for these exploratory events there were some short presentations given at the start of seminars to stimulate the group members thinking and debate. All participants who attended were invited to contribute to this book and chapters included here are by colleagues who responded positively to the invitation.

When examining contrasts between the orientation and expertise of these music practitioners, and the contexts in which their arts health initiatives are developed and practiced, as well as the range of ideas as to what constitutes successful outcomes for these developments, it is possible that confusion might arise. However, it is hoped that the reader's reflection on what is interesting and valuable about each of these approaches to the work represented in the book will enlighten them as to the multiple possibilities for music therapy, music and health, and arts health initiatives for people in hospital.

The provision of music as therapy or as an arts health practice in hospital based services is the main focus for this book. However some wider contexts are included; for example the reports of work with the refugee and asylum seeker community in Ireland (Chapter 10) and music therapy in a post war setting (Chapter 9).

In the opening section, programs in three countries are described. Clare O'Callaghan outlines her work as a qualified music therapist in one of the largest cancer hospitals in Australia. Hilary Moss, a qualified music therapist who works as an Arts Officer in a large Dublin hospital, gives an overview of the ways she has creatively developed arts provision for patients. Joanne Loewy is the director of a successful musicians' wellness clinic, and reflects on developing a role for music therapy in a large hospital service in New York over the past 12 years.

In the next section, Kari Batt-Rawden, Susan Trythall and Tia DeNora provide their sociological perspective on health musicking. Betty Bailey and Jane Davidson present the benefits of group singing.

Researching and evaluating music practices in these contexts is addressed in most chapters however three authors have focused specifically on this topic. Norma Daykin positions music therapy as one type of practice under the umbrella of arts health initiatives in medical care and provides evidence for the ways music therapy and other music practices are perceived in cancer services in the UK. Lars Ole Bonde reports use of a mixed method design in approaching the evaluation of a music therapy project in Denmark with six women who are cancer survivors. Wendy Magee presents her experiences in development of research in music therapy at a London hospital.

The final section provides information about music therapy work with war survivors, older people, and Mothers and their infants from the refugee and asylum seeker community. Susanne Metzner and Constanze Bürger describe music therapy in a post war setting. Alison Ledger presents three cases in which opportunities for musical relating in music therapy addressed psychosocial needs of older adults in long term care. Maeve Scahill, Helen Phelan and I report project work with refugee and asylum seeker mothers and their infants.

The book concludes with a review of some historical sources from the 1890s to the 1940s that have described the use of music in healthcare.

Professor Jane Edwards
Irish World Academy of Music and Dance
University of Limerick

CHAPTER ONE

MUSIC THERAPY INSPIRED TRANSIENT WARD COMMUNITIES IN ONCOLOGY

CLARE O'CALLAGHAN PHD RMT

Fifty-six year old Rachel was sitting on her bed at Peter MacCallum Cancer Centre (Peter Mac), Australia's only sole cancer treatment and research hospital. She had just been told that her cancer had spread to her bones. We arranged that I would return later to play her favourite hymn and other requests. Rachel smiled as her neighbour, who was recovering from surgery and had overheard our conversation in the four bed room, said she that would also like to listen. Brenda told Debbie, 45, who was later admitted into their shared room for intravenous nutrition, and Debbie then told 42-year-old Dan, in another room, undergoing chemotherapy and radiotherapy following partial tongue removal for a tumour. On my return, Debbie found Dan. Another patient, 48-year-old Peter, was sitting in bed hunched over a bowl, vomiting behind his bed curtain. When I approached and asked whether it was alright to play music in the room he turned his head toward me and nodded repeatedly.

After they applauded "Amazing Grace" varying requests were made: Brenda for Buddy Holly, and Dan for the Eagles. All except Dan sang a few words as I played. In amongst joking banter and memories Dan said that he used to regularly sing in a band. He'd had a good voice but added, "That probably won't happen again now." Dan's speech was dysarthric (slurred) and he was drooling.

I suggested that different vocal cavities can be used when singing and that his singing might be clearer than his speaking. "I might give it a go," he laughed. I then noticed that Dan was quietly singing the next song, Elton John's "Daniel". Led by Debbie, Dan was urged by the others to sing more and, eventually, Dan came and sat with me at the piano and sang. Brenda correctly suggested that we slow down to help Dan's singing. With "Daniel," Dan's voice became stronger, his dysarthria barely noticeable, and his face was elated. "I didn't think that I'd sing again," he said. The patients were cheering him, one was crying, and two nurses arrived and joined in with the singing and danced. I popped my head behind Peter's curtain and he lifted his head up from the vomit bowl to say that the music was "great".

Rachel had been smiling and laughing audibly. Her nurse later asked how I "got on" with Rachel. After I described the session, her nurse said, "Well that's great because she has been miserable the whole time she has been here."

Music Therapy and Community

A community can be defined as a group of people united by a cooperative spirit. The foundation for conceptualising how music therapy can inspire adult hospital ward communities was established for me in 1981, when I interrupted my music therapy training to gain a social work degree. When teaching in the subject, "Human Behaviour in the Social Environment", Professor Dorothy Scott showed a family of Russian dolls to illustrate Bronfrenbrenner's (1977) influential paper on how one should consider the "person-in-situation" configuration when aiming to reduce clients' vulnerability, promote their resilience, and help them to be more content within their ecological system context. Bronfenbrenner introduced the idea that health worker's attention should focus on the individual and their sociocultural and political contexts, conceived in four levels: 1) microsystem: that is, relations between the person and their immediate setting such as their family; 2) mesosystem: that is, a system of microsystems, such as how the individual's family interacts with others in their the hospital setting; 3) exosystem: that is, social structures that influence the microsystem and mesosystem (for example hospital institutions); and 4) macrosystem: society values, and ideologies, which can affect music therapy's existence. Bronfenbrenner's theory illustrates how the individual client can be helped through clinical, managerial, or political initiatives at any of these levels. It has remained fundamental to how I imagine, and experience, music therapy helping people with life threatening conditions.

The concept of "community", as used in this paper, is intended to denote the helpful social connections potentially emergent from music therapy being offered in hospital contexts where the focus is on the individual in cancer treatment and palliative care. It should be distinguished from "community music therapy", a widely used phrase in the music therapy literature for depicting varying conceptions of music therapy practices with "goals and interventions relat(ing) directly to the community in question" (Stige, 2002).

My professional music therapy experiences over the past 20 years have included neurological, acute oncology, and palliative care settings. My aim is to offer music therapy methods to help patients, and those close to them, cope with arduous illness and treatment experiences. This may be through "catching the moment", as in the earlier described ward session, but it can also be through long term music therapy relationships. While I have aimed to help patients at the exo- and macrosystemic levels, for example, through lobbying for music therapy funding and actively promoting the improved status of music in health care initiatives in our society, the focus of this paper is on the individual within their micro- and mesosystems. In the cancer and palliative care contexts I have worked, sessions are primarily conducted at patients' bedsides, sometimes in single but mostly in multibed wards. Here beds are close together and conversations seldom private. I usually wheel in an electric piano and offer up to 7000 songs and classical pieces, alongside music therapy methods which include music based supportive counselling, music relaxation and imagery, therapeutic music lessons, and song writing.

Music Therapy in a Cancer Treatment Context

In the cancer hospital, patients can be highly distressed as they a) endure what can be devastating illness and treatment consequences, b) navigate uncertain prognoses, and c) witness their families' attempts to cope with their own fears and possible role changes. For example, a spouse may need to take over the role of family breadwinner if the patient can no longer work. I try and fit into the patients' often busy routines, continuing music therapy sessions as nurses attend to drips, clinical observations, and so on. I usually offer to step out during medical ward rounds and medical specialist visits. Occasionally, however, they say that they will return later, and sometimes even say that what I am doing is more important. Often sessions cease when orderlies come to take patients for X-rays, radiotherapy, and other treatments or tests.

In a multibed ward, if one patient wants music therapy, neighbours who might overhear are consulted for their approval. Alongside receiving music therapy referrals from staff and session observers, I also directly offer opportunities for music therapy to patients, and their visitors, at their bedsides. If other patients also want music therapy, a group session may ensue. However, if the original patient indicated their wish for private time I would sit close to that person and may offer music therapy to other patients in the room later. Negotiating sessions in multibed wards can be a delicate business.

> An 80 year old cancer patient, Angela, welcomed my arrival but Mary, a patient opposite, said she didn't want the music in her room. Angela whispered, "She always gets her way." As Mary did not look in physical discomfort, I asked her whether I could play for Angela very softly for no more than 10 minutes. Mary reluctantly agreed. As I played Angela's song memories, I declined Angela's requests to turn the volume up. But as I packed up to leave 10 minutes later, Mary said, "Please play some more … have you got 'Edelweiss' and can you turn the volume up?" I did. But then Angela whispered in a louder voice, "See what I mean!"

The potential for music therapy to enable ward communities that help people encounter life-threatening conditions has not received much attention. Deborah Salmon (1989) described "Partage", which was an inpatient palliative care group which she developed at Montreal's Royal Victoria Hospital's Palliative Care Unit. In this regularly held structured psychosocial group patients, visitors, and staff shared inspired reflections about their lives through music and other creative media.

Group song writing with people with advanced neurological conditions enabled mutually supportive expressions, including: a) messages of positive regard for each other; b) shared tributes and grief expression when a significant person died; and c) and shared expressions of humour and camaraderie (O'Callaghan, 1994). A group of patients with advanced neurological illnesses wrote and sang a song to celebrate a wine making kit's arrival to their specialised nursing home.

The New Wine Kit

Chorus: Our new wine kit's asleep
And we don't know what to think
At the moment we're having a peep
And hope that we'll get a drink
Verse 3: Don't be thinking it's lemonade
For this brew the roof will raise
Lifting the rafters with all our laughs
It'll suit both us and the staff[1]

---

[1] Altered to protect patient identities, which is acceptable and important when describing clinical practice (Mulder and Gregory, 2000).

The patient composers with recent memory loss also remembered their group songs' lyrics with greater ease than when trying to remember standard conversation. This is a phenomenon reported in varying music and cognitive impairment contexts (O'Callaghan, 1997; Prickett and Moore, 1991; Wallace, 1994), and is likely to heighten the therapeutic outcomes of the sessions, improving self esteem and collective enjoyment.

In 1999 Aasgaard questioned, "What can the role of music therapy be when it comes to creating favourable environments?" (p. 31) and proposed that music therapists, who offer activities in the "open spaces" of institutions, have the potential to both disturb people, as well as to create a "therapeutic environment". In hospice contexts, music therapists might be either involved in "prepared sessions" or need to creatively improvise both musically and environmentally. Aasgaard (1999) described one example where a therapist and patient were singing and playing together in a hospice. Overhearing patients outside the room gradually joined in and sang together, improvising and recording their creation.

"There are no antagonisms between an individually directed music therapy and one mainly directed towards the environment. The best possible music therapy in hospices and in hospital is probably a combination of the two perspectives." (Aasgaard, 1999, 41) "Musical environmental therapy" is

> A systematic process of using music to promote health in a specified environment …. A healthy environment … fosters self-growth and creativity, … and (is) where people are mutually helping one another to experience hope, joy and beauty. (Aasgaard, 1999, p. 34)
>   To measure effects (of "musical environmental therapy") … with quantitative parameters is probably impossible. But to study the *meaning* … seem far more relevant. Any meanings are connected to the experiences of people, (including) … patients, relatives, staff and the music therapist's own subjective knowledge. (Aasgaard, 1999, p. 35).

Aasgaard (1999) proposed that music therapy in open ward contexts can enable unplanned therapeutic interactions whereby people, through coming together, help each other. Similarly, I have also found that music therapy methods can inspire these transient (or temporary) ward community interactions, in oncological and palliative care contexts, that is, supportive and enlightening social interactions, which help the patients', visitors, and staff, biopsychosocially and spiritually (O'Callaghan, 2001).

It is not only music therapy that can enable transient ward communities. An exercise or painting initiative may enable them also. In my experience, however, music therapy methods offered in open wards, where patients, staff, and visitors may stay, or come and go, can be very effective in enabling the development and engagement of transient communities.

Perhaps Aasgaard (1999) and I are describing a comparable music therapy process, but our backgrounds (the Bronfenbrenner system that informs our clinical thinking) lead to semantic differences in how we describe them and how others will also in the future.

Research: Music Therapy Enabling Transient Ward Communities

Doctoral research examining the relevance of my 16-hour-a-week music therapy program, at Peter Mac, provided evidence for both a) how the music therapy program enabled these transient ward communities, and b) how they were helpful (O'Callaghan, 2001; O'Callaghan and McDermott, 2004). Please note that, in this research, I did not aim to investigate these communities in a predetermined manner: their presence emerged in my inductive analysis of the collected data.

Peter Mac comprises mostly three or four bed hospital rooms. In 1999, over a three-month-period, anonymously written feedback about people's perceptions of the relevance of music therapy (that is, what it did and whether it helped) was collected from patients who experienced music therapy (128: 76% response rate), patients who overheard it (27: 50%), visitors (26: 61%), and staff (72 responses). Responses were placed in sealed feedback boxes. I also analysed a 100 000 word clinical reflexive journal, recording my memories and reflections about music therapy's relevance during this time (O'Callaghan, 2005).

Thematic analysis, informed by grounded theory, was used to examine the five sets of data. The textual data was inductively labelled (coded) by me. This means, I did not examine the data for evidence of predetermined labels. Related codes were grouped to inform categories, also developed by me. Related categories were then grouped to inform themes. In this way the vast amount of textual data were systematically condensed into representative themes depicting what varied people thought about music therapy over a three-month period. While these findings have already been published (O'Callaghan and McDermott, 2004; O'Callaghan, 2005), this paper will detail segments of the findings that specifically indicated how music therapy inspired transient, therapeutic ward communities at Peter Mac. These findings can also be used to make logical (but not predictive) generalisations about what music therapy can enable in other comparable cancer and music therapy settings (O'Callaghan and McDermott, 2004; O'Callaghan, 2005; Popay, Rogers and Williams, 1998).

Firstly, anonymous quotes from patients, visitors, and staff that illustrate evidence for the existence, and helpfulness, of music therapy inspired ward communities will be presented. Relevant findings emergent from my clinical journal will then be outlined.

Interestingly, patients and visitors reflected mostly about what music therapy did for themselves as individuals, whereas staff and I reflected more on both individual and ward effects. This can possibly be explained by how health professionals study group therapy (Plach, 1980; Yalom, 1985), rendering it more likely that we would consider group effects as a helpful component of the program.

Anonymous hand written feedback included from patients who experienced music therapy included:

It was a lovely peaceful time that the whole room enjoyed together. (male; 45-69 yrs; 8 sessions)

… I noticed for the remainder of that day everybody in the room was very happy … and it was also talked about a lot that day with interest … we actually had a good sing song also in one room with our nurse of the day and I am sure from our talks with each other that day it brought back memories to them as well. (male, 45-69; 1 session).

Also three of us entered an interesting conversation about illness, feelings, desires etc. I found also soul. … I remembered …. It was great experience! (female; 20-44; 2 sessions)

It brought the whole ward patients and visitors together for a sing-a-long and a dance. (female; 20-44; 1 session)

Marvelous - stimulating – had others in the room communicating with each other. (male; 70+; 1 session)

… Settles your mind and nerves. As a patient make new friends with a sing a long in the room and talk of the past and the friends you made on the day (male: 45-69; ? sessions)

"Patient overhearers" were patients who were in shared rooms while music therapy sessions were being conducted with others. Feedback included:

… Even joined in and sang (male, 45-69; 2 sessions)

The music played seems to bring back positive memories for everyone and most people sing along to the tunes. (female, 45-69, 3 sessions)

> My friend was singing and that made me feel happy. (male: 45-69; 1 session)

> Enjoyed the pleasant atmosphere (male: 45-69; 1 session)

Visitors' comments included:

> ... Had my grand-child with me and to hear "Twinkle Twinkle Little Star" as a request was memorable. (female; 45-69; 1 session)

> It joined myself + my mother (patient) in other aspects of ourselves which are overlooked in the hospital routine; + the seriousness of the illness routine. (female; 45-69; 1 session)

> Good to see the patients enjoy the music – they joined in singing. ... (female; 45-69; 1 session)

> I waited for 2 hrs while mum was elsewhere and hearing the music + people singing along told me that Peter Mac is a sharing + caring place. .... ~ It's great to see the smiles/happiness a person actually playing and singing brings. (female; 45-69; 2 sessions)

> ... Everyone in the ward sang along ... + thoroughly enjoyed themselves. We danced along to "You are my sunshine" + had a great fun singing with each other. (female; 20-44; 1 session)

Staff discussed how music therapy helped them work with patients, as well how they felt it helped the patients and visitors. As mentioned earlier, staff wrote more about the community inspired aspects of music therapy than did patients and visitors, and one of the four themes that their textual responses informed was: Staff found music therapy elicited a range of helpful emotions and self-awarenesses, improving individual and team work life, and the ward environment (informed by 56% of the responses) (O'Callaghan and McDermott, 2004). Their written responses included:

> ... Alters the environment, it softens and humanizes ... It brings joy, especially when staff become actually involved, singing – playing instruments, laughing. Music can be like a catalyst, or "smooth oil" which helps people work together and "work" with patients. Music selection by a patient may help nurses understand more about the patient ... alters the "hospital bureaucratic environment" (nurse: 3-10 sessions)

> I ... have been emotionally moved by its effect on the patients. It seems to ... bring them closer to the patients they share a room with. I have

observed patients say to one another "I'm going to miss you", during a
music therapy session. .... (nurse: > 10 sessions)

I observed patients happily interacting, choosing their own styles of music,
making requests, singing or foot tapping, even reminiscing. Sometimes on
their own or with co-patients and staff. I also observed staff becoming
involved as they worked, humming tunes played by you as they assisted
their patients to also be involved. I felt better ... it gave the ward a happier
atmosphere and I think it improved morale for the patients and staff ....

... We walked in ... just as one of the ladies had begun to sing ... (2
nurses, consultants x 2, resident and registrar), and we stood listening until
she had finished. Her singing was very beautiful and also very moving,
and I felt that we were all very privileged to have witnessed it. (nurse: >
10 sessions)

Many patients are from non-English speaking backgrounds and while
there are language barriers and misunderstandings, there are no barriers
with music. The patients smile, their feet and hands move (where possible)
– they are at one. (administration: 1 session)

... When it (music therapy) ended ... frank discussion took place between
myself, my patient and the two other patients in the Ward. (about) ...
~whether men did wear anything under their kilts! – ... – light laughter
followed amongst these mature age ladies ~ patients began to give short
renditions of other folk tunes...
(allied health: < 4 sessions)

Clinical Reflexive Journal

To examine my own perceptions of the relevance of music therapy at
Peter Mac, I conducted a thematic analysis on a journal that I wrote about
my memories and reflections about my three months of music therapy
practice while the data was being collected from patients, visitors, and
staff. The coded journal resulted in 20 categories which informed one
theme:

At Peter MacCallum Cancer Institute[2], during three months, music
therapy offered patients who engaged in or overheard sessions, as well as
visitors and staff, opportunities to encounter dynamic music spaces
enabling altered intra-awareness and transient community participation,

---

[2] The Hospital's name has altered to Peter MacCallum Cancer Centre since the
study.

although music therapy was not appropriate for everyone. (O'Callaghan and McDermott, 2004; O'Callaghan, 2005)

Codes labelling text depicting how music therapy could inspire these transient ward communities were grouped into five categories: a) patients being with patients and me, in communities; b) "music circles"; c) staff working with music therapy; d) families and visitors sharing music therapy; and e) encouraging patients to participate in music therapy. Space limitations enable only categories a) and d) to be clarified by statements informed by the clinical journal and its codes.

Category: Patients being with patients and me, in communities

"Give him another clap" he said as he slammed one hand up and down on the tray table, because his other arm was immobile (due to a new brain metastasis). He had just watched the patient diagonally opposite get out of bed and play the keyboard.

Patients' life stories, songs, and opinions were shared and validated with families and staff. Staff members' musically inspired stories, dancing, and songs were also shared as they engaged, even momentarily, in sessions while continuing their work. Sometimes music therapy offered a group milieu wherein patients supported each other through their loss experiences and even made practical suggestions for their response.

After one patient sang her song request, "You Don't Bring Me Flowers," she expressed regret about her unfilled life dreams. The patient beside her asked what she was going to do about it and suggested she write them down, take each one at a time, and then she might discover that they are attainable. The other patient said she might just so this.

When reliving memories patients sometimes discovered items that they had in common. Occasionally they became so immersed in their conversations, I felt redundant.

Two patients were sitting quietly in a room and, at the beginning of the session, described different music tastes and did not seem to have much in common. War song requests prompted their discovery that, after the war, they rode the same motor bikes. Much laughter punctuated memories, as they recalled their antics in these machines, with unusual attachments, including machine gun holsters.

The following patient declined music therapy, and then joined his neighbour's session as he witnessed it in their shared room. Upon closure he said:

> It takes your thoughts away from what's on your mind (paused, tears), and it brings people together, the three of us, even though I have different musical tastes to Bob, we could still find something in common and it brought us together (looking at another patient and me).

Some patients seemed to have solitary experiences within the group or a dyad. In one session, a blind patient continually requested his favourite old time songs, alternating with another patient who requested classical pieces in between his vomiting. Occasionally, patients and families asked me to play other peoples' requests, suggested who I should visit, and encouraged others to try music therapy. Patients, however, did not always wish to engage in these transient ward communities. They may have simply observed the others, continued reading or, occasionally, left the room.

Category: Families and visitors sharing music therapy

> You will never believe what's happening. Someone is playing the piano for mum and she is singing. (Daughter on the phone to her brother, at her mother's bedside, three days before their mother died.)

Music therapy provided opportunities for the patients to converse with or to share non-verbal communication with their families. Patients and families possibly identified with the lyrics as, for example, when one couple took each others hands just when the lyrics, "and grace will lead me home" were sung during "Amazing Grace". Tears, eye contact, and hand-holding were regularly observed as patients' and spouses' musical requests were played. Some visitors sat with the patient during music therapy, seeming to offer a supportive presence even if not actively participating, while others enthusiastically danced, sang, and shared stories.

Music sometimes transformed a quiet room, where a patient may have been sitting in bed, with a family member quietly beside, into a forum where their memories were shared, laughed or grieved about, and massaging touch emerged, affirming their significance in each others' lives, verbally, nonverbally, and musically. When people share music, a mutual supportive presence may be cast that transcends words. Distress can be shared.

Lyrics may have also conveyed special messages. On my arrival, one patient requested the song, ("I'll be loving you") "Eternally", just as her husband was about to leave. Patients were also able to share significant moments with offspring through the sessions. A young patient was inspired in music therapy to play percussion instruments with her toddler and borrowed them to play in between sessions.

Category: Negative or negligible effects

Aasgaard (1999) suggested that music therapy in open ward environments could disturb. The research on my journal also elicited the category, "negative and ambivalent considerations about what music therapy did". In my journal, I questioned whether the public music therapy program could reinforce one's "powerless patient identity". Hearing about music therapy one patient said, "Aren't hospitals a place for peace and quiet?" A session was not held in his room. Sessions could also be a forum wherein patients could be denigrated. Someone who had been listening to his classical music requests laughingly stated, "From the sublime to the ridiculous," when another patient requested country and western music. Once a staff member sang in a mocked operatic voice while I played, which seemed to help her, but not the patient. Also when a staff member asked for "happy music" for a patient who was crying, and patients tried to get another subdued patient to choose a request, I thought how the way music therapy was offered in the open wards contexts could potentially invalidate the way that some people just simply needed to "be".

Research Conclusion

Transient ward communities were evident at Peter Mac when music therapy enabled a music space, characterised by people creatively experiencing their musical selves, in supportive and enlightening social interactions. Biopsychosocial or spiritual benefits in patients, visitors, and staff were evident. While group sessions may have been pre-planned, they usually evolved in patients' rooms as patients, visitors and staff became involved for entire, or parts of, sessions, dependent on their personal preferences and treatment requirements. Anonymous feedback from people experiencing music therapy in the cancer hospital, and my personal journal, revealed that music therapy often allowed the human spirit to triumph in a treatment context where the fragility of human mortality was ever present, through these transient ward community interactions.

These findings highlight the profound impact that music therapy could have on staff. The importance of maintaining cohesive team work and reducing stress amongst those who work with patients with life threatening illnesses is often emphasised (Kelso and Turley, 1989; Murrant, Rykov, Amonite and Loynd, 2000; Rezenbrink, 1981; Zollo, 1999). Support sessions, where staff could freely discuss feelings related to their work, was reportedly met with resistance in one hospice because they felt they were being "treated" themselves (Beszterczey, 1977). This research about music therapy, however, illustrates that non-intrusive opportunities for staff support exist though simply providing music therapy on the wards in which they work. This was especially highlighted when a nurse witnessed a very ill cancer patient struggle out of bed to play the piano. With tears she said, "I was thinking about resigning but I don't think I will now."

Final Thoughts

While this paper focused on music therapy inspired ward communities amongst patients, visitors, and staff in shared oncology wards, the scope for such similar co-operative and helpful social interactions, enabled by a music therapist's presence, is evident beyond the four walls of a hospital room. For example, patients and their carers can be helped through their cancer experiences by such interventions as music therapists helping someone to write a song with messages to loved ones, enabling a staff drumming group, and organizing hospital concerts. The question of "What is music therapy?" is inevitable as we consider this potential. A widely held view is that a music therapy relationship is necessary for a music therapy interaction (Suzanne Metzner and Brynjulf Stige, conference paper discussion, 21/9/05). Witnessing the myriad of ways that music therapists can help people through community interactions in oncology (and palliative care), has inspired me to expand my conception of this "relationship", from one denoting only those directly participating in the music based interaction, to also encompass people who witness sessions and choose to engage independently. Such "vicarious" music therapy encounters are evident, I believe, when someone indicates that they have been helped, such as Joan with her grief process:

> Joan had refused music therapy but had watched Mary sing songs from her childhood the previous week. She later found me and asked (concerned), "Did you know that Mary is in Room 6 (single room) and mightn't last long? (smiling) Wasn't it wonderful the pleasure she had with the music last week?"

Also, in the aforementioned research, one of the "overhearer" patient respondents had written that overhearing a favourite piece of music reminded her that she had a lot to live for.

As a music therapist working with people with life threatening conditions, and those close to them, I believe that it is my task to use whatever music and communication skills I have, in a professionally informed manner, to help people directly or indirectly encounter their treatment and illness experiences. This may be through long term therapeutic relationships, or through "here and now" moments with people I may never see again, such as in many of the transient ward communities described above. Enabling a music space in clinical settings, responding to people living with life threatening conditions, in which participants may experience and share joy, laughter, messages, support for loss, and the fulfilment of a special wish, is an important part of my work, and the longevity of these positive effects should not matter in this work. Of the 207 patients who agreed to participate in music therapy at Peter Mac during my research, over one quarter (at least 26%) had died within seven months of the end of data collection, and 58% of the 409 patients who were offered music therapy, had advanced or end-stage illness, that is, they required palliative treatment or care. Good quality moments, especially for these people, matter.

> Frida saw my guitar as I was walking in the radiotherapy waiting area and introduced herself. Eventually I discovered that she was a guitarist and we immediately played together in the waiting area after receiving permission from nearby patients. On hearing us, one of the patients, Hazel's, anxiety was immediately reduced, according to radiation staff. They also said that this made it much easier and quicker for them to prepare her for treatment. Hazel ended up joining a makeshift band just before one radiotherapy treatment, which included Frida and a radiation therapist on the guitar. I drew up a chart so that Helen could play metallophone notes to support the chordal framework. This spontaneous "catch the moment" music making might be ignored by other patients on these waiting areas, but sometimes they really get in the groove. While we were playing there, one very breathless outpatient stood up, hunched over, and requested "Dance of the Seven Veils" (the strippers tune) as she started taking her clothes off, only to be met by humorous cries of, "No, No, No!" from complete strangers in the waiting area. When I rang Hazel, two months after treatment, thanking her for sending me a photo which her husband took of our session, and to ask for permission to use this story, she said.
>
>   ... I was in a real state when I got there. Doing this made me come out of myself. That's how I really am. Best thing I ever did. I was in a real mess. ... Now I think about those good happy times, ...and I have a laugh. I tell everybody (in her community) about the orchestra and how David

(radiation therapist) called it "Hazel and the Nuts" (laughter). It helped me through it all, made me forget about everything else. John (husband) and I kept laughing about it for weeks.

A pastoral care colleague says how Peter Mac seems like an ocean, where "the human tide of suffering just keeps washing in" (Helen Mugg, personal communication, August 9th, 2005). Hopefully, in our work, we can help some people, on their own or with others, to catch a wave and even swim against the tide.

References

Aasgaard, T. (1999). Music therapy as milieu in the hospice and paediatric oncology ward. In D. Aldridge (Ed.) *Music therapy in palliative care: New Voices* (*pp.* 29-42). London: Jessica Kingsley.

Beszterczey, A. (1977). Staff stress on a newly developed palliative care service. *Canadian Psychiatric Association Journal, 22,* 347-353.

Bronfenbrenner, U. (1979). *The ecology of human development.* Cambridge: CUP.

Mulder, J., and Gregory, D. (2000) Transforming experience into wisdom: Healing amidst suffering. *Journal of Palliative Care,* 16: 25-29.

Murrant, G. M., Rykov, M., Amonite, D., and Loynd, M. (2000). Creativity and self-care for caregivers. *Journal of Palliative Care,* 16, 44-49.

O'Callaghan, C. (1994). Song writing in palliative care. Unpublished Master of Music Thesis. University of Melbourne.

—. (1997). Therapeutic opportunities associated with the music when using song writing in palliative care. *Music Therapy Perspectives,* 15, 32-38.

—. (2001). Music therapy's relevance in a cancer hospital researched through a constructivist lens. Unpublished PhD thesis. University of Melbourne.

—. (2005). Creating data for mining: Reflexive journal analysis yields an oncological music therapist's practice wisdom. *Journal of Social Work Research and Evaluation,* 6, 219-231.

O'Callaghan, C., and McDermott, F. (2004). Music therapy's relevance in a cancer hospital researched through a constructivist lens. *Journal of Music Therapy,* 41, 151-185.

Plach, T. (1980). *The creative use of music in group therapy.* Springfield: Charles C. Thomas.

Popay, J., Rodgers, A., and Williams, G. (1998). Rationale and standards for the systematic review of qualitative literature in health services research. *Qualitative Health Research,* 8, 341-351.

Prickett, C. A., and Moore, R. S. (1991). The use of music to aid memory of Alzheimer's patients. *Journal of Music Therapy,* 28, 101-110.

Salmon, D. (1989). Partage: Groupwork in palliative care. In J. A. Martin (Ed.) *Next step forward: Music therapy with the terminally ill* (pp. 47-51). New York: Calvary Hospital.

Stige, B. (2002). The relentless roots of community music therapy. *Voices: A World Forum for Music Therapy.* Retrieved October 8, 2005 from http://www.voices.no/mainissues/Voices2(3)Stige.html

Wallace, W. T. (1994). Memory for music: Effect of melody on recall of text. *Journal of Experimental Psychology: Learning, Memory, and Cognition,* 20, 1471-1485.

Zollo, J. (1999). The interdisciplinary palliative care team: Problems and possibilities. In S. Aranda and M. O'Connor (Eds.) *Palliative care nursing: A guide to practice* (pp. 21-36). Melbourne: Ausmed.

CHAPTER TWO

DEVELOPING MUSIC THERAPY PROGRAMS IN MEDICAL PRACTICE AND HEALTHCARE COMMUNITIES

JOANNE LOEWY DA, MT-BC

This chapter will provide an overview of the institution and development of a medical music therapy program, tracking the growth of a service which began twelve years ago on one unit of a medical center, and which has expanded into a hospital-wide service, and most recently into a Center for Music and Medicine at Beth Israel Medical Center in New York City.

In the hospital environment, there is a commitment to aggressive intervention and a consensus amongst hospital specialists that any test, agent or strategy which will affect the possibility for positive change, should be available and readily accessible to patients. Practitioners keep a careful watch on the patient's physiological response to interventions, as well, in order to monitor shifts and changes. Medicine is thought to be the primary restorative influence that will effect influential change in a patient's ability to heal. The inclusion of music therapy, as an integral component of medical treatment challenges historic conventions in the delivery of hospital services.

As music therapy is a unique discipline, and one that can provide unconventional incentive to the promotion of change in physiological and ego states, understanding its impacts, especially within quality of life parameters is key to the growth of our discipline. This knowledge in turn challenges the profession, and most importantly those who may benefit from music therapy services.

Background

The Louis and Lucille Armstrong Music Therapy Program originated in Pediatrics at Beth Israel Medical Center, in 1994 through an initial five year grant commitment from the Louis Armstrong Educational Foundation, which has continued since that time. Additional grants from foundations and pharmaceutical companies have supported the delivery of music therapy services while additional funding has been attained for research and public symposia[1]. In 1996, the program expanded to include service to HIV outpatient services for children and families and in 1997, music therapy was initiated in the medical center's pre and post operative areas.

Whereas the initial referrals for music therapy in the early work came directly from the medical center's Pediatric staff, the program gradually began to include adults, particularly family members of Pediatric patients. This reflected the way in which an understanding of music therapy was expanding within the hospital and the department was growing. The music therapy team began to provide in-services on other units and also started accepting referrals from adult units.

This ongoing development has been the result of a number of factors. Our day to day music therapy sessions were integral to the development of the service. We documented the effects of individual and family treatment and provided this feedback to the medical team. As well, our team provided frequent in-servicing for staff, and offered experiential groups to staff, particularly for residents in training. On each of the units serviced, we attended ward rounds which increased our referrals. In addition, our assessment form was instituted with a bar code to secure its permanence in the medical record. The studies undertaken in pain management resulted in an eventual reliance on music therapy's presence in procedures such as; veni-punctures, biopsies and circumcisions. We began pilot research that included measuring the impact of music therapy in sedation for tests, both pre-operative, and post-operative (Loewy, Hallan, Friedman and Martinez, 2005).

Our early attention and tabulation of these specific areas of need led us to identify significant lags of service as well as generalised needs within the medical center. These included 1) noise and stress in the Intensive Care Units (ICUs), 2) asthma-non-compliance, 3) high volumes of patients

---

[1] 1997 Music Therapy and Pediatric Pain (Sponsored by Astra), 1999 Music Therapy in the NICU (Sponsored by Con Edison), 2002 Music Therapy in Grief and Trauma (Sponsored by AMTA/The Grammy Foundation), 2004 Music Therapy at End of Life (Sponsored by Smithe).

at end of life with Chronic Obstructive Pulmonary Disease (COPD), 4) unrelieved pain and lack of perceived support amongst patients with Sickle Cell disease, 5) pain and suffering among oncology patients, and 6) secondary stress for MDs and RNs particularly on Oncology units and in the ICUs. Music therapy services were then developed to address these areas of need.

Three key areas we noticed early on in the work included the profound effect that music therapy had in helping children breathe, especially during asthmatic exacerbations. A second area was music's ability to assist in sedation and sleep, especially during medical tests. As a third key area, it was noted that music relieved anxiety, particularly in addressing the fear that children faced when going to sleep or taking resting-times near the end of life. Our team began to be called on to assist in helping terminally ill children die with dignity and to soothe family members during the children's passage from life to death.

During the first decade, we conducted research into pain (Loewy, MacGregor, Richards and Rodriguez, 1997; Loewy, 2000) and sedation (Loewy, Hallan, Friedman and Martinez, 2005). We also initiated a study with in-patient patients with asthma. Our work became further distinguished when in 1999 music therapy was invited to join Beth Israel's new and outstanding Pain and Palliative Medicine service led by Russell Portenoy. The development of medical music therapy, particularly the use of live music in painful procedures, such as the work of Edwards in burn debridement, represents an important clinical intervention that has been influential in the growth of a medical music therapy model (Edwards, 2005). Music therapy became further initiated in the Neonatal Intensive Care Unit (NICU) of Beth Israel, as an intervention of pain relief in 1999. Consequently, the Armstrong program is one of the only medical centers in the world to use live music, including ocean disc and gato box, at the bedside of premature infants.

Model of Integrative Medical Music Psychotherapy

Working closely and collaboratively with my colleague Benedikte Scheiby though the years, together we have developed a model of medical music psychotherapy and have maintained a commitment to working within an integrative medical music psychotherapy approach. Respectively in her work with adults with chronic and degenerative illness, and in my work with patients of all ages with chronic and terminal illness, we have developed a model of integrative practice using music in conjunction with medical practice (See Loewy, 1999; Scheiby, 1999).

The most basic premise of this psycho-spiritual commitment to health is that in addition to our knowledge of medical aspects of treatment, which we seek to enhance with music, the teams we train to provide future music therapy also become committed to treating patients from "within". This means that we use the music process to build from a patient's inner resources, inducing ego function, coping skills and maintenance. This is accomplished through subjectification, and resourcing of both the intra and inter aspects of the music experience. Subjectification is the therapist's use of psychotherapeutic experience, which includes the use of countertransference. This model provides musical mechanisms for patients to draw upon and trust that which they perceive and bring into the medical experience. It challenges the inclusion of that which they desire to strengthen through processes of creativity, motivation and a desired sense of control to build through personal expression via music and through collaborative release.

Live Music in a Music Psychotherapy-based Orientation

A key element that has increased the critical value placed in the efficacy of our medical center program growth in music therapy has been the clinically oriented stance of our day-to-day services and research. In a music psychotherapy approach, it is the clinician that evaluates the relationship of the mind to the body and vice versa. This relationship is key to the institution of a therapeutic service. The therapist's ability to monitor the music is best maintained through an interactive process whereby the therapist can astutely and responsibly make clinical interventions while observing the desired clinical outcomes and the efficacy of music to meet patient's needs.

Some research that has been carried out by RNs and some MDs have described "music therapy" as an intervention, when this inclusion has used only used recorded music without the presence of a music therapist (Heitz, Scamman and Symreng, 1992). Such research presents an ethical dilemma for our professional discipline. As well, there are inherent dangers in using recorded music that is static and delivered through a mechanical device. It is necessary to monitor volume control and to maintain acoustic adjustments. More importantly, a trained clinician can assist a medically compromised patient's reaction and response to music, which should be sensitively navigated.

Although music listening to desired recordings and/or musical mixes via CD recorders or personal stereos may seem to have useful clinical implications in terms of personalising aspects of one's individualised needs derived from a healthy life-world prior to hospitalisation, the psychotherapeutic aspects of treatment may limit therapeutic interventions then to occur outside of the music. It is certainly more expensive to implement a music therapy program headed by a certified music therapist than it is to implement a recording device. Yet, if doctors' first law of practice is "do no harm", the most responsible means of using music is to offer it in a way that is clinically responsible. When recording devices are left at the bedside and no one is monitoring the volumes, or the dynamic shifts that the effect of the music has upon the patient, these circumstances present a myriad of inherent risks especially because of the vulnerability of patients and the potential interface between this vulnerability and the evocative potentials of music experience.

It may be more difficult to generalise and quantitatively measure the results of music psychotherapy, but the safety and mental/emotional status of the patients are thought to be the most critical aspects of music therapy treatmcnt. No one in a hospital environment would argue about issues of safety and comfort and the necessity of having these aspects of care attended to in the critical care environment. Furthermore, most clinically astute researchers recognise the impact of implementing quantitative and qualitative methodologies in their investigations (see Wheeler, 2006). It is entirely possible to quantify and report the effectiveness of an individualised music therapy treatment plan.

The concept of wellness and working from "within" is growing in medical care and this is evidenced by the increase of quality of life measures seen throughout the literature from cancer care to chronic illness (cardiac, respiratory disease) to wellness (Engrebretson et al, 1999; Hollen et al, 1994). Palliative specialists, as well, are writing and treating with growing regard with not so much attention to *how long* a patient will live, but an increasing interest *in how one will experience* the day-to-day living.

The Changing Role of Music Therapy in Medical Practice

Through developing a model of medical music psychotherapy within a large urban institution and within other hospital institutions, I have come to view the success of this growth as integral from two distinct venues. The application of music therapy presented on a continuum that is within the filed of music therapy is critical. Enhancing our own understanding and practice of advanced application of music therapy in medicine is necessary for our growth. This may be thought of as vertical growth.

Horizontal growth is equally contingent to the growth and integration of music therapy in the medical arena. Our colleagues need to understand the impact of what we do, and they are best to comprehend it within the context of how it will serve the mission that they are trying to accomplish, for example music therapy pre-surgery to reduce blood pressure, and how it may serve the areas that they cannot reach, for example emotional fears and anxiety not related to medical per se, but directly impacting treatment effects.

The development of the music therapy program at Beth Israel Medical Center, as well as the other music therapy programs where I have consulted and developed elsewhere are characterised by growth in these two dimensions, the vertical and the horizontal. Without horizontal growth, that is the development of music therapy across a range of areas, it is not possible to grow vertically, that is to have expertise recognised and rewarded.

Vertical Growth

Vertical growth is defined by the way we harvest our unique discipline. One might ask; how does a particular action harvest our profession? What are the central aspects of service and how are we making room for future music therapy to endure? In what aspect of care is the general implementation of our service most needed and how will our growing research expand music therapy practice? We must also pay careful attention to particular aspects of our practice that, at times, we might be compromising in order to provide that which is being asked of us. There is always compromise in growing something new however the way these interactions are negotiated is a particular skill that we at Beth Israel have learned and can teach.

As a music psychotherapist, it is limiting and compromising to the profession when many of our own professionals use recorded music exclusively, and also consult with "lay" professionals who then implement recorded music and title this use of recordings as a music therapy program. It is equally restrictive to follow exclusively medical goals and outcomes that impute strictly medical parameters. As we music therapists working in medical teams learn about medicine and the culture of medical aspects of treatment, we must charge ourselves to remain committed to aspects of care that classic medicine does not typically attend to such as psycho-social parameters and creativity. When adhering to a philosophy of treating from within it is possible to maintain, restore and expand parts of the self which may lose stability or shift where equilibrium might be compromised.

Music therapy has grown professionally here and the early, collaborative research efforts we established with MDs and RNs have been integral to our ability to expand our services. Establishing a program that is initially unit based, beginning in one area and eventually growing to other units, has been critical to successful program growth in the medical centers where I have consulted.

The inclusion of staff needs at each and every juncture has also been essential to their ongoing commitment to program growth. Equally strengthening has been the music therapist's ability to define a model which assigns value to the unique role of the music and the music psychotherapist.

Horizontal Growth

Horizontal growth is the way we harvest areas of care with sensitivity to the needs of the medical venue and the community-at-large. We need to educate ourselves about aspects of disease and how music can effect changes in symptom management, especially in the treatment of pain and in post traumatic stress, where the impact and uniqueness of music therapy to resolve distress is so quickly attainable (Edwards, 1999; Turry andTurry, 1999).

In determining how any health oriented service is most effectively provided, the healthcare professional needs to stay abreast of community statistics. This includes reference to the mortality rate associated with an illness, symptom management, adherence or lack thereof, and perhaps most importantly, a knowledge of the numbers of patients identified as having a particular disease. An important question is to consider how effectively or ineffectively medical care and hospitalisation has served those patients. Included in this tabulation is, length of hospital stay, severity of symptoms, outcome measurements and customer and family satisfaction, which in total present essential data to the health-care professional. These growing trends affect the way costs are managed and determine how services are maintained.

Networking within the community and identifying needs as they present themselves in everyday life is important. From our schools to retirement homes, working in the community can ensure continuity of care as we can access areas of need in wellness and have a holistic view of what may be critical in illness. In this way we seek to avoid Emergency Room treatment and will work more diligently and preventatively by using music in a healthy way. It is a conclusive remark to what has been

presented thus far. It is the philosophy of the changing trend of "sick" and
"well"-in patient to out patient, to preventative care in everyday life.

Defining Key Areas of Care

Through development of music therapy in medicine, there are distinct
areas of medical care where music seems to have immediate and direct
levels of impact. The following sections define areas that represent critical
applications of growth and development.

Winds in Respiratory Care

Asthma is a true example of an "emergency room" illness. It is a
leading diagnosis for children who are hospitalised in the USA. Yet, the
number of routine medical treatments for the child or teenager with asthma
through out patient visits is small (National Center for Environmental
Health (NCEH), 1999). There is an obvious level of avoidance and lack of
compliance that accompanies this disease. When a child is healthy and not
showing signs or symptoms, there is little done preventatively. When a
child or teen is not having asthma, it seems that there is almost a sense of
denial that the asthma occurred. Stated simply, it is easier to forget about a
disease when it is not causing distress.

Chronic obstructive pulmonary disease (COPD) is an illness involving
two lung diseases; chronic bronchitis and emphysema. These diseases
are characterised by obstruction to airflow that interferes with breathing.
Both of these conditions frequently co-exist, hence physicians prefer the
term COPD. It does not include other obstructive diseases such as asthma.
COPD is the fourth leading cause of death in America, claiming the lives
of 128,000 Americans in 2004. In 2004, the cost to the nation for COPD
was approximately $37.2 billion, including healthcare expenditures of
$20.9 billion in direct health care expenditures, $7.4 billion in indirect
morbidity costs and $8.9 billion in indirect mortality costs (COPD Fact
Sheet, 2004; Goetzel, Hawkins, Ozminkowski and Wang, 2003).

Patients with COPD, collectively, represent a group with poor
compliance behaviour. In 2003, 10.7 million U.S. adults were estimated to
have COPD. However, close to 24 million U.S. adults have evidence of
impaired lung function, indicating an under diagnosis of COPD.

Asthma and COPD are diseases that when in crises may have traumatic
effects. To lose one's breath can leave a person feeling quite frightened
and out of control. The treatment of asthma and COPD is largely
pharmacological. There is no known available intervention that

encourages the patient with asthma or COPD to use their breath with a positive outcome and one that might address ways in which the airflow might be strengthened. Exercise may strengthen the body's capacity and incentive to breathe, yet it does not provide direct mechanisms for breath-control. Though some of the medical literature mentions the value of "pursed-lip breathing" in breathing dysfunction, there is little study with regard to wind-playing. The use of training in playing wind instruments may be an important intervention for the music therapist who is treating patients with respiratory disease.

Caring for the Caregiver: Community Music Circles for Staff

Reporting of medical/health care errors is a critical area on which the Joint Commission on Accreditation of Healthcare Organizations in the USA takes an active position http://www.jcipatientsafety.org The Joint Commission on Accreditation of Healthcare Organizations is committed to improving patient safety through its accreditation process. They foresee that meaningful improvement in patient safety will eventually be reflected by a significant reduction in the number of medical/health care errors that result in harm to patients. Achieving this significant reduction is dependent upon careful identification of the errors that actually occur. Careful analyses of causes of medical error are being formulated in order to best determine the underlying factors or "root causes" that, if eliminated, could reduce the risk of similar errors in the future. In order to this, the Commission is requiring that hospitals compile data about error frequency and the type and root causes of these errors. This includes redesigning systems and processes to reduce the risk of future errors. Also, periodic assessment of the effectiveness of the efforts taken to reduce the risk of errors is being encouraged.

Interestingly, a less overt source of medical error that has not been reported in the literature is the tension and stress felt by front line doctors and nurses, which is the result of numerous hours with little or no break. Residents in psychiatry and other specialties endure an onslaught of stress faced by few other people their age. Between one-fourth and one-third of them experience a clinical depression during their training (Evans, Farberow and Kennedy Associates, 2003). Suicide risk also appears to be elevated in medical practitioners (Center, Davis, Detre et al, 2003). Upon observation, one can easily hypothesise that medical staff are behind on sleep and stressed to meet the daily quotas of their shift. Figely (2002) addressed the issue of secondary traumatic stress in his research with professional caregivers. He found that medical staff are often are faced with increased risks of experiencing secondary trauma as the result of inadequate coping skills or supportive resources. He has termed such stress "compassion fatigue" and has developed a standardised compassion fatigue scale for caregivers to monitor their level of stress.

The increase in potential for medical error may relate to the compounding stressors that hospital staff experience on a day-to-day basis. This has important implications for the music therapist. Creating opportunities for staff to participate in drumming circles, or music meditations may ease the level of stress that accompanies their day. Doctors have reported that a mere 15 minutes of drumming can enhance their alacrity and acuity (Personal communication, 2000). Nurses have relished the opportunity to sing amongst one another, especially during times of loss. This has been observed on the oncology unit, where losses may be frequent and there may not be supports to facilitate expression of grief in place for staff.

Caring for the Caregiver music groups (Loewy and Frisch-Hara, 2002) may have subtle, yet lasting effects for professional staff. The importance of this opportunity to experience stress-relief and community amongst staff in the workplace should not be under-rated. It is important to discern, that the music therapist providing such community opportunities for staff is not offering therapy for staff. The music therapist is rather, facilitating music experiences to instil a sense of health and well-being. This, in turn, is perceived to impact the patients, who may experience staff as more alert, and who also are referred more readily to music therapy by staff who, though their lived music experience have a greater understanding about the potency of music.

The role of music and music therapy in healthcare communities is clearly advancing and will continue to grow in new and unique ways. It is helpful for the music therapist to have a conception of the growing medical and community trends that face not only the practice and clinical trials of our profession, but will also understand the challenges in the workplace and community at large.

In this chapter, some of the ways that a music therapy program can address the growing needs of an inner-city United States hospital were exemplified. As part of development of the music therapy program we identified six main areas of need which could be addressed through music therapy services. As discussed above these are 1) noise and stress in Intensive Care Units (ICUs), 2) asthma-non-compliance, 3) high volumes of patients at end of life with Chronic Obstructive Pulmonary Disease (COPD), 4) unrelieved pain and lack of perceived support amongst patients with Sickle Cell disease, 5) pain and suffering among oncology patients and 6) secondary stress for MDs and RNs particularly on Oncology units and in the ICUs. It is hoped that the reader was able to navigate how music therapy can best suit these serious healthcare issues more easily through the context of how we have strategised our development.

The context of growth, whether it is vertical or horizontal is best manoeuvred when we frame it around the musical possibilities for patients and staff, many of which are relatively uncharted, such as winds in respiratory disease. Additionally, the music therapist's commitment to the broad survey of healthcare needs as well as the institution of continuous research endeavours that highlight the use of live music to address these needs will promote and develop the necessity of our work.

References

Center, C., Davis, M., Detre, T., et al. (2003). Confronting depression and suicide in physicians: A consensus statement. *JAMA*, 289, 3161-3166.

COPD Fact Sheet (2005). Retrieved September 9, 2005 from American Lung Association: http://www.lungusa.org/site/pp.asp?c=dvLUK9O0E&b=35020

Edwards, J. (2005). Developing pain management approaches in music therapy with hospitalized children. In J. Loewy and C. Dileo (Eds.) *Music Therapy at the end of life* (pp. 57-64). Cherry Hill, NJ: Jeffrey Books.

Engrebretson, T., Clark, M., Niaura, R., Phillips, T., Albrecht, A., and Tilkemeier, P. (1999). Quality of life and anxiety in a phase II cardiac rehabilitation program. *Medicine & Science in Sports & Exercise*, 31, 216-223.

Evans, G., Farberow, N.L., and Kennedy Associates (Eds.). *The encyclopedia of suicide*, 2nd edition. New York: Facts on File.

Figely, C. (2002)(Ed.). *Treating compassion fatigue*. New York: Brunner-Routledge.

Goetzel, R.A., Hawkins, K., Ozminkowski, R.J., and Wang, S. (2003). The health and productivity cost burden of the "top 10" physical and mental health conditions affecting six large U.S. employers in 1999. *Journal of Occupational and Environmental Medicine*, 45, 5-14.

Heitz, L., Scamman F., and Symreng, T. (1992) Effect of music therapy in the post anesthesia care unit: A nursing intervention. *Journal of Post Anesthesia Nursing*, 7, 22-31.

Hollen, P.J., Gralla, R.J., Kris, M.G., Cox, C., Belani, C.P., Grunberg, S.M., Crawford, J., and Neidhart, J. (1994). Measurement of quality of life in patients with lung cancer in multicenter trials of new therapies: Psychometric assessment of the Lung Cancer Symptom Scale. *Cancer*, 73, 2087-2098

Loewy, J., Hallan, C., Friedman, E., and Martinez, C. (2005). Sleep/sedation in children undergoing EEG testing: A comparison of chloral hydrate and music therapy. *Journal of PeriAnesthesia Nursing.* 20, 323-32.

Loewy, J. and Frisch-Hara, A. (2002)(Eds.). *Caring for the caregiver: The use of music therapy in grief and trauma.* Silver Spring, MD: AMTA.

Loewy, J., and Scheiby, B. (June, 2001). Medical music therapy. Unpublished lecture, Nordoff-Robbins Center for Music Therapy, New York.

Loewy, J. (2000). Music psychotherapy assessment. *Music Therapy Perspectives*, 18, 47-58.

—. (1999). The use of music psychotherapy in the treatment of pediatric pain. In C. Dileo (Ed.) *Music therapy and medicine* (pp. 189-206). Silver Spring, MD: American Music Therapy Association.

Loewy, J., MacGregor, B., Richards, K., and Rodriguez, J. (1997). Music therapy in pediatric pain management: Assessing, and attending to the sounds of hurt, fear and anxiety. In Loewy, J. (Ed.) *Music therapy in pediatric pain* (pp. 45-56). Cherry Hill, N.J.: Jeffrey Books.

National Center for Environmental Health (1999). Asthma at a glance. retrieved March 14th, 2007 from http://www.cdc.gov/asthma/default.htm

Scheiby, B. (1999). "Better trying than crying": Analytical music therapy in a medical setting. In C. Dileo (Ed.) *Music therapy and medicine* (pp. 95-106). Silver Spring, MD: American Music Therapy Association.

Turry, A., and Turry, A.E. (1999). Creative song improvisations with children and adults with cancer. In C. Dileo (Ed.) *Music therapy and medicine* (pp. 167-178). Silver Spring, MD: American Music Therapy Association.

Wheeler (Ed.). *Music therapy research: Quantitative and qualitative perspectives* (2nd edition). Gilsum: Barcelona.

CHAPTER THREE

INTEGRATING MODELS OF MUSIC INTO ACUTE HOSPITALS: AN IRISH PERSPECTIVE

HILARY MOSS

This chapter explores the role of music in a large acute, academic teaching hospital in Dublin, Ireland. The chapter presents a number of methods of using music, such as live performance, music therapy, musician in residence schemes, and using pre-recorded music as part of hospital design. A discussion of the most appropriate use of any one model of music in a hospital setting then follows. Music can be used in many different ways within the acute hospital, and these different methods are presented as a resource from which to select the best intervention to assist a patient or group of patients. Four key features which are essential to selecting the right music for any patient group will be presented and explored. These are 1) assessing patient need, 2) evaluating the benefit of the intervention, 3) insisting on professional training and excellence, and 4) always viewing the use of music in a hospital setting as a therapeutic tool.

The use of these models has evolved from my experience as a music therapist and hospital Arts Officer, both in Ireland and the UK. My professional work experience includes five years working as a psycho-dynamically informed music therapist in a London forensic psychiatry rehabilitation service, research and evaluation as a music therapist in a London stroke rehabilitation service, general psychiatry and nursing home work as a music therapist and health service management in the voluntary sector in Ireland. Following completion of an MBA in Health Service Management I am now currently working as Arts Officer at The Adelaide and Meath Hospital, Incorporating the National Childrens Hospital, Dublin managing a program of arts activities, therapeutic interventions and events across all the departments of a large acute hospital in Ireland.

A key feature of this chapter will be how music therapy and other methods of using music in healthcare context are able to co-exist happily alongside one another. Given the wide range of clinical specialities in acute hospital care, much attention will be given to selecting the right musical intervention for any patient group. Organisation culture and context will be considered, as well as the importance of putting the patient first and designing music program to meet their needs.

The core of this chapter is in taking a broad perspective on music and health, wider than just music therapy, or any one other professional discipline. The chapter provides guidelines for those thinking of using music in hospital for the first time, and also speaks to experienced music and health and music therapy professionals who wish to broaden their working models to suit a specific patient group.

The Adelaide and Meath Hospital, Incorporating The National Childrens Hospital, Dublin, Ireland

The Adelaide and Meath Hospital, Dublin incorporating the National Children's Hospital (AMNCH) opened on the 21st June, 1998. Three inner city hospitals were merged and relocated to a greenfield site in Tallaght, SouthWest Dublin. This new hospital provides adult, paediatric and psychiatric services to a catchment area of 450,000 (including North Kildare and West Wicklow).

The hospital has 587 beds and 2,683 staff. In 2004 the hospital had 21,500 admissions, 74,500 emergency department attendances, 195,000 outpatient-attendances, 19,500 day procedures and 12,500 operating theatre procedures.

In accordance with the Charter of the Hospital, the hospital's mission is to be a public, voluntary and teaching hospital operated in the interests of patients. The aims of the hospital are to:

- Identify and meet the health care needs of the communities we serve so that our Hospital is a Hospital for everyone
- Provide the highest quality health care to all patients
- Undertake and support research in health care
- Educate all staff and students to the highest international standards
- Seek equal opportunities for each member of staff and for each student to fulfil their potential in health care
- Develop voluntary involvement and support for our Hospital to the maximum extent possible

This author was appointed as hospital Arts Officer in September 2003 with a view to developing and promoting the arts in the hospital and to explore the relationship between arts and health. An Arts Committee, made up of senior clinicians and management, was established to oversee the work of the Arts Office. Following consultation with patients and staff, four broad aims were developed for the service, 1) to enhance the environment, 2) to explore the therapeutic nature of the arts through participatory sessions for patients, 3) to raise awareness of the arts and make the arts more accessible to staff, patients and hospital visitors, and 4) to promote local artists and build links with the local community.

Music is used in each of the four aims above, alongside other art forms. Through consultation with patients and staff, the arts office decides which intervention and which art form would best suit the needs of each patient group. In this context, music therapy is used alongside performance, musician in residence schemes and other models, based on assessment of need.

Why use Music in a Hospital?

Healthcare experts, members of the public and financial managers often question the use of music in a hospital. This is the starting point for the arts office at AMNCH. The World Health Organisation defines health as a "state of complete psychological, mental, and social well-being and not merely the absence of disease or infirmity" (http:www.who.int/about/definition/en/2006). We use music in our own lives in a variety of ways, for example to create a romantic atmosphere, to relax, to motivate ourselves in the gym, to express ourselves, to comfort ourselves when grieving, and for many people in religious worship. Our social and psychological health is connected to our access to music and other art forms. One would never live at home without music or pictures and yet in most hospitals such sterile, bare environments are the norm.

Music in a healthcare context is often seen as a fringe activity - a "nice extra" provided by volunteers. However, the preferences, interests, social and emotional needs of patients are increasingly recognised as vitally important to their health, well-being and recovery rate.[1]

Musical preference is highly individual and using music in healthcare can personalise care and enhance the quality of hospital life.

Finally, evidence exists that our ability to respond to sound and pitch is one of the earliest responses in infants and is often retained despite disability or brain damage (The Association of Professional Music Therapists, 1995). As a medium for enhancing communication and self-

---

[1] http:www.who.int/about/definition/en

expression, music can be of particular benefit to some patient groups and deserves to be integrated into patient care rather than be left in the fringes.

Music in Acute Hospitals

When the post of hospital arts office was established, extensive consideration was given to how best to promote and provide musical programs for patients. The methods presented below emerged as important and useful for patients, and are now all used in the hospital.

Live Concert Program

The Adelaide and Meath Hospital, Incorporating the National Childrens Hospital, has, like many others, a program of live performances. Professional musicians are hired to play for patients in various locations around the hospital, including the Age Related Health Care Unit, the psychiatry unit, a number of in-patient wards, and the neurology ward. Performers also give weekly recitals in the hospital atrium. The atrium is a large reception area of the hospital, with a café, main reception desk, banks and shops. All patients and staff pass through this area on their way to the wards, offices and outpatients department. Patients and visitors wait here and staff often use the area for coffee breaks. Patients, visitors, people waiting for outpatient appointments and staff can all enjoy live performance. All performances are financed through fundraising, such as hospital foundations, volunteer fundraising and local council funding.

In my experience as Arts Officer at AMNCH, I have found that a maximum of four musicians works best on a ward, due to space and sound restrictions. Smaller ensembles also have the possibility to create an intimacy between patients and performers. Performances to date have included Irish traditional music performers, a harp duo, string quartets, flautists, and jazz singers. The musicians play for up to one hour - any longer is difficult for patients to concentrate – and they interact with patients, for example, by chatting, describing their music and answering questions. Larger ensembles and choirs can be used in the hospital atrium.

A major issue for the arts office is selecting the right musician. The temperament and personality of the performer is crucial to creating a successful event. Their capacity to be flexible in the environment is crucial. Mistakes have certainly been made in selecting the wrong performers. For example, a cellist once famously performed in the atrium of a large London hospital, and complained about the noise - he even asked if the lifts could be turned off to avoid disturbing him. Our most successful musicians come with an attitude and disposition which is hard to define, but an openness to patients questions, a flexibility regarding performance venue and an empathy with patient's needs are crucial characteristics for this work.

In the USA, some musicians have trained as "Performers in Hospitals", becoming experts in the area of performing to patients (Buenz, 2005). Their work often leads them to playing for very ill individual patients. One such musician told me that the difference between playing his violin in hospital, as opposed to the concert hall, is that in hospital *my performance is a service to the patient* (Buenz, 2005).

In my role as Arts Officer of a large acute hospital, I plan the music program by first assessing which patients would most benefit from hearing live music and what music would be most suitable for that particular group. For example, I have found that long-term neurology and stroke patients can benefit from performances, as some have become depressed and believe that they may never get to a attend a concert again. I also fit in with patients regarding time of day and location. The musician's ego cannot direct music in hospital, but their excellence in performance can dramatically lift a patient's day.

Some of the benefits of bringing live performances in to the hospital include 1) stimulation and distraction for depressed and anxious patients, 2) alleviating anxiety in the waiting room, 3) improving quality of life for longer stay patients, 4) lifting mood in depressed patients, 5) bringing performance to those who cannot access traditional concert venues, and 6) relieving stress and lifting the atmosphere on the ward.

It is most important to ensure that patients can leave the performance if they want to and are not imposed upon in any way. Post-concert evaluation is important to gauge patient reaction and in order to improve future programs.

The Chelsea and Westminster Hospital in England conducted research into the effect of listening to live music on patient's anxiety and depression rates while waiting for chemotherapy and antenatal appointments (Staricoff et al, 2002). Anxiety levels for patients receiving chemotherapy were 32% lower when exposed to live music in the waiting room and pregnant women showed lower blood pressure levels when listening to live music while waiting for antenatal appointments.

Orchestra in Residence

AMNCH has recently forged a link with the Irish Chamber Orchestra, who, for the first time in Ireland, is a hospital *orchestra in residence.*

Members of the orchestra come and play on a monthly basis for patients. An independent evaluation of the benefit of this live music for patients is currently being carried out, and we aim to develop a training program for performers who wish to work in hospitals.

An orchestra (or musician) in residence program allows for development of a strong relationship between the hospital and performers. This allows for programs to be adjusted to suit patients better and to develop the live performance program with the orchestra.

Early indications from the evaluations show that while patients find it difficult to state exactly what music they prefer, they find listening to the music makes them stimulated to move, tap their feet, release worries and help to cope with their hospital stay.

Music Therapy

"Music therapy is the planned use of music to achieve therapeutic outcomes, by a qualified practitioner who has graduated from an accredited university program of study, usually at postgraduate level" (Edwards, 2006, p. 33). By using music creatively in a clinical setting, the therapist seeks to establish an interaction, a shared musical experience leading to the pursuit of therapeutic goals (Bunt, 1994). Ansdell (2002) defines Music Therapy as "moving from playing *to* people to playing *with* them... (using) improvisation to allow spontaneous co-musicing... focusing on interpersonal relationships within the music and modelling the work of other therapies (e.g. psychotherapy, Gestalt)... focusing on emotional issues arising from the music".

At AMNCH, a music therapist is employed in the psychiatry unit, working as part of the occupational therapy department. A music therapy service is also offered as part of the chronic pain management program and a pilot music therapy project has been carried out with neurology patients. A randomised controlled trial (RCT) of the benefit of music therapy in stroke will be carried out later this year.

Three brief case studies follow, showing the benefit of introducing music therapy to selected patients.

Case Study 1 Tina2

Tina was a thirty-three year old patient in the psychiatry unit. She was in a locked ward due to violent behaviour towards staff and fellow patients

---

[2] Names of all patients are changed to protect confidentiality

and she has a diagnosis of paranoid schizophrenia[3]. She had no insight into her illness, her drug use, or her violence, or the relationship between these three issues.

Tina agreed to attend individual music therapy because she wrote song lyrics and wanted to develop her songs. She had a delusion that she was a major pop star and believed she would make a lot of money when she was discharged from hospital. Following assessment, the Music Therapist identified three issues to be addressed in ongoing Music Therapy:

Trust/ Relationship Building

Tina did not trust any therapists or doctors. In the music therapy sessions, she refused to record her music for fear that the therapist would sell her songs and make millions. The early sessions were also characterised by Tina directing and criticising the therapist. Tina would sing, accompanied by the therapist, but continually criticised the therapist's style and technique. It was hoped that by engaging in music therapy, Tina would develop a good relationship with one member of the multi-disciplinary team, and so build up trust in the hospital and her care plan.

Engagement in Therapy/Treatment

The medical team was concerned to engage Tina in therapy. She refused to attend any therapy except Music Therapy and also refused medication. It was hoped that by engaging in a less threatening, enjoyable therapy, Tina might be ready to engage with doctors regarding medication and other therapies.

---

[3] Schizophrenia is a chronic, severe, and disabling *brain disease*. People with schizophrenia often suffer terrifying symptoms such as hearing internal voices not heard by others, or believing that other people are reading their minds, controlling their thoughts, or plotting to harm them. These symptoms may leave them fearful and withdrawn. Their speech and behaviour can be so disorganized that they may be incomprehensible or frightening to others. Available treatments can relieve many symptoms, but most people with schizophrenia continue to suffer some symptoms throughout their lives; it has been estimated that no more than one in five individuals recovers completely. In the paranoid form of this disorder, people develop delusions of persecution or personal grandeur.

Insight into Behaviour

It was hoped that through song writing sessions, there would be opportunities for Tina to develop awareness of how she related to others, in particular reflecting on emotional issues and how to negotiate in a non-violent manner.

Tina engaged in individual Music Therapy and gradually built a relationship with the therapist. The sessions were often fraught, Tina was highly critical of the therapist and untrusting of the situation. They managed to record two songs together, but in both songs the piano accompaniments of the therapist and Tina's singing were strained and disjointed.

Then, sixteen weeks after therapy started, Tina brought some new song lyrics, which she wrote during a time when she was feeling very depressed. This was the most genuine moment of reflection since Tina started therapy. The therapist and Tina improvised a song together and recorded it. Their music integrated well and sounded, for the first time, like a real partnership. It was a small step towards Tina reflecting on her emotions rather than acting out with violence, as well as a step towards really trusting the therapist by sharing her real feelings. This session heralded a new phase in the relationship between Tina and the clinical team.

Tina's song lyrics

I wish I could find a ray of hope
A ray of light as I'm walking
Through the darkness
A ray of sunshine for all time
A ray of happiness

Case Study 2 Cynthia

Cynthia was a seventy-year-old woman who had a stroke and was on a stroke rehabilitation ward in the hospital. She was very quiet and withdrawn on the ward. The hospital was waiting for a nursing home bed to become available for her.

Cynthia attended individual music therapy. She showed no interest in playing the instruments and asked to listen to CDs. Together, the therapist and Cynthia built up a "life review" using music[4]. They talked about Cynthia's life and selected songs and music that were significant to her life. They listened to CDs and sang songs each week. Cynthia enjoyed having a quiet time to listen to her music each week. She found the ward noisy and the television and radio disturbing, as they *never played the music she liked.*

It became clear during therapy that Cynthia was extremely passive and unassertive about her future and what her new home would be like. Cynthia had a vast record collection at home, but had not asked for them to be moved from home to her new nursing home. The team became aware, through music therapy, of her lack of involvement in the move to the nursing home and were able to help her to engage with the process and express her opinions and needs more assertively.

Case Study 3 Sam

Sam was a six-year old boy who attended the children's hospital. He had muscular dystrophy and a learning disability and was an extremely quiet and frail child. He was referred to Music Therapy to help develop his language as he had very few words. The therapist used songs to encourage language development and also used instruments to develop his range of non-verbal self-expression. Through the music he learned new words and showed an energetic and livelier side to his character through expressing himself loudly on drums.

Music as Part of Building Design

One of the most common reasons for using music in any environment is to enhance the atmosphere or create a certain ambience. Restaurants, shops, bars and hotels all use music to create an impression, style or ambience. A number of hospital design projects at AMNCH are using music to enhance the environment. For example, a proposal to redesign the stairwell in the main hallway of the hospital includes solo guitar being piped into the stairwell. As you enter the stairwell, you are transported, momentarily, from the rush outside, or the busy atmosphere of a ward, to a calm, quiet oasis. Coloured balls cast light on the walls, floors are to be changed and handrails will be redesigned.

---

[4] A 'life review' is a musical profile of a person, consisting of selections of music which have special meaning for the person at various stages during life (see Beggs, 1996).

Similarly, the colposcopy treatment room is being redesigned to create a less daunting atmosphere. Currently, as you enter the room you are faced with a frightening treatment table, complete with stirrups and equipment for gynaecological investigations. The new design will calm the atmosphere using softer wall colours, dimmed lighting and comfortable armchairs. A DVD screen above the treatment table will show a calm ocean scene with fish swimming. And finally, music will be playing - gentle classical music, as in a beauty clinic or a massage treatment room. Alternatively, the patient will be able to bring their own music to play while they undergo treatment, to help them relax.

A CD player in a waiting room or treatment room can cost as little as €50 but the effect, and the change in atmosphere, can be immense. Careful selection of CDs is essential and consultation with patients, in other words, finding out what they really want to listen to, can ensure appropriate mood.

Pre-recorded Music in Treatment Rooms

Pre-recorded music is difficult to use effectively throughout society. Marketing experts play music in supermarkets, restaurants and bars to create a certain ambience and to influence shopping habits. Our mood and behaviour can be influenced by music. Yet we often walk into hospital to find no music at all, or worse, inappropriate use of music. Many times in wards and nursing homes for older people I have noticed the music being played is "Hits from the 20s and 30s" or wartime songs. These tapes, while age appropriate and of interest to residents, can easily be overused and inappropriately used. Some patients hate that kind of music and have no way of controlling volume or changing the music.

Music has power - it can create a strong impression and change the atmosphere. Music can be used with a hyperactive child to help them to calm down. Music can provoke tears that were being held in. A string quartet in the atrium of a hospital can provide a strong corporate impression of professionalism, and of caring about the waiting experience. But music is not always appropriate either. Silence is also important. Health professionals often assume too much about what a patient wants to listen to, or they pay too little attention to the ambience of a bedroom or day area. Quality of care can be greatly enhanced by taking care of the physical environment and creating a pleasant atmosphere for patients.

Wherever possible, pre-recorded music needs to be individualised. Every single person finds different music relaxing. For example, a group of teenagers in hospital once told me that they find listening to heavy metal music relaxing.

In the radiography department of our hospital, patients are sent an appointment letter for MRI scans. An MRI (magnetic resonance imaging) scan is an investigation that produces pictures of the inside of the body. It is performed as an outpatient procedure and takes up to one hour. The procedure does not require an anaesthetic (except in the case of small children) although some people are given medication to help ensure that they are relaxed and comfortable during the procedure. Having an MRI scan may involve being enclosed in a fairly narrow space, and for some people this feels quite claustrophobic.

At AMNCH, when a patient is sent their appointment letter, the letter includes the line *Please bring a CD you enjoy listening to, which we will play during your scan.* Patients use their own music to provide distraction and alleviate anxiety. The patient is also given control over their environment. In a ward for older people, we bought four CD/tape players and headphones. These machines were lent out to patients who could listen to their own music. We also developed a music library, staffed by volunteers, so that patients could access a wide range of CDs while in hospital.

Our musical choices are informed by factors such as personality traits, language, past experiences, culture and education. The specific piece of music utilised in clinical procedures is not as important as the associations that have been developed by the individual patient with the selection (Standley, 1992).

Menegazzi, Paris, Kersteen, Flynn and Trautman (1991) carried out a randomised controlled trial in an Accident and Emergency department. They found that listening to music through a headset significantly reduced the pain and anxiety associated with laceration repair. Patients undergoing the procedure were given a headset, from which they could choose from 50 available styles and artists and they controlled the volume. A control group received no music. 89% of patients using the headset rated the music as "very beneficial" and 100% said they would use music again.

Selecting the Right Music at the Right Time

One of the main goals of using music in this hospital context is to try to relieve the anxiety and pain children suffer as a result of the intrusive procedures to which they are subjected.
(Preti and Welch, 2004, p. 334)

The methods of using music set out above are, to me, a tool kit from which I can select interventions to best assist a patient or group of patients. Whichever model of using music is adopted, I have found it most important to carefully select the right model according to clinical need. My training as a music therapist, and initial work experience in forensic psychiatry, was predominantly psychodynamic. This stood me in good stead as a basic training, but led me to believe that music is a toolbox that should be used more widely to achieve greatest therapeutic benefit for patients, for example in the many ways outlined above. I believe that music therapists are well placed, as specialists in both music and health, to carefully select the right method of using music for their patients.

Four key features stand out when selecting the right music for any patient group, 1) assess patient need, 2) evaluate the benefit of the intervention, 3) insist on professional training and excellence, and 4) always view music as a therapeutic tool.

It is of key importance to first assess patient need. This can be done by verbal consultation with staff, patients and family members, or through more formal assessment tools. A sample assessment form is presented in Appendix One. Once a model of using music has been selected and used, it is also critical to evaluate the benefit. A sample evaluation form, used for the orchestra in residence program, is presented in Appendix Two. Finally, it is crucial, as a hospital manager, to insist on excellence in both musical and health service terms, and to do so, professional training and excellence should be sought when employing any musicians. Musicians who work in the hospital have to demonstrate excellence both as performers and, just as importantly, in their understanding of the heathcare environment. In looking for such specialists, I would view music therapists, who have post-graduate training in music and health, as the specialists who can best provide such a service. However, there is a large arts and health movement, both in Ireland and the UK, that has grown alongside music therapy. I believe this is partly in response to a perceived lack of flexibility on the part of music therapists. I have experienced a number of music therapists who identify their role as similar to that of a psychoanalyst, who felt that if they were to perform, or organise performances, in hospital this would be compromising their role as a therapist.

A similar approach is sometimes taken towards musical instruments - if a nurse asks to borrow a keyboard so that a patient can play at the weekend, I have seen this refused on the grounds of breaking therapy boundaries. I believe that some music therapists are resistant to expanding their role to fit the hospital culture and can be inflexible in their approach to meeting patient needs. I have also found that focusing on what is best for the patient and assessing the particular ward culture and environment, can lead one to be more flexible about how one uses music in the organisation and provide a more successful service.

Music can easily be used inappropriately in healthcare. For example, music might be played on the radio on the ward, with no way for patients to control the channel or volume. Alternatively, individual music therapy might be offered on a ward where staff are too stressed and pressured to be able to cope with the extra work of getting patients ready and moving patients to the therapy room. It is vitally important to weigh up which music to use with which patients and what the hospital or ward culture needs, and to view music as a therapeutic tool which can help patients and staff to achieve enhanced health and well being.

Sometimes, music and health practitioners offer a short-term project that is very positive for patients. However, it is important that a therapeutic approach is taken towards initiating music projects and ending them properly, as the impact of withdrawing a positive activity from vulnerable patients can be more significant than we would often realise. Sometimes arts and health projects are very focused on an "end product" (such as a performance or recording) and it is often more important to live through the process with patients, even if this diverges from the intended end place.

Three examples follow which show how I have used the four criteria 1) assess patient need, 2) evaluate the benefit of the intervention, 3) insist on professional training and excellence and 4) always view music as a therapeutic tool)to select the right music for a particular patient group. The fourth example is one where music was not appropriate at all.

Example One: Stroke Rehabilitation Ward, London

When working as a music therapist in a London stroke unit, I wanted to offer individual music therapy to patients. However, the ward was one of the most difficult I had worked on. Staff verged on abusive, disinterested, rough, talking negatively about patients in front of them, and disrespectful of visitors. I realised, after some weeks in the unit, that there was a need to alleviate staff stress, in order to improve the well being of patients on the ward. So I brought my keyboard and a few hand held percussion instruments to the day room of the ward, despite feeling that perhaps this "wasn't exactly music therapy". My own instincts seemed to be at odds with what my training had led me to believe was "proper" music therapy. I began a weekly "singalong" session with patients and

visitors. Staff joined in, patients sang solos, some clapped, and some
tapped their feet. A very elderly patient, in the late stages of dementia,
sang the last line of "My bonny lies over the ocean" and the nurses, who
had described him to me as "useless, away with the fairies" realised that he
still had a contribution to make. He became a central figure in the singing
group and his wife was able to participate with him.

I found that music and health professionals have to be flexible to the
needs of patients. Sometimes, patients want music therapy, they want to
express themselves and explore their emotions. At other times patients
want music to be a therapy-free zone, to just be the "thing they enjoy
doing", rather than being "therapy". As music therapists, teachers,
performers and practitioners we need to be willing to be flexible. We need
to be willing to move outside the traditional boundaries of our professional
identity to meet patient need, and yet retain professional integrity in our
approach.

Example Two: The Chronic Pain Program, Dublin

Chronic pain is defined as pain that lasts longer than six months. Many
people who have been suffering from chronic pain in the back or in other
areas may think they are permanently disabled and will never be able to
have an active life. Many give up work and withdraw from most forms of
activity because of their pain, their perception of what they can and cannot
do as a result of the pain, and due to the fact that they have not had much
success with the treatments they have tried. At AMNCH a new four-week
program was developed in 2001 and has had impressive results with
patients with chronic disability, mostly resulting from back pain. The
program is run by a multidisciplinary team of anaesthetist/pain specialist,
physiotherapist, occupational therapist, psychologist and psychiatrist, all
of whom provide an integrated care plan. Recent data from the program
showed that 53% of participants who expressed a wish to return to work or
training did so post-completion of the program.

I was invited to provide a pilot music therapy group, once a week on
the program, to explore how music could help people cope with pain.
When I joined the program I soon realised that patients were very sceptical
and uncomfortable about playing instruments. The program was highly
structured with the other therapists providing worksheets and structured
discussion around specific topics. It became clear that I needed to develop
some simple, non-threatening arts activities to engage the group and break
down fear. So I devised a music relaxation session for week one, to

introduce patients to the idea of music therapy and to alleviate some high levels of anxiety in the patient group.

Through feedback and evaluation, this program actually developed into a "creative" therapy group, using creative writing, music and visual art to explore and address coping with pain, relaxation, self belief and coping mechanisms. The changes in my part of the program came directly from feedback from patients who had completed the program. The music component of the program now addresses relaxation, using music to lift mood and using music as motivation for exercise.

Patients identify their own individual musical preferences and compile a CD of "their" music as a tool to use when the program finishes. Developing this program has again been a challenge to my own ideas about what music therapy is and my perceptions about my profession's definition of "proper" music therapy. Again, the need to be flexible to the patients needs is of paramount importance.

Example Three: Psychiatry unit, Dublin

When I became Arts Officer at AMNCH I was invited to meet the occupational therapists in the psychiatry unit to see whether the arts could contribute to patient care and quality of the environment. The occupational therapists already ran a full group program including art groups, relaxation and craft sessions. The team was keen to have music therapy as they currently did not use music as a therapeutic medium and patients expressed an interest in this medium. I offered a weekly music therapy group on the ward on a pilot basis for twelve weeks.

Given the very short stay of most patients on the ward, and the nature of their illnesses, the group was an open group for any patients who wanted to attend. Patients were able to leave during the group if they needed to. I provided a basic structure for the group, which included introducing ourselves using a drum, exploring the instruments, improvisations and song writing. Due to the acute nature of patients' illnesses, and the short stay, the group was a "moment" in the week, for relaxation, self expression, conversation, singing or whatever the patients needed that week.

The patients often used the group as the "fun" part of the week. The release and energy in the group was high and the group was large (normally eight to ten patients attended). The group did a lot of singing. We wrote songs and also took turns to suggest our "favourite" songs. This group at times made me question, again, what "proper" music therapy was… these patients seemed to be having fun, were not addressing any serious issues and I wondered if I needed to change the focus of the group? However, I realised that the patients had a hard week with a challenging group program and they were telling me that they needed a space that was FUN! The skill of the therapist was, I felt, in supporting the patients, keeping the group safe and boundaried, and not avoiding the moments when reflection was needed. For example, at Christmas we sang a lot of Christmas carols in the group and at one point a patient became angry that he had to stay in hospital for Christmas. I made reference to Christmas not always being fun, and that perhaps as well as being a time for carol singing, the group could also be a place for people to bring sad thoughts and feelings about what they would miss by being in hospital for Christmas.

The occupational therapy department now funds a music therapist to run this group, individual sessions and a session in the new high dependency unit. When the Irish Chamber Orchestra became the hospital's orchestra in residence, ward staff were also keen to have them perform for patients in the psychiatry unit. In addition to having music therapy, patients now also receive regular performances from the orchestra.

Example four Renal Dialysis Unit, Dublin

I was asked to develop an arts program for patients in the Renal Dialysis unit. Dialysis is a medical process through which a person's blood is cleansed of the toxins the kidneys normally would flush out. It is generally used when a person's kidneys no longer function properly. The patient is hooked up, via a tube in the veins, to a machine that circulates blood through a machine, through semi-permeable filters that take out the toxins in the blood. The procedure usually takes three to four hours and many patients attend the unit three times a week. Dialysis is a life-saving procedure, and patients must show great commitment to their regular visits to hospital.

Patients attend the unit up to three times a week, they are wired up to machines for up to four hours each day and often complain of boredom. I approached the unit with assumptions ready... these patients would benefit from live music being performed on the unit each morning. I imagined a jazz guitarist in the corner of the unit, entertaining patients as they passed a boring day. A day spent observing and talking to patients challenged that assumption completely! Patients said that no, they wouldn't want music performed on the unit, because some patients like to sleep and it would be too disturbing. Instead, those who wanted to listen to music brought their own music with them and listened on headphones. Further discussion and observation led to a group of patients saying that they would like to try painting, while in bed. Staff were unsure, as all patients have at least one arm restricted by their treatment and there was concern that the sessions would be disruptive to the work of the staff. However, the patients had spoken and expressed this wish, so we brought in a visual artist with experience with patients, and gradually some patients started to paint. Two years later, there are three artists working on the unit and staff are involved and supportive of the initiative. This year eight patients, who had never painted before they tried during their dialysis, exhibited their work in an art exhibition in Dublin. The hospital also won a National Health Service Innovation Award for the art groups on the renal dialysis unit. So much for providing music on the unit! Consultation with patients and staff led to the development of a successful visual art program instead.

Organisational Context and Culture

When setting up a new music in healthcare projects or services, one has to consider the organisational culture and the context of the hospital. For example, at AMNCH the hospital had only a little previous experience of arts and health but a very open culture towards piloting new services. As Arts Officer, I could not walk into the hospital and expect management to provide high level funding for arts programs and arts therapists. Instead, I piloted some projects to show the benefit of using arts in the hospital, worked with volunteers for some projects and applied for grants to fund other activities. Staff throughout the hospital were extremely supportive and collaborative so it was easy to get a number of supported projects off the ground and to build organisational experience of the arts and health. The wider context of the Irish health service was important too - at the time I was appointed Arts Officer there was a freeze in spending on health service posts and there were a number of national health priorities that urgently needed more funding. The attitude of the wider society towards music and health is also relevant. Spending money on arts in hospitals had received a couple of negative media reports during the year I was appointed and it was important for me to at least part-fund arts projects from outside core health spending.

In an acute hospital, a musical practitioner, including the music therapist, can only really offer a transitory "moment" to a patient, due to the short stay of the majority of patients. Many of the methods described above have been used at AMNCH because I have found it best to offer patients a one-off space, a good "moment" in an otherwise frightening visit to hospital. For example, a patient attending an outpatient appointment might be nervous about the test they are about to receive, and the arts office offers live performance to distract and relax the patient. In the psychiatry unit, patients normally stay only a couple of weeks, so an open music therapy group is offered as a one-off space for patients to use in whatever way they need to. For example, sometimes patients "let off steam" on the drums, other times they sing songs and have fun, other times we use music to reflect on memories or what is happening for patients in the unit.

However, in a London forensic rehabilitation service patients stay for long periods of time, and so it has been more appropriate to develop an arts therapies department with a psychodynamically informed approach to music therapy groups and individual work. This approach works well in this context and type of setting. The culture of the organisation is one which accentuates the importance of patients engaging in therapy and gaining insight into their illness and offending behaviour before being discharged. This service, where I worked for four years, has informed my practice and my perspective on broadening out what music therapy is, and can be, in different settings. In the acute hospital, however, there are less opportunities to develop long term work with a patient, due to the short stay of most patients, and this drives the development of the music service. However, for patients with long term complex illnesses it may be a very appropriate approach to have available in an acute hospital.

Concluding Thoughts

One can never assume to know what music another person wants to listen to, play or explore. Wherever possible, music needs to be within the control of the patient. Often on wards, the TV or radio is on too much. If it is out of reach of our control it can be highly irritating and inappropriate. When you are in pain, extra noise can be difficult to bear. Choice about attending musical activities or therapy should always be given to the patient and respected.

Using music in a healthcare setting is a highly specialised activity. Making music can be a social activity, bringing together staff and patients and breaking down the traditional hierarchies in hospital. Music therapy can be used, I believe, as a specialised, professional resource within a variety of models of using music in hospital.

Ansdell (2002) argues for a broader practice of music therapy, which he calls Community Music Therapy … "a context-based and music-centred model that highlights social and cultural factors influencing music therapy". The model of the arts office at AMNCH seeks to integrate music therapy and other methods of musical intervention. Above all, it seems important to develop flexibility towards all methods of using music in healthcare and to focus on patient quality of life, rather than battling for territory or professional recognition. Roberts (1994) asks that health professionals "redefine their primary task … to enable patients to live out, their lives in as full, dignified and satisfying a way as possible."

My Best Practice Guidelines for Using Music in Healthcare Settings

1. Assess carefully which type of musical intervention is best used in any clinical environment
2. Develop high level of skill and knowledge in your organisation regarding ALL of the above ways of using music in hospital
3. Develop and insist on the highest standards from musicians working in your organisation.
4. Select your musicians carefully
5. Look for flexibility in approach at all times and be willing to be flexible yourself
6. ASK PATIENTS continually what they need and prefer
7. Talk to staff regularly
8. Evaluate all interventions
9. Above all, BE CREATIVE!

References

Ansdell, G. (2002). Community music therapy and the winds of change [online] *Voices: A World Forum for Music Therapy*. Retrieved March 18, 2005 from
http://www.voices.no/mainissues/voices2(2)ansdell.html
Association of Professional Music Therapists (1995). Music therapy and mental health information booklet, Second Edition, UK.
Beggs, C. (1991). Life review with a palliative care patient. In K. Bruscia (Ed.) *Case studies in music therapy*. Gilsum: Barcelona .
Buenz, J. (2005). Professional Musician speaking at the Society for the Arts in Health International Conference in Edmonton, Canada, June 2005. Retrieved from: www.stanfordhospital.com/forPatients/
Bunt, L. (1994). *Music therapy: An art beyond words*. London: Routledge.
Edwards, J. (2006). Music therapy in the treatment and management of mental disorders. *Irish Journal of Psychological Medicine*, 23, 33-35

Menegazzi, J. J., Paris, P., Kersteen, C., Flynn, B., and Trautman, D. E. (1991). A randomized controlled trial of the use of music during laceration repair. *Annals of Emergency Medicine*, 20, 348-350

Preti, C., and Welch, G.F. (2004). Music in a hospital setting: A multi-faceted experience. *British Journal of Music Education,* 21, 329-345

Roberts, V. (1994). Til death do us part: Caring and uncaring in work with the elderly. In O. Obholzer and V.Z. Roberts (Eds.) *The unconscious at work.* London: Routledge.

Standley, J. (1992). Clinical applications of music and chemotherapy: The effects on nausea and emesis. *Music Therapy Perspectives,* 23, 56-122.

Staricoff, R., Duncan, J., Wright, M., Loppert, S., and Scott, J. (2002). A study of the effects of the visual and performing arts in healthcare. [online] Retrieved 23rd January, 2006 from www.publicartonline.org.uk/archive/research/documents/Chelwesteval .rtf

World Health Organisation definition of health [online] Retrieved 23rd January, 2006 from http:www.who.int/about/definition/en

Appendix One

Assessment Tool - Music and Health

Consider:

Age and sex of patient group

The age and sex of your group will affect what kind of music is most appropriate and what sort of intervention to offer. For example, children will need a structured session whereas a group of older men and women might be more used to a tradition of singing songs together. Men and women may demonstrate a different approach to group work.

Social/cultural context and background

Music appropriate to the person's culture can personalise a health service care plan. For example, one service in London had a predominantly African-Caribbean and Greek patient population, yet the music therapy department was predominantly white English. Introducing musicians from other cultures might provide a more relevant social life on the ward and break down barriers between different cultural groups.

Nature of illness (for example pain levels, motor function and psychological issues)

A group of patients with dementia might benefit from a music therapy group as an alternative means of communication, whereas patients receiving rehabilitation after a stroke might use music to help motivate them to exercise. Some patients will have shorter concentration span and require short sessions; others might be dealing with a neurological diagnosis and need 1:1 therapy to cope with emotional issues surrounding their condition.

Context: Ward culture, staff needs, financial and space restrictions in the environment, group size, time of day, specific location

What is possible in your unit? What money is available? Is the ward culture open to individual music therapy or would they like music performance on the ward? Is there a space suitable for concerts or will musicians need to be flexible and play on the ward? Do ward staff want to improve the atmosphere using pre-recorded music?

Service priorities What are the priorities of senior hospital management? Do these affect your music program? What kinds of music projects will attract funding? What do management need from your service?

Needs of staff, management, visitors and patients: Preferences of staff and patients. Ask patients what they would like, talk to staff to see what is possible and practical.

Appendix Two

Sample Patient Evaluation Form - The Live Music Project

Thank you for agreeing to participate in this evaluation, this questionnaire will take approximately 5 minutes to complete. Your opinion is important to us and therefore all answers are valid. Your information will help to plan future music programs and performances at AMNCH and your confidentiality will be maintained.

Please TICK or CIRCLE the answer(s) that you agree with most and WRITE other answers in the spaces provided. If you require any help, or would like someone to fill the evaluation form in on your behalf please ask one of the volunteers for assistance.

1. Are you   MALE □ or FEMALE □
2. Are you a   Staff member □ Patient □ Visitor □ Other□_____
3. If you are a patient, how long is your hospital stay/visit to date approximately?
4. Were you aware of the live music program at the AMNCH?
Yes □   No□   Unsure □
5. Have you experienced music at the AMNCH before today?
Yes □   No□   Unsure □
6. Please tick the age band you belong to
10–20 □ 20-30□ 30-40 □40-50□ 50-60□   60-70□   70-80□   80-90□
     90+□
7. What type of music to you normally/typically listen to? _____
8. How did you feel *before* the live music performance?
9. How did the live music performance make you *feel*?
(Please circle as many words as you want here)
*Happy *Sad *Depressed *Confident *Relaxed *Stressed *Cared for *Ignored
*Anxious *Hopeful *Bored *Creative *Lonely *Nervous *More pain *Less pain *Negative *Positive *Tired *Energised *Part of an audience *Isolated *Valued *Devalued *Understood *Misunderstood
If there are any *other words* that describe how the music made you feel please write them below
10. Did the music performance make you *do* any of the following?
(Please circle as many words/sentences as you want here)
*Laugh*Cry *Smile *Frown *Dance or Move to the music *Sigh *Hum *Sing

*Clap *Tap your foot/feet *Relax your body *Tense-up your body *Release your worries *Become worried or anxious *Forget your worries temporarily *Bring back/Evoke memories *Distract you from your state of health

*Bring your attention to your state of health *Give you peace of mind *Clutter/confuse your mind *Help you cope with your hospital stay *Make your hospital stay more difficult *Talk to a patient/staff member/visitor/musician you hadn't spoken with before.

11. What did you *most enjoy* about the music performance?

12. What did you *least enjoy* about the music performance?

13. Was *the length* of the music performance?

Perfect □   OK □   Too long □   Too short□

14. What was your impression of the AMNCH *before* the live music performance?

15. What is your impression of the AMNCH *after* the live music performance?

16. What was your *favourite piece of music* that you enjoyed most at the performance?

17. What was your *least favourite piece of music* at the performance?

18. What type of live-music performance would *you personally* like in the hospital if you could chose?

19. What type of live-music performance do you think *other people* would prefer in the hospital?

20. Please give any other comments, suggestions or feedback here.

Thank you for taking time to complete this questionnaire, your answers will be carefully considered and help to inform future music programs at the hospital. Please return this questionnaire to ****.

CHAPTER FOUR

PSYCHOLOGICAL AND PHYSICAL BENEFITS OF PARTICIPATION IN VOCAL PERFORMANCE

BETTY BAILEY AND JANE DAVIDSON

This chapter presents the positive value of musical engagement by reporting descriptions of active, individual, adult participation in group singing activities. Information from three brief case studies show that whilst physical benefits are reported by singing participants, it is the psychological aspects of the activity that are perceived to be particularly important. In summary, this chapter suggests the power of singing as a significant form of multi-layered interpersonal communication for mental and physical well-being.

Background

The science of music therapy, along with the specialist role of the music therapist, has tended to place the health, well-being and curative values of music in a professional domain, which unfortunately has underplayed the everyday benefits of musical participation (Bruscia, 1998). We suggest that this more medicalised approach has marginalised ordinary musical activity from the discourse surrounding the function of music in health and well-being. In a discussion of these matters, Ruud (1997) has usefully identified music "as a potential resource for obtaining a better quality of life" by proposing that music may help individuals achieve greater life satisfaction through stimulating emotional awareness, fostering social and/or task competency, encouraging social and spiritual connection, and strengthening their sense of self. This chapter provides some support for this argument for the role of music. It reports individuals with no health professional training who use music to support many aspects of their personal well-being.

Some of the recent music therapy literature has shown an increased interest in the importance of music as it is commonly integrated into our everyday lives. Aasgaard (1999) has advocated the use of music as an inherent component of institutional and non-institutional settings. He has suggested that when opportunities to engage with music are built into the environment, music can enhance the well-being of those inhabiting the space. Similarly, Aldridge (1999) described how the simplistic gesture of singing to and with a dying friend heightened intimacy and understanding in a situation where words were too painful, too awkward, or inadequate. From a community perspective, Stige (1993) discussed the importance of culturally defined musical practices in shaping the health of the community.

In the academic domains of sociology and psychology, the notion of the therapeutic effects of everyday uses of music is also beginning to receive attention (Bull, 2000; DeNora, 2000; Sloboda, O'Neill and Ivaldi, 2001). The research demonstrates how individuals use music listening as a form of self-administered therapy to adjust the personal environment to meet diverse needs. For example, personal stereos are used to block out intrusive sounds, avoid unwanted affiliation, create an idealised milieu to counteract the mundane living routine, and maintain or alter mood.

The existing literature demonstrates that the therapeutic effects of music may be realised in many diverse, yet ordinary, music experiences, where music becomes a vehicle for positive personal, cultural, and communal expression. One commonplace music activity that is enjoyed in many cultures is singing.

Positive Attributes of Singing as Self-therapy

Psychological benefits of singing have been found, with participants reporting profound emotional experiences, positive self-mood regulating effects, and increased self-esteem (Davidson, 2002). Singing also appears to be a very satisfying activity for the shared emotion and sense of group cohesion reported (Clift and Hancox, 2001). The satisfaction derived from singing does not appear to be dependent on level of expertise, as many amateurs have very limited music training.

The intensity of the positive psychological effects of singing can be seen in a wide range of investigations that have included activities with hospitalised psychiatric patients, through to reports by members of a university choral society. Participants perceived that group singing not only enhanced emotional and social expression, but also physical health, with reports of increased vigour and better breath control (Bunt, 1994; Beck, Cesario, Yousefi and Enamoto, 2000).

Physiological Effects of Singing

A small number of contemporary physiological studies have advanced understanding of the effects of vocal performance through the measurement of levels of 1) secretory immunoglobulin A, and 2) cortisol. Secretory immunoglobulin A (sIgA) is an endocrine defence against bacterial infection in the upper respiratory tract and cortisol is a measure of stress. Generally, increases in levels of sIgA and decreases in levels of cortisol are considered favourable. Studies have shown a significant increase in sIgA following group singing conditions. The cortisol results were variable, with one study reporting a significant decrease occurring during practice but not during performance, and the second study revealing that cortisol decreased significantly between pre and post passive group listening but not between a pre and post group singing condition. Clearly this type of research needs replication to test the robustness of previous findings, however, the increase in sIgA levels suggests that active participation in singing may enhance immune system functioning (Beck, Cesario, Yousefi and Enamoto, 2000; Kreutz, Bongard, Rohrmann, Hodapp and Grebe, 2004).

Previous Research

Over a number of years, we have collected sufficient data and published enough material to be confident that our own lines of investigation in the domain of singing for well-being are both valuable and necessary. Below is a summary of our findings.

Improving the Quality of Life

Three qualitative studies reveal that a range of individuals, including homeless men and other marginalised individuals, used participation in a choral group to facilitate social interaction, and that the activity of performance led them to develop concepts of self-worth and pride which had been formerly annihilated owing to trauma in earlier life (Bailey and Davidson: 2005, 2003, 2002). There were also some indications that whatever a person's former experience, the activity of singing motivated concerns about living better, for example:

Dan: (Participating in the Choir) helped me to stop drinking, get off the welfare and be off the street.

Joan: The choir had about 70 to 75 percent of me being determined and able to lose it (weight) easier, you know, I belong somewhere, like they've accepted me.

The most important results, however, were obtained from two large scale quantitative investigations which look directly at the overall perceived health benefits of singing. Data were collected from over three hundred participants from as far a field as Australia and Iceland (Bailey, 2005).

Perceived Health Benefits

In the first of these two studies, three different types of choirs were investigated, and the effects of 1) group singing, 2) isolated listening (listening to music alone), and 3) social listening (listening to music with others) were compared, utilising a research instrument containing a battery of questions relating to specific cognitive, emotional, physical, life-satisfaction, spiritual and social attributes (Bailey, 2005). Participation in group singing was found to be more beneficial than either isolated or social listening on the majority of test items. These items included: group singing improves my concentration, group singing is an exhilarating experience, group singing gives me a kind of high, and singing improves my mood. However, isolated listening did result in more positive responses to items such as: music helps to suppress emotions, reduce stress and makes me feel mentally rejuvenated. Generally, the research indicates that the activity of group singing promotes heightened arousal on a variety of behavioural dimensions; whereas, isolated listening promotes stress reduction and restoration of a homoeostatic state. It is important to note that all effects were independent of type of choir, years of choral singing, years of music training, age, level of education and gender.

Value of Participation

The second study (Bailey, 2005) compared perceptions of participants from Australia, Brazil, Canada, Hong Kong and Iceland regarding the holistic health effects of 1) group singing, 2) listening to music, 3) watching television, and 4) each participant's preferred activity. Probes to explore the holistic health effects of each of these four activity categories assessed cognitive, emotional, physical, social and spiritual effects. The results indicated that group singing was regarded as being significantly more holistically beneficial than the other activity categories. Similar to the previous study, the effects of music background were negligble, as were gender and home culture. Even when the activity of choice was a physical and group activity like playing volleyball, participants believed that group singing was a more holistically beneficial activity.

Valuing Participation

Another important aspect of the research we wish to emphasise is that related to performance. In our exploration with homeless and marginalised individuals, participation appeared to create a comfortable distance from which the marginalised choristers could begin to develop a relationship with the public and demonstrate that they were much more than their dishevelled appearance might suggest. The public performance arena additionally provided a platform to instruct the larger society about the world of poverty and homelessness. Regardless of socioeconomic status performance seemed to promote feelings of pride for social contribution and personal recognition. In a world in which we are often surrounded by people, but have few opportunities to "stand out" or be noticed, it seems that performance opportunities offered by group singing provides a platform to be noticed and praised within the community, without being too pressurised, as would be the case in a solo performance context.

Summary

The vast majority of the participants in our studies, whether marginalised or privileged, indicated that singing gave them the sense that they were sharing something of themselves with others. This finding demonstrates a key potential positive psychological health benefit of singing. Thus, the existing research, including our own special contribution, shows the positive effects of singing on a number of psychological and physiological measurements. The studies also indicate that health effects including feelings of being more "fit" and "better exercised" are reported by choristers and soloists.

We shall now present three brief case studies to highlight these points. Unlike our previous work where the emphasis has been on fairly conventional choirs, where membership may be the result of an audition or a membership fee, or some sort of other "bonding" arrangement (as was the case with the homeless people), these individuals sing in different types of communal singing contexts. We offer examples of three women of different ages, and life experiences.

Case Studies

The data collected is from three women who discussed the value of singing in their own lives. Their responses are important here for they highlight both the psychological and physical aspects of self-regulation and identity maintenance, and show how these in turn seem to contribute to feelings of "health" and positive sense of wellbeing, especially in the context of performance. They mirror our previous studies, but offer depth with their personal views, and portray singing groups other than the more regular part-song choirs our previous work drew upon.

Approach and Methodology

Smith is eager to remind us that life-history texts depend strongly on the interpretations of the story-teller's memory. Since memories are stored for reasons that are important to someone, where details are rich, the memories are genuinely important to the storytellers. So, the subjectivity of the life-history we report here is its significance. The life-history interviews comprised the following structure: the interviewee was encouraged to describe her vocal-life in her own words, in an extensive and informal interview. The interviewee adopted a chronological approach, though she did not just describe the facts, but also reflections on personal feelings and meanings related to her singing. Interviews were transcribed, before being subjected to coding and "verification" by a third party. To respect confidentiality, pseudonyms are used.

Nancy

Nancy is 46 years old and is married with two young daughters. She is a high achieving professional white woman, holding down a full-time job in the City of London. Her husband has a busy and very well-paid job in an allied field. They have a part-time helper who takes their children to and from school and takes care of many domestic arrangements such as meals and housekeeping. Prior to her current job, Nancy was a primary school teacher and during this time, she became part of a parent-teacher singing group which focuses on Afro-Caribbean popular singing such as reggae, folk, and work songs. Ten years since leaving teaching, she still sings with the group. It rehearses once a week at the school, and gives three concerts a year: one at the school, as a fund-raiser for the school; one at the local community centre, along with several other groups; and one at the local church just before Christmas, joining with the gospel group there.

Marilyn

Marilyn is 63 years old; she is a widow with one grownup daughter. She is a working class woman, and though now retired, she was a sewing machinist in a dress factory. She is active in her church, and besides regular attendance, she participates in the gospel group which sings every Sunday, and rehearses on Wednesday evenings. She is of Afro-Caribbean origin.

Eleanora

Eleanora is 16 years old. Her mum and dad run a delicatessen store, and work long hours. Ellie is still at school and hopes to study hairdressing. She loves pop music, and sings in two groups, 1) a "girl band", comprising herself and three school friends, and 2) a Greek Cypriot folk/rock band. The "girl band" has been formed recently, and though it practices regularly, so far it has not given a concert. The folk-rock band often plays at the Greek restaurant next door to her parents' shop.

The second author, Jane, met these three women as they all happened to be performing in the same community centre event. They were selected at random from the performing groups at the event. Although the women are of different ages, experiences, cultures and class backgrounds, their thoughts, feelings and experiences as singers are similar, mirroring many themes from our earlier studies.

Echo themes: Improving the quality of life; Perceived health benefits; Value of participation; Valuing participation

There were many instances of these echo themes, and for illustration, one substantial quoted excerpt from each interviewee is offered as an illustration.

Perhaps, not surprisingly, Marilyn offers reflective comments on what singing has offered her:

> Well, as a little girl, I was always singing because it was just a part of being a kid in Trinidad: in the street singing with friends and for games; at school, in church, round at Auntie's. You name the place, and we were singing at it. I never had opportunities to learn a musical instrument, but I don't think that was important because I had my instrument with me all the

time. It was me, a core part of me, and it still is. I could make my music whenever I wanted [...]

I'm quite a shy person, so I would never dare to be a leader sort of person, and really my husband used to take care of most things. But, when he died, I decided that I would involve myself much more with my music. So I got a lot more involved at church, and especially in the Gospel group. Since I've got back to singing, I feel like things are better; my life is more complete [...]

Of course, it [singing] gets me out of the house, and I'm always with my friends, but for me, the important thing is that I feel better about myself, and so my life. Doing singing is like my daily fitness routine. Imagine me doing the dusting and singing all those fantastic songs. I get a buzz in my mind and my body![...]

If I tell you the truth, when I sing I feel that Bert [her deceased husband] can hear me [her eyes well with tears]. [Pause.] I think I sort of send him my love in my singing.

Ellie values many similar physical, emotional and spiritual aspects of singing:

Music at school is BAD. It has no life: you know, those boring assembly things [...]

Singing with my friends is great. Well, we feel together, close. Sometimes we start messing around making up songs and then we'll all be laughing or even sobbing with it all. I mean, singing let's your heart fly [...]

I quite like the Greek singing because it reminds me of Cyprus and stuff like that. The other thing is that you just can't keep still when you hear those tunes – they're like, so cool. I just want to dance and dance. None of the girls in the band are Cypriot, so they think it is kinda good that my music is so fun and it just gets you dancing and crazy stuff like that [...]

Music moves me. It shakes me. You could say it is good for you – gets you active [...] It is much better than watching TV and that sort of thing.

Singing is also vital to her sense of self, certainly as a performer:

When I stand up and sing I feel good. I feel special. I am a better person when I do my singing.

Nancy:

I can't believe I've been in this group for 10 years now. Mick [her husband] says it "keeps me sane", and I think he's right. It is such a good de-stressor. There's something special about making harmony together with other people: it sort of improves me. I feel so much more "together" after the singing. I suppose I could just do it alone – sort of in the bath – but being with those people who are all so different. I mean we just come together in the music. I like it […]

I think singing should be compulsory. Seriously, I wish my girls did more singing generally, but especially at school ! […]

Oh, but in addition to singing, you need to get out there and perform. Singing out loud for others, that gives you a chance to show off, without using spoken words!

As for singing for physical health, Nancy intriguingly adds:

Oh, I'm a bit of a health "nut". I try to play tennis at the local club with my friends. I think we're a "fit" sort of family. I mean we eat "whole" foods, and try to go for walks in the parks round here at the weekends. The difference between really doing a thing like tennis as opposed to singing is that the tennis focuses mainly on the physical thing: the sort of dexterity, mental agility thing. It can also be competitive, which singing is not for me. Singing is about being with people, not trying to beat them.[…]

In singing you need physicality, even fitness, but it ALWAYS has this sort of meaningful empathy thing with the other people: being in it together. Also, your singing voice is a sort of different aspect of you. It is a bit only people experience when you decide to sing. It's not like walking or running or speaking. I mean all that stuff is just "boring and normal". Singing has a special "flying" quality to it.

Nancy's ideas about singing and physical health are intriguing. Clearly, the psychological aspect of this being a way of extending yourself physically, without being in competition with your collaborator was important, however, we were particularly interested in the "special" sort of offering the activity of singing gave Nancy. It is as if singing, though a normal activity – in the sense that everyone is capable of singing – had the potential to make her feel special, to transport her sense of who she is or who she can be to a different place. This could be a comment of a similar type to Marilyn's parallel between singing and spirit: she speaks about the spiritual nature of singing to bring her "closer" to her deceased husband. The singing voice seems to transport Marilyn to a different dimension.

Though these are ideas, and imagined constructs of the women, the metaphors used to describe the experience of singing such as "flying" imply the transporting/transformational aspects referred to by all the participants in our previously mentioned studies. Perhaps there is a beneficial psychological and even physical function of singing; and one that makes it so potentially powerful. That is, besides enabling emotional release, physical arousal, social communion; perhaps it also offers a personal sense of transformation: a shift of the sense of what you experience.

It is significant to note that the three singers are adamant about the value of the vocal activity and the group setting, especially performance itself. No doubt social dynamics have a strong role to play in the experiences the women report, however, we cannot ignore the fact that the vocal activity per se is of great significance to them. In addition to the mirrored themes raised in the opening of this chapter, Marilyn, Ellie and Nancy permit us to note how singing offered a means of developing personal identity. Singing offers a niche, and connection that made each woman feel special and valued.

Concluding Note

The interview data presented in this chapter reveals that singing offers individual participants a positive sense of well-being. This well-being seems to include spiritual and emotional feelings, cognitive and physical arousal, and satisfying social connection. In addition to this, group singing (whatever the type explored here – gospel, pop, folk and choral) provides a performance forum that is exciting and uniting without being stressful.

Davidson (2002) has spoken about the performer's personality, and how offering an outwardly focused communication of self to an audience can be an empowering and importantly validating part of self-identity. If singing in a group can offer an individual participant this, as well as, the sense of closeness and sharing between other singers, it seems to have very powerful benefits at the social level.

We hope that this brief chapter has offered food for thought about the power of singing. A concluding thought is that we have developed cultural contexts in which we use singing as a means of regulating our personal and group behaviours: singing at ceremonies of various kinds; singing to aid work patterns and increase productivity; singing to excite or sooth physical activity – fighting, sleeping etc. According to Trevarthen (1999; 2000), the root of these positive culturally mediated effects of singing lies in the mother-infant interaction which enables mutual emotional soothing and consonance, social interaction and communication. It is regrettable that in our currently high-pressured career-oriented world that many people do not permit themselves the time or opportunity to engage in an activity that is affirming and holistically beneficial. More pitiful is that in many Western cultural contexts where high achievement and professionalism often remove people from activities such as singing, people become afraid to sing or to use their singing voices when it is such a natural and self-regulating force. When we think of music, health and therapy, it would seem necessary to also integrate the concept of group sharing and performance.

References

Aasgaard, T. (1999). Music therapy as milieu in the hospice and paediatric oncology ward. In: D. Aldridge (Ed.) *Music therapy in palliative care: New voices* (pp. 29-42). London: Jessica Kingsley.
Aldridge, D. (1999). Music therapy and the creative act. In D. Aldridge (Ed.) *Music therapy in palliative care: New voices* (pp. 15-28). London: Jessica Kingsley.
Bailey, B. (2005). Singing out of tune and in tune: An investigation of the effects of amateur group singing from diverse socio-economic and cultural perspectives. Doctoral dissertation, University of Sheffield.
Bailey, B., and Davidson J.W. (2005). Music as adaptive behaviour. *Psychology of Music*. 33, 269-303.
Bailey, B., and Davidson, J.W. (2003). Amateur group singing as a therapeutic agent. *Nordic Journal of Music Therapy*, 12, 18-32.
Bailey, B., and Davidson, J.W. (2002). Group singing as adaptive behaviour: Perceptions from members of a choir of homeless men. *Musicae Scientiae*, VI: 221-256.
Bailey, B., and Davidson, J.W. (2001). Singing as adaptive behaviour. Proceedings of Phenomenon of Singing III, Festival 500: Sharing the Voices, St John's, Newfoundland, Canada, June, pp. 25-29.
Beck, R, Cesario, T., Yousefi, S., and Enamoto, H. (2000). Choral singing, performance perception and immune system changes in salivary immunoglobulin and cortisol. *Music Perception*, 18, 87-106.
Bruscia, K. (1998). *Defining music therapy* (2nd ed.). Gilsum: Barcelona.
Bull, M. (2000). *Sounding out the city*. New York: Berg.
Bunt, L. (1994). *Music therapy: An art beyond words*. New York: Routledge.
Clift, S., and Hancox, G. (2001). The perceived benefits of singing: findings from preliminary surveys of a university college choral society. *The Journal of the Royal Society for the Promotion of Health*, 121, 4, 248-256.
Davidson, J. W. (2002). The solo performer's identity. In: R. MacDonald, D. Hargreaves and D. Miell, (Eds.) *Musical identities* (pp. 97-113). Oxford: OUP.
DeNora, T. (2000). *Music in everyday life*. Cambridge:CUP.

Kreutz, G., Bongard, S., Rohrmann, S., Hodapp, V., and Grebe, D. (2004). Effects of choir singing or listening on secretory immunoglobulin A, cortisol, and emotional state. *Journal of Behavioral Medicine*, 27 (6), 623 - 635.

Ruud, E. (1997). Music and the quality of life. *Nordic Journal of Music Therapy, 6*, 86-97

Sloboda, J. A., O'Neill, S. A., and Ivaldi, A. (2001). Functions of music in everyday life: An exploratory study using the experience sampling method. *Musicae Scientiae*, 5, 9-32.

Stige, B. (1993). Changes in the music therapy "space" - with cultural engagement in the local community as an example. *Nordic Journal of Music Therapy*, 2, 11-22.

Trevarthen, C. (2000). Musicality and the intrinsic motive pulse: Evidence from human psychobiology and infant communication. *Musicae Scientiae, Special Issue, 1999-2000*, 2, 155-215.

CHAPTER FIVE

HEALTH MUSICKING AS CULTURAL INCLUSION

KARI BATT-RAWDEN, SUSAN TRYTHALL AND TIA DENORA[1]

At Exeter, there are a number of on-going projects concerned with the arts, especially music, identity and action within a research group in arts sociology.[2] In this chapter we will describe two of these studies that deal explicitly with music, the self and well-being. Both focus on innovative forms of musicking, (Small, 1998) and both explore the affordances of musical activity for communicative action and for the care and restoration of the self. These forms of musicking provide resources for the recovery of self-identity; understood here as musically afforded opportunities for 1) interaction, 2) reminiscence, and 3) the adoption of roles and emotions through musical activity.

We begin by considering the social disruption posed by illness. We then present material from the two studies which we use to highlight a "grey" but increasingly emerging area in music provision/participation, between "therapeutic" and "everyday" musicking (Aasgaard 2002; 2004; Stige, 2003; Davidson and Bailey; 2004; Pavlicevic and Ansdell; 2004; Edwards; 2005; O'Callaghan, 2004; Rolvsfjord, 2004; Ruud; 2004; 2005; Magee; 2005). Our aims are 1) to highlight how this musicking employs culturally innovative strategies designed to engage individuals who are otherwise isolated through illness, and 2) to describe how music is not

---

[1] Thanks for comments to Sophia Acord and Arild Bergh.
[2] Sophia Acord, *Unearthing the Code*; Kari Batt Rawden, *Music and Health Promotion*; Arild Bergh, *Music and Conflict Transformation in three cultures*; Simon Procter, *Music Therapy: What is it for whom?* Ian Sutherland, *Music and Genocide: composers' strategies in Nazi Germany*; Susan Trythall: *Music, Well-Being and Health Promotion: An ethnographic study of the work of Music in Hospitals*.

only a vehicle of identity maintenance but a medium through which social connections are forged. We conclude by suggesting that the ambiguities highlighted by these practices challenge our very notions of what counts as music and musical participation.

Illness as Isolation and Exclusion: Musicking as Inclusion and Health-Promotion

Illness, as many have observed, is doubly disruptive. First, it is debilitating, it disrupts the individual's ability to complete ordinary routines (for example, to move freely and be mobile, and in some cases, to live in a non-medicalised dwelling). Second, illness is often estranging: it partitions friends and loved ones and sequesters the sick from their everyday life worlds and social networks. This sequestering is spatial but it is also temporal; it divides the "sick" individual from the on-going social times and thus from the opportunity of sharing and shaping those times in the flux of here-and-now.

Illness imperils our ability to make, communicate and share meaning, pleasure, and emotion. To speak of this matter points in turn to critical questions about cultural participation and the ways in which illness acts as a barrier to continued participation.[3] Participating in culture – whether through consumption or production[4] is, we believe, the means through which we connect with others, the way we tell each other that we are not alone but are *together*.[5]

Our research looks specifically at the important role that participation in music, and with reference to the arts in general, is able to play in fostering opportunities for participation in the on-going making of meanings when capacities for ordinary forms of cultural participation may be impaired. Our research suggests that, through these quasi-therapeutic forms of musicking, individuals may construct ontological security (Giddens, 1991), regaining a sense of coherence (Antonovsky, 1986;

---

[3] In recent years, these matters have been broached through a focus on health, social capital and cultural participation (e.g., Putnam 2000), and through a growing body of research attuned to the interaction of health and environment (Freund 2001)

[4] We do not view these activities as distinct, since watching a film but then talking about it with others is active meaning production.

[5] This issue is perhaps most pressing when, as in the case of chronic and progressive illness, the optimistic and future oriented narratives of illness and outcome cannot be used so as to bracket illness as "a phase".

1996) and community when life is disrupted by illness or disease (Batt-Rawden and Tellnes, 2005).

Normally, when we think about arts distribution (as opposed to the arts therapies) and the question of social inclusion, we think about how to deliver "disabled" or socially "disadvantaged" people to sites of cultural participation. Looking at the "problem" this way round, the "solution" is pursued by various adaptations to *physical* access – the installation of ramps, elevators, sur-titles, and hearing loops for example in arts performance contexts. Setting aside here the fact that many seriously ill people cannot, practically and without risk to their health, be brought to these sites, strategies of inclusion that deal only with physical access tend to conceive of the challenge in material-technical, rather than, more radically, social and presentational terms. No thought, in other words, is given to the question of what forms of artistic media, and what forms of presentation of these media, might be best suited or most "fit" for constituencies of "sick" people

And yet, if illness disrupts many of the *non-physical* capacities that otherwise allow us to appropriate culture, then, no amount of audio-technology, concert hall redesign, or wheelchair accessibility, for example, will ensure that music or a conventional gallery display will actually manage to "reach" people with Alzheimer's disease or severe depression, or whose attention fluctuates because they are in pain, or those with partial sight (Hetherington 2002; 2003). Something different – adaptation, innovation – is called for in these cases where the delivery of "ordinary" music-presentational formats (for example, staging an opera or performing a symphony) may not meet the needs of these "audiences". Just as we might not set a tough-textured meal in front of an invalid who can no longer chew, so too, we might need to redesign the ways that the arts, as opportunities for cultural participation, are offered to the seriously ill, but in ways that stop short of traditional "therapy".

As we describe below, we have been investigating how it is possible to reverse the "problem" of how to make musical culture accessible to the seriously ill, by thinking about how to adapt musical forms themselves, in particular, how to adapt the modes through which music is presented to these constituencies. In short, much greater attention should be devoted to what we consider to be a new or at least different mode of musicking (Small, 1998), one that occupies the currently grey area in between ordinary, everyday life forms of musicking (for example, private listening, concert attendance, amateur musical performance) and music therapy. We think this ambiguity of what we will now describe is attractive – is it "therapeutic" or is it "ordinary culture consumption"? – precisely because uncertainties such as these help to erode the barriers between the specialised enclave that "therapy" (treatment)[6] occupies and the open territory of "everyday" musicking (for example, having some fun). For example: we are probably all engaged at times as recipients or providers of therapeutic musicking (sometimes both simultaneously).

Two Studies - Musical Participation in and out of Hospital

The first study (Trythall 2006; Trythall on-going) is organised around the work of the UK's Council for Music in Hospitals.[7] It examines live music performances in alternative venues – hospitals, hospices and care homes. The study focuses on care-centre concerts as specific types of musical-social event, and on the experience of this event by patients, carers, their families and others (including the researcher herself). The research has consisted of participant observation at concerts in hospitals, care centres and hospices, observation of auditions, interviews with musicians, Music in Hospitals Staff, carers and medical staff and, where possible, patients and analysis of the Music in Hospitals media and documents.

A sub-aim of the study that we will emphasise here, is to identify some of the many and varied skills mobilised by hospital musicians in the crafting of this event and this deployment provides resources that helps residents convert themselves from "patient" to "audience member" to "participant" during the temporal course of the concert event. How, in other words, do musicians adapt concert conventions so as to "reach" their audiences?

The second study (Batt-Rawden and Tellnes 2005a; Batt-Rawden and DeNora 2005; Batt-Rawden, DeNora and Ruud 2006; Batt-Rawden and Aasgaard 2006; Batt-Rawden, 2006) deals with musical participation as a strategy for health promotion. A piece of action research, the project drew together a sample of 22 Norwegian participants[8] who were interviewed

---

[6] and all the power dynamics associated with this term (see Procter 2004)
[7] The idea for the Council for Music in Hospitals was conceived in 1946 by Shelia McCreery and, after gaining financial aid and much advice from the medical profession, became established in 1948.
[8] Participants in the study were between 34 and 65 years of age, nine men and 13 women, of different socio-economic status. These were people suffering or recovering from some form of chronic illness (muscular disease, neurological disease, cancer, anxiety or depression, chronic fatigue), all of whom had previous experience of active music making (though some had to curtail musical activity

eight times over the course of a year. During this time, each participant was asked to contribute to the production of a series of CD compilations in which they shared, through the researcher as mediator, their musical loves, associations and memories. The point of the project was less to find out about "how" they experienced music then to use this question as a springboard into a project of informal learning, to help participants discover and rediscover how to use music as a "technology of the self" (DeNora, 1999, p. 46) and thus also as a "cultural immunogen" (Ruud, 2002).

In both these cases, we understand music to provide a medium that *can be adapted to afford* particular types of *connections*. The shape these connections take is potentially unlimited. They may include connections between: a) ill individuals themselves, b) ill individuals, musicians and other people (such as carers, family members, friends, medical staff), c) ill individuals, music and musical activity and meaningful/emotional responses (memories, values), and d) individuals, music and musical activity and embodiment (for example, breathing more easily during music, toe-tapping or finger snapping, relaxing, falling asleep, energised).

We think it is important in these cases that the musicking is decidedly *not* identified as therapeutic – though undoubtedly functions therapeutically and, as we describe in the next session, partakes of the music therapist's craft. Framing this therapeutic interaction as "ordinary" is, we believe, vital to its ability to provide bridges back to "normal" cultural participation and to the aspects of identity that exceed a person's illness.

Getting Music to People

The following passages are taken from Trythall's field notes and deal with one concert, which took place before lunchtime in a hospice. We think they are self-explanatory in the way that they chronicle the musicians' attempts to afford group experience and to forge an occasion – a concert, here, for us – in real time. We begin with the perhaps inauspicious circumstances under which the concert began. How, then, do musicians, through their conduct as particular types of musicians at a particular type of concert manage to draw individuals in to a shared event?

> 10.55… We then walked into the room where all the noise had been coming from and I was, once again, hit by the nauseating smell…As I

---

due to illness – ten played or sang, the remaining twelve were involved in folk clubs, choirs, concert attendance and home-listening.

looked around the room I noticed that of all the patients who I could see, almost all of them had catheter bags visible.....There were twenty people in the room, more women than men, many of them were asleep and one woman was singing hymns loudly. The television was on, the volume was loud, and it was showing a well known daytime programme.... I sit next to the door, looking into the room, and am beside two patients, one female, one male, who are both asleep, the woman is snoring.

11.00 The two musicians ("Helen' and "David")[9] arrive. After saying hello to me [they knew the researcher from a previous concert and interview at this stage] and having a general chat about how things are going, Helen starts setting up the instruments, David is taking his 'cello out from the case in the hall. A few patients wake up and as Helen is sorting her violin out, she talks to the woman who is still singing a hymn.

11:05 Some patients in the front row, all women, are talking to each other. A few others are shouting out randomly and the TV is still on...

11:10 Helen turns the TV off, David checks his guitar tuning and the woman is still singing although it is hard to make out exactly what. David then introduces them and talks about where they are from etc. Woman still singing as they are talking. Helen says they are going to play some Celtic music and "please feel free to clap along, stamp your feet, even have a dance". A male patient asks why they have turned the telly off, David laughs and then Helen says laughing, "it's because we don't like being ignored" (a few people laugh), David then says they will "turn it back on after the concert". The man says, "ok but don't forget please."[10] Helen starts playing and immediately gets up and walks/dances around the room smiling at all the patients. Two female patients in front row start clapping albeit not in time, and the woman with the balloon is smiling and starts waving the balloon in time. This seems to upset the man sitting next to her, he keeps frowning at her and trying to move his head, the balloon keeps blocking his view. The singing woman starts becoming more vocal, again just random "notes" another patient shouts "wee-hooo". Helen smiles back at him and echoes him using her voice, he smiles....

11:15.Helen, who has raised her voice (gently however) to talk above the noise, says that they are going to play a song which might help the sun come out, she then immediately starts strumming the intro to "Summertime", announces the song and tells everyone to sing along even if they don't know the words; David accompanies her on 'cello. Most of the patients seem calmer and are either watching them or focusing on their plastic beakers of tea. The atmosphere seems more relaxed....

---

[9] These are pseudonymns.

[10] When a carer asked him at the end whether he had enjoyed the concert he said, "no, I don't like music".

Note that over the roughly twenty minutes that have passed so far, Helen and David have begun to prepare a social situation. They have a) socially acknowledged the woman who is singing to herself (which Helen tells us, when asked later about the incident, that she probably did by asking the woman if she was willing to join in with some group singing), b) negotiated the turning off the television, c) supplied quite a bit of information about themselves and what they are about to do (transparency; reciprocity), d) chosen an opening number suitable for masking the disparate sounds that otherwise pose a threat to establishing a shared musical situation ("please feel free to clap along, stamp your feet, even have a dance"), and e) provided visual material also oriented to this goal - Helen in motion, walking and dancing around the room (so as to greet everyone [showing respect] and also make a bid for attention).

Within this same period of time, having managed to establish a degree of collective focus, they perform a second piece "Summertime", that takes the energy level back down, allowing the nascent "audience" to begin to focus on itself *as* a "focused audience". Under very difficult circumstances, these musicians found their way through to what is emerging after fifteen minutes as an audience, a group of people with a collective focus of attention, individuals being (in and among music) together.

This minor miracle did not happen by chance. It was achieved in and through the ways that Helen and David presented themselves to and interacted with this group of, initially, disparate people, through their selection of appropriate pieces of music for the local circumstances, and through how they, and Helen in particular,[11] used their performance to redefine that situation, to bring it from seeming chaos into partial order. We see this particular combination of musical performance plus attention to care needs repeatedly in Music in Hospital concerts.[12] An example from the same observation puts this in context:

> 11:25. ...The woman at the back covered in the blanket was still sleeping. Helen was walking around the room singing and making lots of contact with those at the back of the room who had their backs to us; from where I was I could not see if there was any visible response from them. She also

---

[11] Helen functions as the 'front person' of the group, tending to move around more than David who plays the cello and therefore needs to sit. He also plays piano and guitar. . Note the versatility of these musicians.
[12] In her work-in-progress, Trythall describes the rigorous process of a Music in Hospitals audition and their 'ground rules' for performance (e.g., no reading music, all from memory, make eye contact, etc).

smiled at the sleeping woman and I noticed she sang more quietly in that area of the room....

We see that attention to care needs again in the next passage, when Helen insures that mugs are not tipped over and then offers contextualisation cues (DeNora, 1986) about how one might participate in the next piece, which helps to coalesce the event as an occasion, as participation, inclusion. She does this by modelling a "mood" and mode of action for her "audience" (see the passages emphasised below in italics):

11:29. After a short hushed conversation with David, Helen jumped up and said, "right, here's one for you all to join in but only if you have finished your tea". She then walked over to the carers and then they started to remove then empty cups and mugs. While they were doing that, David was playing a rhythmical plucked bass line ("Fever")on the 'cello, the man sitting next to me started humming along and tapping his arthritic hands on his knees, Helen *was sitting down, smiling and tapping her feet.* David kept changing the key getting higher with each section and you could see this was getting the attention of more patients, some were tapping their feet, another man was clicking his fingers, the atmosphere was changing through the bass line to one of expectancy and anticipation. Now that all the cups had been removed, Helen *suddenly jumped up and loudly said "FEVER!" and starts singing immediately.* Most of the able bodied patients were now clapping and singing along, the lady at the back was still asleep under her blanket. Many people were smiling. This felt good.
Every time Helen sang the word "fever" she thrust her arms up into the air in a dramatic way. By now, the rain was teeming down outside, Helen *said loudly, "we'll have to do better than this if we are going to drown the noise of the rain out" (it was beating down on the plastic roof). She then started dancing round the room, singing more enthusiastically,* David was moving in time and had a smile on his face. Finally, it seemed that this was a good time, a good place to be in, the atmosphere was happy, even the patients seemed to be interacting with each other more. *She then danced to the back of the room, once again making sure that everyone is involved in the concert.* Suddenly, the woman under the blanket sits up and seems aware of where she is but not awake. The room was full of applause at the end and [one woman] bangs her hands on her knees and shouts "more". Many people were smiling. Helen then sat down, looked at David and grinned....

At this stage, half an hour in, and halfway through the concert, Helen, David and the participants have established a collective event, a mutual tuning in. People have also had fun, pleasure, exercise, and opportunity to engage in reflection, remembering and emotional experience. This is collective effervescence in Durkheim's sense (1965 [1912]). This social emergence was, we venture, known to all, the musicians and the researcher, as seen in the field notes, included. It was now a feature of the newly constructed context that could be used as a resource and, in their choice of the next piece – slow, "classical", quiet – David can be seen to hold, as it were, a musical mirror up to this collective, enabling perception of the focus that is now a characteristic of this "community":

> 11:36 David (who had been re-tuning his cello quietly while the room became quieter), then tells us he is going to play something classical, "The Swan". He explains where the piece comes from and shows, using his bow in the air, how the melody makes the shape of a swan. The room is very still, people are focused on David, some even seem to be swaying in time with him including Helen.....

Note how David also uses bodily techniques to help his audience relate to (connect with) and appreciate this cello piece. As bodily beings, we do not need to have scholarly knowledge of this music to be able to relate to it in terms of how a swan – and David – move. We can find ways of relating to the music very simply, and perhaps in ways that reflect initial creative impulses of the composer and the embedding of the body in these strands of musical discourse which the composer taps: the shape of the swan, its gliding motion, and perhaps many other *possible* connections and sensations.[13]

It is at this stage, we think, that the musicians begin to be able to tap the resources of this group's situation, for example, in the next excerpt we think we see how individual's "dis"-abilities [sic] are actually mobilised by Helen to give the music a meaningful (and for us at least, poignant) frame – this music, indeed, "our" music, music that could not be more "fitting" for this place, here, now:

> [around 11.43] The room was silent when the piece was over and almost immediately, as if sensing the atmosphere David started the introduction to "Moon River" (11:45am)....A couple of patients were singing along.

---

[13] See Sophia Acord (2006) who describes how high level curators understand their work often in bodily, pre-verbal, pre-cognitive terms but, when asked to 'explain' that work to others, including members of the public, they turn to more formal, theoretical accounts. Indeed, their first 'glimmers' of how something might take shape are often linked to particular gestures or fleeting – and often mundane – images that serve as holding forms for what they then seek to elaborate through their work (see Atkinson forthcoming also on this point). The embodied codes, however, have potential – if explored in depth – to draw arts appreciation/understanding out to new constituencies.

Helen stands up and sings as she is walking slowly around the room, looking each patient in the eyes, touching their hands or shoulders. One nurse walks over to the back of the room, looks out of the window and sings along. [around 11.46] Helen's voice [she is singing "Moon River"] is very quiet and gentle and she sits down next to the now sleeping woman. The nurse looks at her and smiles, she winks back. Gentle applause at the end and one female patient said "lovely".

Perhaps the greatest skill of these musicians is how they enable/encourage their "audience members" to be skilful themselves, for example, to be musicians also, and to be able to engage in creative musical/social strategies that add important dimensions to the performance. All of this happens using what ever is to hand, it is improvised and seems to occur spontaneously but the confidence to be active, and to help to make/shape these musical times has been established with great craft, a craft that involves featuring opportunities for focus, expression, pleasure and back-grounding or erasing those things that detract from these opportunities:

11:47. "Now for a reel, I want to hear you all clapping along". Helen dances over to the back of the room, playing her violin, and faces David. People start clapping and smiling, a nurse dances into the room and the smartly dressed man sitting next to me walks over to a male nurse in the doorway, speaks to him and comes and sits down again with a smile on his face. Helen makes full use of the room dancing and playing, the room was alive again. The male nurse comes into the room and hands the man two spoons!, more people were clapping and smiling. He then, with a pained look on his face, carefully places the spoons in one hand and begins to play them first on his knee then on his hand and then on his knees again, by this time Helen has walked over and they are playing a duet together. Helen gives him solo passages, this is so much fun. He then becomes more cheeky and plays them on the leg of the female nurse who is now sitting next to him, she grins! This was infectious, energising and happy. Patients were smiling, even those who had just been sitting with their eyes closed and/or asleep seemed to be reacting. The woman who had been asleep next to me looked at me and smiled. The piece seemed never ending, and I certainly did not want it to end, there was an atmosphere of fun, party-like, everyone involved. There was incredible applause and cheers at the end, and the man stood up and took a bow. He then gave the spoons back to the nurse and sat down smiling. Helen shook him by the hand.

It also involves knowing how and when to use musical genres, and particular pieces, to afford ambience and mood. And this in turn is a vital part of what makes for successful beginnings, good middles and good endings, since part of what marks an occasion as an occasion is its temporal structure:

> 12:03 Helen sits down, picks up her guitar and says, "I'm going to sing a slow country song now, if you know it (here she looks across and me, smiles and winks) don't be shy, please sing along." "Speed the sound of loneliness" (we had talked about this song on a previous occasion when I mentioned that it is one of my favourites). The room is mostly quiet aside from a few people humming, me included!, people swaying in time to the pizzicato bass line, faces looking contented. A few more nurses quietly walked into the room, one very young male nurse went and took over from the nurse who was holding the woman. Two more nurses come in and start giving patients medicine however this does not seem to disturb the room, thank goodness. The woman on my right started making grunting noises. Helen, who is walking round the room singing by this time, walks over, kneels down in front of her and immediately the woman goes quiet. A room alarm is sounding down the corridor but no one in the room seems to notice it (aside from the nurse who leaves to attend).Helen then gets up and continues walking around the room acknowledging, touching, smiling at every single patient even if they had their eyes closed. It was incredibly moving to watch her give so much care to so many, even though the concert, as they said afterwards, had been incredibly hard work. Not one patient or nurse was left out, or me for that matter. There was no break; at the end of the song, they went straight into "Wonderful World". She continues to walk round the room, some patients were singing and even the young male nurse was singing along. Some patients seemed to be falling asleep, some were looking sleepy, most of those who were awake were smiling. It felt calm, it felt as though everything was going to be alright. A very different feel from other parts of what had been, for the musicians, a very difficult concert….

Music Listening as Participation and Reconnection with "Self" or "Others"

We now turn to Batt-Rawden's study also about providing user-participant appropriate opportunities for musical participation, albeit this time with a virtual community and focused mostly around private music listening. As described above, this study was developed through a series of eight in-depth interviews with 22 participants over the course of one year. Methodologically this time period enabled rich data sources but in action research terms it was also to forge relationships between participants and the researcher, and, virtually, through the mediator of the researcher and the CDs produced, between participants themselves).

During the year, each participant received, at bi-monthly intervals, four double CDs and two single CDs. The project began with the presentation of CD 1: "Keepsakes and Memories". This was a CD compiled by the researcher and combined eight tracks representing one of four typical musical tastes in Norway (folk/country, pop songs, classical music, jazz and blues) all of special significance to the researcher herself (for example, reflecting childhood memories, and "happy moments" of music performing and music listening. Choosing pieces significant to the researcher was also a way of "showing" how musical narratives were part of the researchers' own "care of self" and to offer up something personal to the research participants, thus seeking to establish reciprocity. The first CD acted as an icebreaker and a diversion which provided a pretext for further talk, show-and-tell and started to unfold participant's interests, opinions, and values at a very early stage.

From this point on and starting with interview number two; every other interview would involve the distribution of a new CD. With the exception of the final CD (a "farewell" gift from the Researcher at project's end), these CDs featured tracks chosen by *each participant* (in other words, all participants were equally active in designing the content of these CDs, and came to know of each others' existence through each others' musical choices as "shared" virtually with the group). Each CD was oriented to a particular "theme". Themes two through six were:

CD 2 (double): Music, its significance for me and why

Music selected by participants for inclusion that had some special significance for them. They were asked to explain that significance and the reasons for their choice.

CD 3 (double): My Mood

Participants were asked: Would you be able to describe your mood when you chose which piece of music to go on the CD 3? Why? Is it possible to connect your current life situation with your choice of music? If so, why? How? Are there any events since last time we met that might relate to the chosen piece of music?

CD 4 (double): Feeling at Your Best

Participants were asked: When you have been feeling at your best these last few weeks, could you tell me what piece of music you have been using? How? Then select a favourite. Why? What is it about the piece of music you have been using?

CD 5 (double): All Time Best

Which piece of music makes you feel better or creates an increased sense of well-being? How or in what way is this experienced and why?

CD 6 (single): Parting Gift (chosen by the Researcher)

From stage to stage, as the CDs were distributed and discussed, the participants were encouraged to think about and describe musicking and the ways they used it to promote their own health. The various stages in this process highlight how participants' came to produce *for themselves but with resources and models offered by the researcher* modes of conscious awareness of music's "powers" and skills of musical use over the course of the year-long project phase and, in the process, adjusting themselves and changing their environments and habits in light of this new consciousness, this new skill set for musicking.

It is important to note that, as in the music in hospitals, it was not music, per se, that achieved the outcome of connecting, of social recovery. Rather, that was the collective product of the musickers involved (performers, interviewer, participants) though it was greatly enabled by the facilitative work of those who were responsible for bringing (performing, distributing and talking with/about) music to these people.[14] In the hospitals study, individuals emerged from their apparent isolation to help produce the music, singing along, playing percussion, tapping their feet and became, at times, connected to each other through shared and collaboratively produced emotional situations, and structured opportunities for remembering. In the music listening study, participants engaged in a process of informal learning about how to "tell" about music's meaning and uses in their lives, thus creating for themselves (and for fellow participants) pointers and tips on how to use music so as to promote health and well-being, connection to others (specific and generalised) and self-empowerment, that is, the ability to determine self-conditions, and also how to active music such that it might "work" in health-promoting or otherwise beneficial ways.

In both studies participants referred to their musicking experience in terms of "high points" and something to be valued, treasured. And in both it was possible to see bridges been made between music reception (listening) and music production (performing). For example, a male participant in the listening study who had just recovered from depression here explains how his singing and playing guitar at several hospitals or care centres seemed to be a key to communication and vitality for his "audiences", and simultaneously for himself:

---

[14] See Bonde's (2005) study of Guided Imagery in Music and how imagery (narratives) developed over time. Here music can be seen to provide resources through the ways it is connected to images, metaphors, scripts and narratives, cultural repertoires for rehabilitation. Again, this work was accomplished by participants themselves, albeit facilitated by, in this case, the Music Therapist.

When I play for old people I can sometimes see the fire in their eyes, they love to participate in singing the songs they know, particularly those with Alzheimer's disease. I have also noticed that if elderly people don't participate, I find it difficult to hold their attention. Through musical participation they get "alive"

Participants also spoke of how their involvement with music lead them to want to renew connections with others in live music making contexts and in this sense, music listening in private space came to be connected to social and active music participation or it promotes a deeper understanding which assists the handling of difficult life issues:

What I have gained through this project is to reinforce my belief that the strongest effect I gain from music is through playing and singing with other people, this synergy effect is like an encounter of love, it is so mysterious, just like somebody connects you to heaven, it is so strong this playing together, you know... (Male, 53, recovered from depression)

and:

The situation of being isolated from the work situation is not very pleasant. Through this project I have been able to contribute a lot and that means a lot to me. It has been very inspiring and also a huge contrast to being "unable to work". It has been very important to me that I have been able to focus on my resources and the kind of resources I have through music...huge contrast to my feelings of weariness and tiredness. This project has actually made me make contact with a folk-music group in my community and now I am feeling so good. I have regained control and well-being in my life. It is great... (Female, 52, recovered from depression and severe back-pain two months before final round of fieldwork)

Conclusion: Music and Health Promotion:
The Role of Resources

Musical participation engenders self-awareness, may retrieve fond memories of "happy times" and to memories of self as a more capable agent. It also provides resources for converting music recipients into music actors. These heightened and renewed forms of agency, which are achieved through the connections that musicking may afford, may include feelings of self-recovery, self-change, pleasure, connection to others, new lifestyle patterns and many other means of enhancing well-being or "wellness".

Stige (2003) has described music in therapeutic contexts as health musicking, that is, the shared and performed establishment of health-promoting relationships. The musicking processes that we have described above would not, normally, be described as "music therapy" (no trained therapists for example). However, Stige's proposal of the following notion of health as relevant for Community Music Therapy is, we believe, directly relevant also to the quasi-therapeutic forms of musicking we have studied:

> Health is a quality of mutual care in human co-existence and a set of developing personal qualifications for participation. As such, health is a process of building resources for the individual, the community, and the relationship between the individual and the community (Stige 2003:207).

Through the culturally adaptive practices of mutual music making and musical care we have just described, individuals are enabled to find, build and learn how to cross bridges between themselves and others, thus regaining control over environmental and social circumstances and control over the meaning and quality of time.

Our emphasis above on the ambiguity of therapy/non-therapy helps to highlight, we think, how health musicking may take myriad forms, may occur on a continuum from "therapy" to "ordinary cultural participation". Indeed, care might be taken to think about how these forms of musicking may be coordinated in mutually supportive way and how music is used to re-establish *wholeness between mind and body*, making the participants feels healed. In Batt-Rawden's study musical narratives seemed to play a vital role in the participants' everyday life relating to memories of happy times and meaningful moments, which created access routes into emotions and feelings. Aasgaard (2004; 2002) argues how important it is to experience and look forward to occasional pleasurable and enjoyable moments for people being ill and a healthy environment is one that fosters growth and creativity. From this perspective, sharing personal narratives in a comfortable and safe field setting, with music on the agenda, may promote health or well-being for people who are experiencing illness.

The CDs might have been a contributing factor in helping to uncover or explore *new* or hidden topics or issues on health and illness, through reference to their own personal music or musicking, thus increasing their consciousness and emotional competence. For example, Batt-Rawden's use of CDs as an interactive and dialectical tool could be used in hospital or institutional settings in conjunction with "live" performances (Trythall, 2006) as a way of sustaining or providing a musical "echo" of a "peak experience" (Gabrielsson and Lindstrøm, 1994), for example, of previous live musical performances.

In this way, the live musical event and its collective effervescence – music's social reverberations - may be sustained after and in between musical events, allowing the "moment" to be stretched (Aasgaard 2001: 203-208). [15] To prolong a sense of well-being, health professionals could encourage "musicalised" dialogues (Bennett, 2000) as means of achieving a salutogentic effect (Ruud, 2005), encouraging patients to reflect over *their* musical biographies enforcing a holisitic "art of caring" (Gagner-Tjellesen, Yurkovich and Gragert, 2001). The increased awareness and consciousness resulting from musical narratives and participation at live performances may develop a solid lay skill and lay expertise in music's use and power as a "folk-healing practice" - its role as a behavioural immunogen (Ruud, 2002). So too, one might consider coordinating more traditional forms of (dyadic) music therapy with "everyday" musical activities. We offer these merely as examples of multi-dimensional health-musicking strategies.

Finally, thinking about this grey area also prompts us to think about cultural change. For example, as variants of health musicking (for example, music performed in hospitals and hospices) becomes more prominent, it will be poised to have an impact on musical practices in the wider community of the town or region and, to the extent that this happens, health musicking may play an active role in aesthetic politics – perhaps having an impact upon what we take to be "good" music and indeed, what counts as music, performer, audience conduct, and so on. It should also be a priority to expand the belief in music as a "healer" through extended use of "therapeutic" musicking in the Health Service and with that, to expand our musical consciousness so as to foster musical inclusion. Meanwhile, we believe that it is within local communities and via locally sensitive adaptations to the ways that music is offered that this empowerment (social healing) may occur. In short, musicking is an inevitably political issue (Procter, 2004) because music provides resources and opportunities for our being in society.

---

[15] As Aasgaard puts it: "When the act of recalling or waiting for music therapy activities is linked with a pleasant memory or an expectation of something nice to happen, the symptoms-sickness-diagnosis-treatment-outcome panorama fades for a while and a different focus of mind is temporarily substituted....Also every moment of pleasurable remembrance or waiting is a means of expanding the present life world..." (2002:203-4). Looking forward or back at good times with music, in other words, imbues time with retrospective and prospective orientations that foreground health, pleasure and connection over time.

References

Acord, S. (2006). Beyond the code: New aesthetic methodologies for the sociology of the arts. *Sociologie de l'Art : OPUS, 9 (Questions du méthod)*.

Aasgaard, T. (2004). A Pied Piper among white coats and infusion pumps: Community music therapy in a paediatric hospital setting. In M. Pavlicevic and G. Ansdell (Eds.) *Community music therapy*. London: Jessica Kingsley.

—. (2002). Song creations by children with cancer – process and meaning. Doctoral Dissertation, Aalborg University.

Antonovsky, A. (1996). The salutogenetic model as a theory to guide health promotion. *Health Promotion International*, 11, 11-18.

Atkinson, P. (2005). *Everyday arias: An operatic ethnography*. Austin, TX: AltaMira.

Bennett, A. (2000). *Popular music and youth culture: Music, identity and place*. Great Britain: Palgrave.

Batt-Rawden, K.B, and DeNora, T. (2005). Music and informal learning in everyday life. *Music Education Research*, 7, 289-304.

Batt-Rawden, K.B., and Tellnes, G. (2005a). Nature-culture-health activities as a method of rehabilitation; an evaluation of participants' health, quality of life and function. *International Journal of Rehabilitation Research*, 28, 175-180

Batt-Rawden, K.B, and Tellnes, G. (2005b). Music and health promotion. A case study. In G. Tellnes (Ed.) *Urbanisation and health: New challenges to health promotion and prevention*. Oslo: Academic Press.

Batt-Rawden, K.B., DeNora, T., and Ruud, E. (2005). Music listening and empowerment in health promotion; a study of the role and significance of music in everyday life of the long-term ill. *Nordic Journal of Music Therapy*; 14, 120-136.

Batt-Rawden, K.B., and Aasgaard, T. (2006). Music a key to kingdom. *Electronic Journal of Sociology*; *http://www.sociology.org/inque.html*.

Bonde, L. O. (2005). "Finding a new place…" Metaphor and narrative in one cancer survivor's BMGIM therapy. *Nordic Journal of Music Therapy* 14, 137-154.

DeNora, T. (1999). Music as a technology of the self. *Poetics*, 27, 31-56.

DeNora, T. (2000). *Music in everyday life*. Cambridge: CUP.

—. (1986). How is extra-musical meaning possible? Music as a place and space for 'work'. *Sociological Theory*, 4, 84-94.

Durkheim, E (1965 [1912]). *The elementary forms of religious life*. New York: The Free Press.

..

Edwards, J. (2005). The role of the music therapist in working with hospitalized children: A reflection on the development of a music therapy program in a children's hospital. *Music Therapy Perspectives*, 23, 36-44.

Freund, P. (2001). Bodies, disability and spaces: The social model and disabling spatial organisations. *Disability & Society*, 16, 689-706.

Gabrielsson, A, and Lindstrøm, S: (1994). Can strong experiences of music have therapeutic implications? In R. Steinberg (1994). *Music and the mind machine*. Berlin: Springer-Verlag

Gagner-Tjellesen, D., Yurkovich, E. E., and Gragert, M. (2001). The use of music therapy and other ITNIs in acute care. *Journal of Psychosocial Nursing and Mental Health Care*, 39, 26-37.

Giddens, A. (1991). *Modernity and self-identity*. Cambridge: Polity Press.

Hetherington, K. (2003). Accountability and disposal: Visual impairment and the museum. *Museum and Society*, 1, 104-115.

Hetherington. K. (2002). The unsightly: Visual impairment, touch and the Parthenon Frieze. *Theory, Culture and Society*, 19, 187-205.

Magee, W., and Davidson, J. (2004). Music therapy in multiple sclerosis: *Music Therapy Perspectives*, 22, 39-51.

Magee, W. (2005). Music therapy with patients in low awareness states: Approaches to assessment and treatment in multidisciplinary care. *Neuropsychological Rehabilitation*, 15, 522-536

O'Callaghan, C. (2004). Music therapy's relevance in a cancer hospital researched through a constructivist lens. *Journal of Music Therapy*, 41, 151-185

Pavlicevic, M. and Ansdell, G. (Eds.)(2004). *Community music therapy*. London: Jessica Kingsley.

Procter, S. (2004). Playing politics: Community music therapy and the redistribution of music capital for mental health In M Pavlicevic and G Ansdell (Eds.) *Community Music Therapy* (pp. 214-222). London: Jessica Kingsley.

Putnam, R. (2000). *Bowling alone*. New York: Simon and Schuster.

Rolvsjord, R, (2004). Therapy as empowerment. Clinical and political implications of empowerment philosophy in mental health practices of music therapy. *Nordic Journal of Music Therapy*, 13, 99-112.

Ruud, E. (2002). Music as a cultural immunogen – Three narratives on the use of music as a technology of health. In I.M Hanken, S.G Nielsen and Nerland, M. (Eds.) *Research in and for Higher Music Education. Festschrift for Harald Jøregensen*. Oslo: NMH Publications.

—. (2004). Foreword: Reclaiming music. In M. Pavlicevic and G. Ansdell (Eds.) *Community music therapy*. London: Jessica Kingsley.

—. (2005). Music: A salutogenic way to health promotion? In G. Tellnes (Ed.) *Urbanisation and health: New challenges to health promotion and prevention*. Oslo: Academic Press.

Stige, B. (2003). *Elaborations towards a notion of community music therapy*. Doctoral Dissertation, Faculty of Arts, University of Oslo.

Trythall, S. (2006). Live music in hospitals: A new 'alternative' therapy. *The Journal of the Royal Society for the Promotion of Health*, 126, 113-114.

CHAPTER SIX

CONTEXT, CULTURE AND RISK: TOWARDS AN UNDERSTANDING OF THE IMPACT OF MUSIC IN HEALTH CARE SETTINGS

NORMA DAYKIN

Music making in health care settings takes place in a rapidly changing context in which a number of trends can be identified. First, there is increasing interest in the broad field of arts and health care. This means that there are a growing number of stakeholders entering the debate on the impact of arts as well as a proliferation of arts projects and practices in diverse health care settings. The second major trend is the growth of the evidence based health care movement. Hence along with increased recognition of the role of arts in health has come a requirement to demonstrate through robust research the effectiveness of arts interventions. This chapter begins by examining the implications of these broader trends for music and health research before exploring some of the specific challenges that face music researchers and practitioners.

A key challenge is the pressure to identify positive effects of music and arts interventions. Outside of the specialist domains of art and arts psychotherapies there is sometimes a perhaps naïve assumption that creativity can only be an uncomplicated benefit. Further, there are also strong pressures on those involved in arts and health activity to justify their use of scarce resources. This can lead to an emphasis on outcomes rather than a focus on complex social processes that can help us to understand the impact of music and arts. It can also lead to the underreporting of negative outcomes. These pressures can therefore limit conceptual frameworks for the understanding of risks as well as benefits in arts and health practice.

A further challenge is that of how to research the role and contribution of music and arts to health and wellbeing. While there is growing recognition of the need for a stronger evidence base for arts and health interventions, there is no real consensus about the appropriate methods to use. A wide range of methodologies are available but the underlying conceptual models and theories that shape these are not always fully explored. As well as understanding the impact of arts, researchers face the challenge of theorising appropriately the mechanisms by which arts can affect health. Sociological research has examined the role of music as a "technology of the self" (DeNora, 2000, 1995b; Frith, 2003). However, it can be difficult to translate the findings of such research into health care settings. Hence at present, medical and biological models tend to dominate the debate. Here I argue for a broader focus. While considerable progress has been made in identifying measurable outcomes of arts interventions, particularly music, there is also a need to address political, organisational and cultural processes in order to understand complex experiences of music and arts in health care.

The rest of this chapter outlines these challenges in more detail, drawing on research I have undertaken with colleagues as part of the Arts and Health Research Programme at UWE, Bristol.

Arts and Health: A Perspective from the UK

The role of music in health care is influenced by the broader context of arts for health, which is currently undergoing rapid expansion. Within the UK this field is diverse and pluralistic, encompassing established disciplines such as music and art therapies as well as emergent fields such as medical humanities and arts for health. The latter encompasses a broad range of activities from art and music therapy to visual arts, music, performance, drama, poetry and creative writing. While these disciplines and activities have developed separately, they may share similar concerns and face some similar challenges. It is useful to consider some aspects of this broader context before going on to examine some of the challenges facing those researching music and health.

Within the UK a growing number of agencies with divergent agendas are currently engaged in sponsoring arts and health initiatives. The benefits of arts are construed across a broad continuum that has, at one end, individual health and wellbeing and, at the other, social and cultural impacts. Hence as well as clinical outcomes, issues such as social exclusion and community cohesion are emphasised (DCMS, 1998, 1999). This perspective suggests that the arts contribute to individual and social wellbeing through community participation as well as therapeutic benefit (SEU, 2004). Within the National Health Service, there is also increasing interest in the broader field of arts and health. Hence use of participatory arts is seen as a means of reducing stigma and discrimination against vulnerable groups within the community (DoH, 2006). Further, arts are seen as enhancing health care environments and contributing to the wellbeing of patients and staff (Ulrich, 1991; Ulrich et. al 2004). Guidance on building design from the Department of Health Estates and Facilities Directorate reflects this, hence the emphasis on the use of arts to create healing atmospheres and encourage civic pride (NHS Estates, 2002a, 2002b).

While arts and health projects are proliferating, this work is not evenly spread across all sectors of the health care system. The perceived benefits of arts and health work in relation to psychological well being may make arts and health seem particularly appropriate in areas where emotion plays a part (Hecht, 2005). Hence there are relatively high number of arts and health initiatives in areas relating to drugs and alcohol use as well as mental health. Nevertheless, at the 2006 conference of the UK Public Health Association there was a great deal of interest expressed in extending the scope of arts and health initiatives to encompass broader public health concerns such as obesity and coronary heart disease. This reflects a strategic goal of Arts Council England to broaden the remit for arts and health to include healthy living and well-being (ACE 2004).

The entry into the debate by a growing number of powerful stakeholders has highlighted a number of issues that may affect the future development of arts and health. One of these is the complexity of the division of labour of arts and health provision. This includes an array of groups and individuals including artists, musicians and performers in hospitals, service user groups, health care staff working with music and arts, community arts workers and musicians, and art and music therapists. While there are examples of local partnerships between these groups, the lack of national level partnerships is identified as a concern for policy makers (ACE, 2004). Further,

> ... there is, in general, a lack of understanding between arts therapists and arts in health practitioners about the unique contribution that each makes to improving and enhancing health services, and what they can learn from one another's practice (ACE, 2004, p. 6).

The way these various practices are organised could make it difficult for particular groups to contribute to the development of strategies for arts and health. On the one hand music and art therapy professions are recognised as established groups with their own frameworks for regulation, professional development and quality assurance. Yet their apparent focus on individual and medical models of health has meant that

they are not always included in arts for health initiatives where these are
underpinned by social and holistic approaches. This could lead to the
possible marginalisation of art and music therapy professions from broader
initiatives where they could offer valuable experience and expertise, such
as in relation to the development of supportive frameworks for artists
involved in arts and health work.

Differentiating the role of different contributors to arts and health has
therefore emerged as a key task for the professions. In relation to music,
researchers have sought to identify the particular contribution of qualified
music therapists as opposed to other groups providing music in health
care. A key distinction is that offered by Bruscia (1988) between music *in*
therapy, in which music might contribute to the care environment, and
music *as* therapy, in which music is the main agent of therapeutic change
(see also Wigram, Pedersen and Bonde, 2002).

There is a need for further exploration of these distinctions in practice.
A recent study of music activity in UK cancer care examined music
provision by 80 organisations providing supportive care (Daykin, Bunt
and McClean, 2006). A survey examined patterns of provision and open-
ended questions were used to elicit the perceptions of care providers about
the role and contribution of music and music therapy in cancer care. The
study found a wide range of music practices at points along a continuum
ranging from "music in the background" to "music as therapy". The study
also revealed a complex division of labour in which unpaid carers,
volunteers and performing musicians as well as professional music
therapists all contribute to music activity in cancer care environments. For
some of these organisations music therapy provision was a relatively new
venture, viewed as a part of a supportive care package that included other
arts activities and complementary and alternative therapies (CAM).

Our research found the managers of care did not always clearly
distinguish between music and other forms of supportive care. While
practitioners in each of these areas may bring different perspectives and
frameworks to their work, these differences may not well understood or
accepted by those responsible for care provision. Hence there was an
absence of a developed discourse surrounding the benefits of arts and
music participation as distinct from other forms of supportive care. This
may account for the fact that while the majority of organisations provided
some music activity for patients, a much smaller number employed
professional music therapists to engage patients in musical experiences. Of
the organisations surveyed, 52 initially described themselves as offering
music therapy. Yet less than a quarter of organisations employed a
professional music therapist: over half of organisations providing music

therapy in adult cancer care did not employ a professional music therapist for this activity.

This discussion reflects the fact that organisational contexts and local policy making processes and can influence the development and impact of therapeutic interventions as much as knowledge about the outcomes from clinical research. The study therefore demonstrates the importance of understanding local organisational and political contexts in which arts for health activity takes place. Further research on these local and national contexts is needed along with research focusing on patient and staff experiences.

Researching Music, Arts and Health

While there is a growing evidence base supporting arts and health, this is still at a relatively early stage of development. There have been repeated calls for more robust research and evaluation (DCMS, 1999, SEU 2004, ACE, 2004). Within arts and health there are diverse approaches to research and evaluation, although the policy developments discussed above and the common need to strengthen research cultures may encourage a convergence of research agendas in the future.

Music is the most well researched art form in health care. Music is widely used in health and social care in a complex and diverse array of practices, a proportion of which is undertaken by professional music therapists (Aldridge 2003; Pothoulaki, MacDonald and Flowers, 2005). Evaluation methodologies in music therapy in recent years have risen to the challenges of the evidence based health care movement (Edwards, 2005). These challenges were outlined by Watt, Verma and Flynn (1988) in an early review of wellness interventions. They include the relatively small numbers of people participating in music activity, making it difficult to recruit sufficiently large samples for research, and the difficulties of standardising interventions. The lack of both control groups and randomisation in many studies, together with a lack of agreed outcome measures, have also been seen as limiting research on supportive interventions such as music in health care. More recently, considerable attention has been paid to the development of increasingly robust experimental research designs (Gold 2004; Pothoulaki et al, 2005; Vink and Bruinsma, 2003), although not all music therapists agree that this is the only or best way to evaluate the impact of their work (Edwards 2005).

The evidence base for music and health is outlined by Staricoff (2004) in a review commissioned by the Arts Council England. This review selected music therapy and other music studies that included pre and post-test measures from which a range of effects of music are identified. For example, in relation to mental health Staricoff's review notes outcomes including improved wellbeing and quality of life; enhanced communication; improvements in behaviours such as agitation, aggression, co-operation, eating and sleeping; and improvements in cognitive function linked to music. A recent systematic review of music interventions in oncology settings by Pothoulaki et al (2005) identified 24 studies from USA, Canada, Australia and Europe. Over half of these used experimental methods including two randomised controlled trials. These studies report a range of outcomes including effects of music on the immune system as well as on psychological dimensions including anxiety, communication, expression and behaviour.

   Where clinical outcomes are claimed for arts interventions there is a clear need for high quality research in order to assess these specific aspects. Nevertheless, there is an ongoing debate as to whether outcomes based research offers the most appropriate means of evaluating arts interventions (Aldridge, 2003, Edwards 2005, Angus 2002, White and Angus 2003). This form of research is seen as incapable of identifying the complex and subtle effects of music: "elusive and subtle qualities such as joy, release, satisfaction and simply being, are not readily susceptible to rating scales" (Aldridge, 2003, p.20)

   The problem is not simply addressed by emphasising psychological as opposed to the physiological outcomes and variables. In the area of cancer care for example, Aldridge (2003) also identifies spiritual and communal needs of patients that could be addressed through music. Qualitative research has identified a range of phenomena relating to these needs, such as feelings of "aliveness" (O'Callaghan and McDermott 2004; O'Callaghan, 2002).

   These issues and debates are echoed in the wider, emergent arts for health field where both quantitative and qualitative research methods are less well established than in music therapy. A number of challenges have been identified in relation to the development of the evidence base for arts and health. These include the one-off nature of funding arrangements for projects, leading to a lack of sustainability and associated difficulties of establishing long term evaluation programs (Hecht 2005). A more fundamental difficulty is the lack of agreement about what constitutes robust evidence. A review of arts and mental health provision by White and Angus (2003) notes that many projects are characterised by a lack of clarity about aims as well as uncertainty among arts for health practitioners about what evaluation methods to use. Further, the authors note a concern among some that quantitative outcomes evaluation may be damaging to projects.

As Angus (2002) suggests, while many arts for health initiatives take place within the health service, their aims are quite different from those of medicine. Medical models of health and wellbeing, measurement and assessment cannot therefore be simply transposed onto arts for health projects. There is a need therefore for improved methods and practices of research and evaluation in arts for health based on explicit models of health and wellbeing.

The review by White and Angus (2003) notes that many current arts for health interventions seek to address psychological, social and spiritual dimensions of health and wellbeing rather than clinical indicators of health improvement. The review identifies three general approaches to research and evaluation currently in use in arts for health. These include health-based approaches investigating the contribution of arts to self-esteem and well-being; socio-cultural approaches including impact assessment of the arts; and community based approaches adapted from social capital theory on health improvement. Nevertheless, the authors note that relatively little empirical evidence exists to support these approaches. Further, the qualitative research that does exist is seen as being anecdotal and not sufficiently robust to inform policy development. Hence the authors conclude with a call for more robust qualitative research on arts and health:

> ...more grounded research and greater engagement with projects over long periods is necessary to explore impact and evidence in these complex interactions (White and Angus 2003, p. 6).

It is easy to see how the challenges described above could lead to calls for the development of a qualitative tool of evaluation equivalent to randomised controlled trial – the "gold standard" in quantitative health research. While initially appealing, such calls overlook the pluralistic nature of qualitative approaches with their diverse ontological and epistemological frameworks. However, these frameworks are not always well developed or made clear in arts and health research and evaluation, and the use of them requires skills that may be unfamiliar to some practitioners, particularly those who are new to the health sector and/or research. Hence collaboration between practitioners and researchers represents an important strategy for strengthening the evidence base for arts and health.

Understanding the Impact of Arts: Some Mechanisms by which Arts can Effect Health and Wellbeing

A key challenge for arts and health researchers and practitioners is that of understanding the mechanisms by which arts can affect health. Different disciplinary traditions approach this question in different ways. For example, social and holistic models of health that draw on notions such as cultural capital can be contrasted with biomedical approaches that identify physiological and neural pathways of reception (Angus, 2002; Staricoff, 2004). Smith (2003) presents a typology of approaches whose foci include the intrinsic benefits of creative expression; individual health well being; creative learning and social cohesion; community and social relationships; and cultural processes and experiences in understanding the role of arts.

The impact of music and arts on health is most often explained with reference to biomedical and psychology discourses. While music therapists emphasise the importance of personal and interactive processes such as self-expression, reminiscence and communication (Bunt and Hoskyns 2002) the quantitative evidence, such as that included in Staricoff's 2004 review, reflects the dominance of the medical model. Hence studies that discuss biological pathways of reception and the effects of music on the brain greatly outnumber studies of cultural factors that mediate reception of arts and health (Staricoff, 2004). This is paralleled in the broader arts for health movement where it is suggested that a focus on outcomes has limited the development of social science approaches even though many projects and interventions draw implicitly on notions from the social sciences (White and Angus 2003).

A useful alternative approach may therefore be to draw on concepts and theories from the field of the sociology of health and illness in the study of music, arts and health. A key concern for researchers in this field is that of the meanings of illness and health. An important notion that has emerged from this literature is that of illness as a "biographical disruption" (Bury 1982, 2001). Researchers have built on this notion, using techniques of narrative analysis to examine the role of illness and healing in the construction of identity (Becker, 1997; Frank, 1995; Riessman, 1993). Hence narrativisation is seen as one way in which people can attempt to redress the effects of illness on identity.

Research has also identified the importance of storytelling and meaning making in arts activity (Aasgaard, 2001; Staricoff, 2004). In music therapy, this is seen as occurring through engagement with music in the context of a therapeutic relationship; hence music therapy can offer opportunities for healing by affirming identities otherwise subsumed by illness (Aasgaard, 2001). Narrative analysis may therefore offer a useful means of exploring the impact of music and arts on health and well being.

Consideration of the theoretical premises of narrative analysis and the cultural basis of stories raises some interesting questions about music when this is added to the frame. A starting point for narrative researchers is that individuals have a basic need to impose order on experience (Becker, 1997; Riessman, 1993). Making sense of the life course is not just an individual process but draws on cultural scripts, which in Western societies emphasise linearity, development and progress (Becker, 1997). These scripts are often severely challenged by illness.

Illness can also be stigmatising and within narrative analysis story telling therefore takes on a moral as well as a cultural dimension. By disrupting the expected life course, illness can represent a moral challenge to identity (Bury, 1982; 2002; Frank, 1995; Riessman, 1993). These authors suggest that people with serious illness can face a need to restore moral status and "authenticity" as individuals. It is through the process of narrativisation that individuals re-work their understandings of the self and the world, redefining the disruption and re-evaluating the meaning of their lives (Becker, 1997). This process can also allow people to redress the effects of stigma and marginalisation that often accompany the experience of illness.

Sociological research on illness narratives recognises that scripts and stories are cultural and not just individual resources. Story telling involves engaging with repertoire such as metaphors that are widely available within a particular culture (Becker, 1997; Bury, 1982; 2002; Frank; 1995; Riessman, 1993). Further, core narratives can emerge from storytelling that themselves represent powerful cultural metaphors: these can both limit or facilitate change (Bury, 2001; Frank, 1995).

A sociological understanding of the role of music in health demands that attention be paid to wider cultural contexts and meanings of music. If engagement with music during periods of illness triggers processes of storytelling and affirms identity, the cultural scripts and repertoire that support such processes of narrativisation are worthy of examination. Research and writing on the cultural meanings of music from the 1980s onwards reveals some of these scripts. Such writings recognise as their starting point that music and aesthetics do not have intrinsic meaning; rather musical meanings are inextricably linked with social processes (DeNora, 1995; Leppert, 2003; McClary, 2000; Williams, 2001).

For example, the role of personal and public consumption of music in reinforcing social divisions and hierarchies has been examined (Leppert,

2003; McClary, 2000; Williams, 2001). An historical study by Weber (1992) of the early establishment of the classical music canon in England shows how this process provided moral legitimacy and a means of cultural leadership to a ruling class that was increasingly threatened by political crises. Similarly McClary (2000) in her analysis of the historical role of tonality in European art music likens tonal composition, with its pattern of progress from the tonic key through a series of modulations before a return home to the tonic key, to a quest narrative. By drawing listeners into these apparently natural musical structures tonal music was both reflective and productive of 18th century ideologies of progress, rationality and the emergence of the rational self. While the meaning of music is complex and cannot be simply reduced to aspects of its context (Shepherd, 2003), the importance of musical metaphors in driving home extra musical ideas is widely recognised (Kingsbury, 1998; Leppert, 1993; Williams, 2001). Of relevance here is Bourdieu's notion of taste as a form of social distinction, with music and arts offering individual and communal resources for cultural capital (Bourdieu, 1984).

In Western societies, engagement with music has been seen as offering an important means of articulation of the self (Andsell, 1997; DeNora, 2000; 1995; Frith, 2003). This research draws on notions of reflexivity, with apparently mundane consumption of music seen as a form of reflexive practice through which individuals constitute themselves and their biographies, using music for emotional management and ongoing identity work. Research on music and identity in health care settings may therefore offer a useful avenue for investigation of the impact of arts processes.

The Cultural Context of Music Narratives

In my own research I have explored notions of music and health in the narratives of professional musicians. This research examines the role of cultural scripts surrounding music in the face of biographical disruptions caused by illness and risk (Daykin, 2005). These scripts seem to reflect a number of paradoxes. On the one hand, music making, particularly for professional musicians, is often seen as a privileged space for gifted individuals. Yet there is a mismatch between the high levels of training and preparation that professional musicians undergo and the low pay, chronic insecurity and risks that many of them encounter. Artistic labour markets are characterised by high levels of self-employment, freelancing and contingent work (Menger, 2001). Ill health in this context is a serious threat and there is an extensive literature documenting the high levels of ill health among this group (Daykin, 2005; Harper, 2002). For example, research has revealed the devastating nature of playing related injuries for performing musicians (Zaza, 1992; Zaza, Charles and Muszynski, 1997; Zaza and Farewell, 1998). Hence while music work can be highly rewarding it is often insecure, combining high psychological demands with low levels of control and support (Karasek and Theorell, 1990).

Some of the cultural scripts concerning music and creativity may not be conducive to supporting health and well being. For example, research by Alford and Szanto (1996) suggests that musicians are socialised to accept high levels of risk, encapsulated in the phrase "no pain no gain". Their study identified two common scripts that in combination rendered engagement with creativity dangerous for musicians. On the one hand they identified a common assumption that virtuosity cannot be achieved without some level of pain and discomfort. On the other hand, they identified pressures arising from competitive environments, peer groups, teachers and mentors to deny pain as well as strong disincentives to acknowledge and seek help for difficulties. They suggested that young pianists develop in an isolated atmosphere and are trained to think of themselves as psychologically and physically unique and different from other people. This may be in part a legacy of the romantic period in which the separation between artist and society was emphasised, with the artist seen paradoxically as on the one hand visionary and heroic and on the other marginalised and rejected (Boyce-Tillman, 2000; Williams, 2001).

The world of music education is changing, with broader influences such as world music, jazz and popular music increasingly embraced alongside the traditional canon of western classical music. Yet it has been suggested that the basic training and socialisation of musicians continues to reflect traditional ideologies of musical talent and risk (Boyce-Tillman, 2000; Green, 2003). Further, these ideologies continue to influence popular perceptions of creativity. O'Neill, Ivaldi and Fox (2002) point to the widespread belief in Western societies that possession of innate "talent" is what explains exceptional musical accomplishment, despite evidence that early musical opportunity and experience provide better indicators of eventual musical expertise. Their research on the narratives of young female musicians explores the gendered construction of notions of talent. The young women in their study reflected an assumption that boys who engage with music have more "natural" ability than girls, who were viewed as having to work hard in the absence of any "real" talent (O'Neill, Ivaldi and Fox, 2002).

In my own small study of musicians whose biographies were challenged by illness (Daykin, 2005) I sought to explore the way in participants talked about music as work. The influence of hegemonic notions of creativity on biography emerged as an important theme. Hence the accounts often took as a starting point the ideal of the expected life course of the musician. The notion of musical ability as a "gift" was often invoked, and frequently linked with the idea that musical talent needs to be discovered in childhood in order to be fully exploited. Respondents used these notions both to legitimise their claims to creativity as well as to distance themselves from the norm, with the some citing "late" entry to music as a cause of trouble later on.

Within these accounts musical creativity was accepted as an essential component of identity rather than a cultural practice influenced by particular contexts and experiences. As a consequence, professional music making was seen as very different from "normal work" in a number of ways. For example, professional musicianship demand higher levels of risk taking and personal sacrifice other forms of employment. It also seemed to require physical and emotional mastery. Hence physical and psychological vulnerability were viewed as weaknesses to be ignored or overcome. While the perception that being a musician involves a high personal cost was present in many accounts, there was a noticeable absence of alternative discourses associated with "normal" work, such as entitlement and rights.

The denial of physical and psychological vulnerability was not sustained by the musicians in this study, hence their agreement to take part in the research. The performance of hegemonic creativity is difficult to maintain in the presence of frailty. The research examined the scripts and stories that emerged during a process of biographical reworking in which individuals engaged to different degrees in response to illness and other difficulties. Of interest here are those scripts that emphasised healing and therapeutic values. Hence some individuals spoke about the ways in which their creative practice had changed in recognition of physical and psychological needs. Notions of embodiment and pacing, as well as balance and limitation, were all invoked. Further, some stories emphasised the need for connection with others and collaboration as survival strategies in maintaining creative identities. Other powerful stories emerged, such those focusing on recognition and valuing of the mundane aspects of music as "normal work" (Daykin, 2005).

A finding from this study was that several of the musicians had changed their working patterns in response to their illness experiences. A number had started to engage with therapeutic and arts in health work as part of the process of re-evaluation following personal injury and ill health. In some instances, this had changed the nature of the music they produced. Among arts and health practitioners Angus (2002) identifies a concern about the quality of arts. For some of these practitioners, linking arts projects too closely with social or educational "messages" is seen as a mistake: using art to deliver specific health outcomes will simply result in bad art. At its most extreme this concern reflects an essentialist view of aesthetics. As we have seen, notions of quality in art and music are difficult to separate from the cultural contexts from which these forms emerge. This is recognised by those artists also identified by Angus (2002) who seek to develop their roles as responsible citizens, and so perhaps to produce different kinds of art and music.

As well as highlighting the dangers in over emphasising the distinction between "real art" and "therapy" this discussion has highlighted the links between those providing care and those receiving it. Further research is needed into these experiences, including the health and wellbeing of those who provide art and music as a service in health care. Not only are these issues important in themselves, but they are also a key influence on the environment and provision of health care.

Experiences of Participants of Music Therapy

The experiences of professional performing musicians discussed above may be far removed from those of musicians and artists involved in health care. Yet cultural meanings of creativity may affect the ways in which patients and service users engage with arts. The cultural meanings and associations with creativity that individuals bring to therapeutic processes may be an important factor mediating their effects. This discussion challenges the simple notion that creativity is good for health. A number of risks associated with music and health have been identified (Edwards, 2005; O'Callaghan, 1996) and it is recognised that interventions such as music therapy may not be appropriate for some groups of service users (Edwards, 2005). Staricoff (2004) draws attention to difficulties for participants that might arise from the psychological demands of being engaged in arts activities as well as the possibility of physical injuries to both patients and staff. This has implications for the knowledge, training and support required by artists and musicians engaging in the health sector as well as care staff engaging with the arts.

Angus (2002) also notes the complex emotional issues that can arise from participation in arts and music. There is a concern that these issues are adequately supported and followed up if necessary, this support being seen as important for workers as well as for participants:

Art for health workers may become deeply involved in people's lives
around times of great stress, distress and disturbance and are bound to be
affected by these experiences. It is important that they look after
themselves (Angus, 2002, p.11)

In established areas such as music and art therapy these issues are
recognised and supported through extensive processes of education and
training. This is not necessarily the case for arts and health workers
providing more fragmented input into health care. Concerns about risk
management can lead health care staff to assume that art for health
contexts should be "safe" and have a calming effect. Angus (2002)
suggests that this view is not necessarily shared by, or beneficial to,
patients. While some art and music can have a calming effect, careful use
of more challenging material may be useful for stimulating thought,
activity and dealing with difficult emotions. Successful use of diverse
forms of arts and music in health care therefore requires a high level of
training and interpersonal skill on the part of the worker or therapist.

Some of these complex challenges were explored in a qualitative study
of the accounts of music therapy given by people with cancer (Daykin,
McClean and Bunt, 2007; McClean, Daykin and Bunt, 2005). The study
sought to examine the different ways in which participants engaged with a
one off process of group music therapy as part of a one week program of
supportive care that included a range of complementary therapies. The
research identified cultural notions of aesthetics and music scripts that
influenced the responses. One of these was that of talent. Hence
participants often began their accounts with statements along the lines of
"I'm not musical, but". However, these were often followed with, albeit
modest, claims to creativity.

Another script that influenced the accounts was that of musical
biography. Hence the extent to which participants were able to draw on a
musical biography influenced their responses to improvised music making
in a therapeutic context. It was not necessarily the case that those with
more musical experience got more out of the therapy. Rather, their
engagement with the therapy was contingent on their sense of musical
biography.

The notions of talent and biography worked together to influence
responses to the therapy. Further, the music therapy session provided a
space where these notions were negotiated and constructed. Hence the
notion of "latent" creativity stimulated by the session emerged as
important. Some participants were able to use the music making process to
successfully construct creativity as part of themselves. These participants
often reported that this discovery had knock on effects after the therapeutic

process was over, and there were several examples of individuals going on to join choirs, drumming groups and engage with other forms of communal music making. These individuals also often took the creativity metaphor into their personal lives, integrating this into their accounts of healing.

While these effects were of course linked to the group process and the role of the skilled therapist they were also influenced by other factors. One of these was that of external cultural notions of creativity. Hence it seemed important to the participants that the music was both "good" and "meaningful". In discussing this, participants made references and comparisons between the improvised "pieces" created by the group and established music genres or the style of music that could be heard on particular radio stations. Personal biographies also seemed mediated participants' judgements about "good" or "meaningful" music. Most participants were able to use the session in a reflexive way, emerging from it with a sense of hopefulness and a commitment to including creative arts and music in their future lives. For a small number the session threw up some difficult challenges relating to the role of music and creativity in their biographies. Hence for some the process invoked unhappy memories of music making. These accounts were characterised by cynicism and lack of enjoyment of the group music therapy session and, at worst, by regret and hopelessness about the future.

The discussion highlights some of the complexities that can arise when using art and music in work with vulnerable people. In the context of a supported music therapy session led by a skilled facilitator there is an opportunity for debriefing and working through some of these issues so that participants can continue to reframe the meaning of illness in their lives. The discussion draws attention to the need for ongoing support for both participants and workers in arts and health. It also indicates that further research on the construction of art and music narratives may offer a useful way forward for understanding some of the complex processes involved in arts and health.

Discussion

This chapter has explored some of the issues facing researchers and practitioners within music and health, drawing on the wider arts and health agenda. Recent policy developments in the UK have on the one hand encouraged the use of arts in health care and, on the other, raised key questions about the future development of the diverse arts and health disciplines. Arising from these is a need to understand the different roles

of the various contributors to arts and health as well as a need to challenge
naïve assumptions about the role of arts in healthcare.

The need to strengthen the quantitative and qualitative evidence base
for arts and health has also been identified. Music is the most well
researched art form in health care and there is a growing body of
quantitative and qualitative research exploring the benefits and risks of
music and music therapy in health care settings. Nevertheless, there is still
a debate about what constitutes robust evidence and within the broader arts
for health field there is an identified concern that too much emphasis on
quantitative outcomes research may inhibit recognition of, or even
damage, important arts processes. There is a need therefore for research on
arts for health based on social models of health and wellbeing. Rather than
suggesting that this can be addressed by the development of universal
qualitative research and evaluation tools it may be more worthwhile to
recognise the diversity of qualitative research approaches. Collaboration
between practitioners and researchers from a variety of traditions
represents an important strategy for strengthening the evidence base for
arts and health.

Understanding the ways in which arts can affect health represents a
key challenge for arts and health researchers and practitioners. Critics have
suggested that these frameworks are underdeveloped within arts and health
research, inhibited by the emphasis on quantitative outcomes research.
Hence biomedical and, to a lesser extent, psychology discourses have
dominated the debate with relatively little attention given to the cultural
factors that influence experiences of arts in health care.

Drawing on my own research and research undertaken with colleagues,
I have discussed narrative research as an example of a framework for
investigating experiences of arts and health. This is not to suggest that this
is the only useful framework available. However, narrative approaches
allow the study of individual accounts of wellbeing to be combined with
an understanding of the social and cultural nature of arts and health
processes. By focusing on issues of identity and biographical construction
within particular cultural contexts, narrative research may offer a useful
means of exploring the impact of the arts on health and well being.

In relation to music, the cultural context of western music and its
influence both on musicians and service users has been explored. While
music worlds are diverse, there are some central cultural scripts
concerning music and creativity, particularly those that emphasise innate
talent, hedonism and risk, that for many are not conducive to supporting
health and well being.

The process of music making as a cultural practice influenced by particular contexts and experiences is well illustrated in cancer patients' accounts of music therapy. Yet some arts and health practitioners still see a trade off between cultural engagement and quality, with "social" or "therapeutic" art valued less highly than "real" art. These tensions were also reflected in the participants' accounts of music therapy in the study described above (Daykin, McClean and Bunt, 2007). The majority of these participants emerged from a supported group process with a strong sense of personal creativity that they felt had been only latent before the experience. Yet others found the music they made was meaningless, referencing their comments to a range of scripts including those of aesthetic quality and judgement as well as personal musical biography.

The discussion has highlighted some links between the experiences of performing musicians, musicians and artists involved in health care, and participants in arts and health activity including music therapy. It has also highlighted the complex challenges that can face those delivering arts and health projects, particularly when working with vulnerable groups. Some arts and health stakeholders take the view that art for health should be "safe" and calming. Our research supports the argument made by Angus (2002) that this approach does not always bring out the potential benefits of arts and health. It may underestimate the ways in which people can engage with arts process reflexively in order to reconstruct biographies challenged by illness. Successful use of a range of arts and music in health care therefore requires that therapists and art for health workers receive appropriate levels of training in interpersonal skills.

This chapter indicates a number of directions for future research on arts, music and health. The development of robust conceptual frameworks and qualitative methodologies has been identified as a key priority for the broader arts and health field. Specialist areas such as music therapy have led the way in terms of the development of evidence and understanding of the impact of the arts on health. Approaches that develop social and cultural understandings of the broader meaning of arts and health activity, as well as the experiences of arts and health providers and participants in specific contexts, may also offer an important contribution in future.

References

Angus, J. (2002). *A review of evaluation in community-based art for health activity in the UK*. Centre for Arts and Humanities in Health and Medicine, University of Durham.

Arts Council England (2004). *Arts, health and well-being: A strategy for partnership*. Draft for consultation, November. ACE, London.

Aldridge, D. (2003). Music therapy references relating to cancer and palliative care. *British Journal of Music Therapy*, 17, 17-25.

Alford, R. and Szanto, A. (1996). Orpheus wounded: The experience of pain in the professional worlds of the piano. *Theory and Society*, 25, 1-44.

Andsell, G. (1997). Musical elaborations. What has the New Musicology to say to music therapy? *British Journal of Music Therapy*, 11, 36-44.

Becker, G. (1999). *Disrupted lives: How people create meaning in a chaotic world*. California: University of California.

Bourdieu, P. (1984). *Distinction: A social critique of the judgement of taste*. Cambridge, MA: Harvard University.

Boyce-Tillman, J. (2000). *Constructing musical healing: The wounds that sing*. London: Jessica Kingsley.

Bruscia, K. (1998). *Defining music therapy* (2nd edition). Gilsum: Barcelona.

Bunt, L., and Hoskyns. S. (Eds.)(2002). *The handboook of music therapy*. Hove: Brunner-Routledge.

Bury, M. (1982). Chronic illness as biographical disruption. *Sociology of Health and Illness*, 4, 167-182.

—. (2001). Illness narratives: Fact or fiction? *Sociology of Health and Illness*, 23, 263-285.

Daykin, N., McClean, S. and Bunt, L. (2007). Creativity, identity and healing: participants' accounts of music therapy in cancer care. *Health: An interdisciplinary journal for the social study of health, illness and medicine,* 11, 349-370.

Daykin, N., Bunt, L., and McClean, S. (2006). Music and healing in cancer care: A survey of supportive care providers. *The Arts in Psychotherapy*, 33, 402-413.

Daykin, N. (2005). Disruption, dissonance and embodiment: Creativity, health and risk in music narratives. *Health: An Interdisciplinary Journal for the Social Study of Health, Illness and Medicine,* 9, 67-87.

DeNora, T. (2000). *Music in everyday life*. Cambridge: CUP.

—. (1995a). The musical composition of social reality? Music, action and reflexivity. *The Sociological Review*, 43, 295-315.

—. (1995b). Music as a technology of the self. *Poetics*, 27, 31-56.

Department of Culture, Media and Sport (1998). *Bringing Britain together: A national strategy for neighbourhood renewal*. London, DCMS.

—. (1999). *Policy Action Team 10: Report on Social Exclusion*. London, DCMS.

Department of Health (2006). *From segregation to inclusion: Commissioning guidance on day services for people with mental health problems*. London: DoH.

Downer, S. M., Cody, M. M., McCluskey, P., Wilson, P.D., Arnott, S.J., Lister, T.A., Slevin, M.L. (1994). Pursuit and practice of complementary therapies by cancer patients receiving conventional treatment. *British Medical Journal*, 309, 86-9.

Edwards, J. (2005). Possibilities and problems for evidence-based practice in music therapy. *Arts in Psychotherapy*, 32, 293-301.

Featherstone, M. (1991). The body in consumer culture. In M. Featherstone, M. Hepworth and S. Turner (Eds.) *The body: Social processes and cultural theory*. London: Sage.

Frank, A. (1995). *The wounded storyteller: Body, illness and ethics*. Chicago: University of Chicago.

Frith, S. (2003). Music and everyday life. In T. Herbert, M. Clayton and R. Middleton. (Eds.) *The cultural study of music*. London: Routledge.

Furnham, A., and Vincent, C. (2000). Reasons for using CAM. In M. Kelner., B. Wellman., B. Pescosolido and M. Saks (Eds.) *Complementary and alternative medicine: Challenge and change*. Amsterdam: Harwood.

Gold, C. (2004). The use of effect sizes in music therapy research. *Music Therapy Perspectives*, 22, 91-95.

Green, L. (2003). Music education, cultural capital, and social group identity. In T. Herbert, M. Clayton, R. Middleton. (Eds.). *The cultural study of music*. London: Routledge.

Hecht, R. (2006). *Shared territories: Audit and analysis of the arts and health sector in the south west*. Arts Council England and Arts and Health South West, June 2006

Harper, B. (2002). Workplace and health: A survey of classical orchestral musicians in the United Kingdom and Germany. *Medical Problems of Performing Artists*, 17, 83-92.

Karasek, R., and Theorell, T. (1990). *Healthy work: Stress, productivity and the reconstruction of working life*. New York: Basic Books.

Kingsbury, H. (1988). *Music, talent and performance: A conservatory cultural system*. Philadelphia: Temple University.

Kruse, J. (2003). Music therapy in United States cancer settings: Recent trends in Practice. *Music Therapy Perspectives*, 21, 89-98.

Leppert, R. (1993). *The sight of sound: Music, representation and the history of the body*. Berkeley: University of California.

McClean, S., Daykin, N., and Bunt, L. (September. 2005). "More than just a good old bash on the drums": Reflections on identity, creativity and illness in cancer patients' accounts of performing group music therapy. *BSA Medical Sociology Conference, University of York*, 15-17 September 2005.

McClary, S. (2000). *Conventional wisdom: The content of musical form*. Berkeley: University of California.

Menger, P. M. (2001). Artists as workers: Theoretical and methodological challenges. *Poetics*, 28, 241-254.

NHS Estates (2002a). *Advice to Trusts on the main components of the design brief for health care buildings*. Leeds: The Design Brief Working Group, NHS Estates.

—. (2002b). *Better health buildings: Good design is a commitment to a better quality of life for all*. Leeds, Centre for Health care Design, NHS Estates.

O'Callaghan, C. (1996). Pain, music creativity and music therapy in palliative care. *American Journal of Hospice and Palliative Care*, 13, 43-9.

—. (2002). Identifying comparable therapeutic foundations between "musical re-play" and improvisation: Cancer research inspires a hybrid perspective. *Nordic Journal of Music Therapy*, 13, 127-142.

O'Callaghan, C., and McDermott, F. (2004). Music therapy's relevance in a cancer hospital researched through a constructivist lens. *Journal of Music Therapy*, 41, 151–185.

O'Neill, S.A., Ivaldi, A., and Fox, C. (2002). Gendered discourses in musically 'talented' adolescent females' construction of self. *Feminism and Psychology*. 12, 153-159.

Pothoulaki, M., MacDonald, R., and Flowers, P. (2005). Music interventions in oncology settings: A systematic literature review. *British Journal of Music Therapy*, 19, 75-83.

Rider, M. (1987). Treating chronic disease and pain with music-mediated imagery. *The Arts in Psychotherapy*, 14, 113-120.

Riessman, C. K. (1993). *Narrative analysis*. London: Sage.

Roset-Llobet, J., Rosines-Cubells, D., and Salo-orfila, M. (2000). Identification of risk factors for musicians in Catalonia (Spain). *Medical Problems of Performing Artists*, 15, 167-174.

Shepherd, J. (2003). Music and social categories. In T. Herbert, M. Clayton and R. Middleton. (Eds.) *The cultural study of music*. London: Routledge.

Silverman, D. (2001). *Interpreting qualitative data: Methods for analysing talk, text and interaction*. London: Sage.

Smith, T. (2003). *An evaluation of sorts: Learning through common knowledge.* CAHHM, Durham. Retrieved from *www.dur.ac.uk/cahhm*, 5 April 2005

Social Exclusion Unit (2004). *Mental health and social exclusion.* Social Exclusion Unit Report, Office of the Deputy Prime Minister, UK.

Sollner, W., Maislinger, S., DeVries, A., Steixner, E., Rumpold, G., and Lukas, P. (2000). Use of complementary and alternative medicine by cancer patients is not associated with perceived distress or poor compliance with standard treatment but with active coping behavior: A survey. *Cancer*, 89, 873-880.

Sparber, A., Bauer, L., Curt, G., Eisenberg, D., Levin, T., Parks, S., Steinberg, S. M., and Wootton, J. (2000). Use of complementary medicine by adult patients participating in cancer clinical trials. *Oncology Nursing Forum*, 27, 623-630.

Standley, J. (1995). Music as a therapeutic intervention in medical and dental treatment: research and clinical applications. In T. Wigram, B. Saperston and R. West (Eds.) *The art and science of music therapy: A handbook.* Amsterdam: Harwood.

Staricoff, R. (2004). *Arts in health: A review of the medical literature.* London: Arts Council England, Research Report 36.

Ulrich R. (1991). Effects of interior design on wellness: Theory and recent scientific research. *Journal of Health Care Interior Design*, 3, 97-109.

Ulrich R., Quan X., Zimring C., Joseph A., and Choudhary R. (2004). *The role of the physical environment in the hospital of the 21st century: A once in a lifetime opportunity.* College of Architecture, Texas A & M University.

Vink, A., and Bruinsma, M. (2003). Evidence based music therapy. *Music Therapy Today* (online), 4, http://musictherapyworld.net

Watson, M., Haviland, J., Greer, S., Davidson, J., and Bliss, J.M. (1999). Influence of psychological responses to breast cancer and survival rates: A population based cohort study. *The Lancet*, 354, 1331-1336.

Watt, D., Verma, S., and Flynn, L. (1998). Wellness programmes: A review of the evidence. *Canadian Medical Association Journal*, 158, 224-230.

Weber, W. (1992). *The rise of musical classics in eighteenth century England: A study in canon, ritual and ideology.* Oxford: Clarendon.

White, M., and Angus, J. (2003). *Arts and adult mental health literature review.* Centre for Arts and Humanities in Health and Medicine, University of Durham.

Wigram, T., Pedersen, I.N., and Bonde, L.O. (Eds.)(2002). *A comprehensive guide to music therapy.* London: Jessica Kingsley.

Williams, A. (2001). *Constructing musicology*. Aldershot: Ashgate.

Zaza, C. (1992). Playing-related health problems at a Canadian music school. *Medical Problems of Performing Artists*, 7, 48-51.

Zaza, C., Charles, C., and Muszynski, A. (1998). The meaning of playing-related musculoskeletal disorders to classical musicians. *Social Science and Medicine*, 47, 2013-2023.

Zaza, C., and Farewell, V. T. (1997). Musicians' playing related musculoskeletal disorders: An examination of risk factors. *American Journal of Industrial Medicine*, 32, 292-300.

CHAPTER SEVEN

USING MULTIPLE METHODS IN MUSIC THERAPY HEALTH CARE RESEARCH: REFLECTIONS ON USING MULTIPLE METHODS IN A RESEARCH PROJECT ABOUT RECEPTIVE MUSIC THERAPY WITH CANCER SURVIVORS

LARS OLE BONDE, PHD

Research Vignette

Mrs. M. attended music therapy one and a half months after discharge from hospital for the treatment of breast cancer. Her baseline pre-test score on a Quality of Life dimension in the intake questionnaire was 7; on a scale with anchors titled 1 (very poor) to 7 (very good). In a later interview, she explained her result thus: "I was not given the option of answering a question like 'How many times during the last week or period have you been really down?' As the instruction said the answer should only address the last week, it was not possible to report feelings of 'depression' from the week before that." I asked her: "According to two of the questionnaires the music therapy had no effect for you. But now you tell me that it did?!" Mrs. M.: "Yes, it has been... well if not the most important outcome in my whole life, then at least in the later part of my life. That's for sure."

In other words: at the time of the intake score Mrs. M. was free of pain and reported her quality of life at the maximum at baseline. Six months later, at follow-up, that is 6 weeks after post-test and the last music therapy session, Mrs. M scored herself at 6 on both questions. From an empirical viewpoint she indicated a deterioration following music therapy. The interview however, tells another story. In the interview Mrs M indicated that the music therapy experience had profound impact on her life. The only way she could express this in the questionnaires was to add personal comments in the margin, for example, she scored the question in the anxiety scale: "Do you enjoy things as much is you did before?": with the highest score "as much as before" but included her own comments written in the margin "even more than before", and "also other things than before".

Introduction

In this article I will share some of my experiences with and reflections on using multiple methods[1] in a music therapy research project with cancer survivors (Bonde 2005a). The project will be outlined briefly, as background for a discussion of some of the methodological and epistemological issues in the project, including the reporting of findings. Some general reflections on the rationale of using multiple methods will be included as well as a discussion of core concepts in the study. Some of the results are presented with a focus on advantages and disadvantages of combining standardised questionnaires with qualitative interviews. Critical issues emerging from the evaluation of the study will be presented in order to broaden the perspective, and finally I will discuss the question of multiple methods and validity, including some reflections on "truth" in research.

A Rationale for Using Multiple Methods

I classify myself as a humanistic researcher, as I was trained as a musicologist in the qualitative traditions of hermeneutic inquiry and critical theory. I have published many purely qualitative studies in music education and music therapy .However, in this study of the use of Bonny Method of Guided Imagery and Music (BMGIM) with cancer survivors one important purpose was to communicate with professionals in the health care systems, or more specifically: professionals in oncology, that is, doctors, nurses and consultants. Based on preliminary dialogues with some of these professionals and on the demands and standards of funding agencies I knew that a purely qualitative study would not open doors in Danish hospitals to music therapists. In order to establish a dialogue I would have to include a quantitative dimension to my study, knowing that this would demand that I developed new statistical skills..

---

[1] 'Multiple methods' and 'mixed methods' are terms covering the same phenomenon.

For many years I have been teaching music therapy students theory of science, including the question of paradigms and methodologies, and my explicit stance has always been that "quantitative and qualitative are not scientific paradigms, but complementary research methods". Also from a more pragmatic point of view I considered multiple methods useful for music therapists working in multi-disciplinary teams, especially methods which combine descriptive statistics, phenomenological descriptions and hermeneutic interpretations.

Robson (2002) proposed that the scientific world is in a multi-paradigmatic stage, and there is almost never only one method to answer a specific research question. However, the three major research cultures of 1) natural science, 2) social science, and 3) humanistic science, still have a tendency to emphasise certain research strategies and evaluation standards, which are not identical. Qualitative research is still a rare approach in natural science, and quantitative research is still only a niche in humanistic science. The broadest scope of research approaches is actually found within social science. Social scientists have developed a wide spectrum of both quantitative and qualitative strategies and methods, and reflections on when, why and how to combine methods. Robson has suggested that the terms "fixed vs. flexible design" is a more appropriate way of understanding the relationship between paradigm and methods. He also supports the use of multiple methods: "Using more than one [method] can have substantial advantages, even though it almost inevitably adds to the time investment required" (Robson, 2002, p. 370). The epistemological advantages may be 1) the reduction of inappropriate certainty (nice, "clear-cut" results may not be "right"); 2) multiple methods permit triangulation (of sources, methods, investigators, or theories); 3) they may be used to address different but complementary research questions within one study; and 4) they may enhance the interpretability of the results.

Robson has summarised eleven ways in which qualitative and quantitative methods can be combined. Within the music therapy community standards of both quantitative and qualitative research and research reporting have been discussed extensively (Wheeler, 1995; 2005). Standards of quantitative research are well-known and often described, while the lesser known basic requirements of qualitative music therapy research may be expressed in the acronym ERIC (Stige 2002). ERIC reflects that qualitative research must be dealing with relevant and solid empirical material, address the problem of representation, acknowledge the primacy of interpretation, and accept the obligation to produce permanent critique[2]. The basic standards and requirements of the researcher are expressed in Bruscia's analysis of integrity (Bruscia, 1998). Robson (2002) also presented guidelines and a checklist for qualitative research reports. Other sources of inspiration from the music therapy literature have been Aldridge (1996), Bruscia (1995), Smeijsters (1997), as well as Ansdell and Pavlicevic (2001).

However, the music therapy literature has little to say about multiple methods. The issue was not included in the first edition of the music therapy research book (Wheeler 1995), and in the second edition (Wheeler 2005) it is only addressed in one chapter (Wheeler and Kenny, 2005). Edwards (1999; 2005) emphasises the importance of explicating epistemological and ontological considerations of the researcher, relying less on overarching methodological concerns (such as "qualitative and quantitative"), more on underpinning the researcher's beliefs and their influence on the choice of method. Yet, many music therapy research discussions have separated quantitative and qualitative methods as if they are epistemologies[3].

The following describes how I brought quantitative and qualitative methods together in one study.

BMGIM with Cancer Survivors – Questions, Method, Results

Question: What is the influence of ten individual BMGIM sessions on mood and quality of life in cancer survivors?
The study addressed the following sub-questions:

1. Can ten BMGIM sessions improve the mood of the participants?
2. Can ten BMGIM sessions improve the quality of life of the participants?

---

[2] Stige's proposal was based on the four elements of Reflexive methodology, as presented by Alvesson and Sköldberg (2000): 1) Systematic techniques in research procedures, 2) Clarification of the primacy of interpretation, 3) Awareness of the political-ideological character of the research, and 4) Reflections in relation to the problem of representation and authority. The forum discussion included Aldridge's presentation of an "Evaluation tool for qualitative studies", and Stige revised his acronym EPICURE to include comments from both the forum and the Bergen symposium (Wheeler and Kenny, 2005).
[3] Ansdell and Pavlicevic (2001) for example introduce their 'researcher protagonists' (quantitative Franz and qualitative Suzie) as representatives of separate research cultures. They only meet at cafés and barbecues, trying hard to understand each other.

3. Can music and imagery help the participants in their rehabilitation process?
4. What is the experience of the participants of BMGIM and its influence on mood and quality of life in the rehabilitation process?
5. What is the specific nature of the imagery/image configuration of cancer survivors?
6. How does the imagery develop and/or is re-configured during BMGIM therapy?
7. What elements are there that describe the relationship between the music and the imagery transformations?

Sub-questions 1-3 were addressed in a quantitative investigation with 10 hypotheses. Sub-questions 4-8 were addressed in a qualitative investigation in three parts: 1) with focus on the participants' experience of the BMGIM therapy, 2) with focus on the imagery, and 3) with focus on the interrelationship between music and imagery.

Method

The quantitative investigation was a Clinical trial/Pre-Post-Follow-Up-design/Multiple case study design. The participants were six women, 40-65 years old, in cancer rehabilitation 1.5 to 18 months after discharge from hospital who volunteered to receive 10 biweekly, individual BMGIM sessions conducted by a GIM therapist. The setting used was the standard BMGIM format, and the standard GIM music repertory of programs and selections was used. In the data sampling the following questionnaires/self reports were used: A) The Hospital Anxiety and Depression Scale (HADS) (Snaith and Zigmond, 1994) plus (A1) four specific music therapy questions, B) The European Organization for Research and Treatment of Cancer Quality of Life Questionnaire (EORTC QLQ-C30) (Fayers, Weeden et al, 1998), and C) Antonovsky's Sense of Coherence Scale (SOC) (Antonovsky, 1987).

After every session questionnaires A), A1) and B) were filled in. After termination and 6 weeks later all questionnaires were filled in. two to four weeks after follow up, all participants were interviewed by the researcher. The qualitative investigation had five elements: 1) grounded theory analysis of interviews with the six participants, 2) grounded theory analysis of images and metaphors in all sessions, 3) two case studies – a hermeneutic/mimetic analysis of the imagery and its development in two participants, 4) event structure analyses of the interrelationship of music and imagery in four music selections, 5) grounded theory inspired categorisation of the music used in the project.

Results

The quantitative investigation: Inferential statistics (Wilcoxon Signed Ranks Test) and Effect Sizes were calculated on (selected) scores of the three questionnaires: 1) HADS: A significant effect was found at pre-follow up on the Anxiety subscale: .045 (Effect size: 1.33), 2) QLQ-C30: No significant effects found, 3) SOC: Significant effect found Pre-Post: .028 (Effect size: 0.62) and pre-follow up: .027 (Effect size: 0.41)

The qualitative investigation: In the analysis of the semi-structured interviews with the six participants the following core categories emerged as descriptors of their BMGIM experience: 1) Enhanced coping, 2) Improved mood, 3) New perspectives on past/present/future, 4) Enhanced Hope, 5) Improved self understanding, 6) Coming to terms with life and death, 7) Opening towards spirituality (Bonde, 2007).

The imagery of the participants was analysed based on the principles of grounded theory (Strauss and Corbin, 1995), and hermeneutic investigation (Ricoeur, 1978; 1984). The outcomes of the analyses showed that core metaphors and self metaphors emerged with all six participants and that configuration of metaphors in narrative episodes or longer, coherent narratives could be identified in 5 of the 6 participants (Bonde, 2005; 2007)

The interrelationship of music and imagery was analysed. Three types of music were identified, and a grounded theory on the therapeutic function of music in BMGIM was suggested (see Bonde 2004; 2006; 2007). An in-depth investigation of one participant's BMGIM process is presented in a case study (Bonde, 2005b).

Core concepts: Anxiety, Depression, Quality of Life

The psychosocial oncology literature clearly demonstrates that anxiety, depression and quality of life (QoL) are core issues, both in the life world, and in the psychosocial treatment of cancer patients, from the phase of curative medical interventions to rehabilitation and eventually palliative or end of life care.

In this study, I wanted to include a replication of Burns' small-scale randomised controlled trial (Burns, 1999; 2001), thus I wanted to use the same standardised questionnaires that she used, the POMS (McNair, Lorr and Droppleman, 1971) and the QOL-CA (Padilla, Grant, Ferrrell and

Presant, 1996). However, as I wanted to communicate with clinicians in the Nordic countries I had consultations with oncologists in Denmark and Sweden on the choice of questionnaires. It became clear that there are different preferences in the US and Scandinavia and other questionnaires were recommended: the HADS and the EORTC-C30 (see above). I also included the SOC, because it has been used in related BMGIM research (Körlin and Wrangsjö, 2001; 2002), and its salutogenic perspective on health is related to quality of life (Antonovsky, 1987). No matter which questionnaires are chosen, and how the core concepts are operationalised for quantitative processing, the researcher should always reflect on other ways of understanding them, especially when the core concepts include or "mean" more than specific side effects or pathological symptoms. The core concepts of my study illustrate this.

Anxiety

In HADS, anxiety is defined as a concept covering "the general state of anxious mood, thoughts, and restlessness". This operational definition allows the researcher to ask specific sub-questions, measure the self-perceived level of anxiety and perform a pre-post-test. Participants answer 7 questions on a 4-point Likert scale within a spectrum from "Not at all" to "Very much" (or similar). The total score is placed in one of four groups: normal (0-7); mild (8-10); moderate (11-14); severe (15-21).

However, a very different understanding of anxiety, actually a totally different paradigm, can be found in existential philosophy, and/or psychology, and/or psychotherapy. As the Danish philosopher Kierkegaard has stated, anxiety is a basic human condition, what he called a "constituent characteristic" of the human being. It is object-free, at the core of existence and, as such, is not a pathological symptom.

Depression

In HADS, depression is defined as "the state of loss of interest and diminished pleasure response (lowering of hedonic tone)", and it is operationalised in the same way as anxiety. In contrast, in existentialism depression is not understood as a "disorder" but as a natural, human reaction to a life crisis, such as facing mortality, experiencing lack of meaning, or feeling abandoned.

Quality of Life

In QLQ-C30, quality of life is not even defined, but it is covered by two questions: How do you rate your Global Health / QoL? Participants answer on a 7-point Likert scale, ranging from "Very poor" to "Excellent". In contrast, quality of life is a multi-dimensional concept in contemporary health psychology, including issues such as emotional awareness, sense of agency and belonging, life experienced as having meaning and coherence (Ruud, 1998). In other words: questionnaires can only cover very limited uni-dimensional aspects of a phenomenon. It is understandable that participants' may find them both reductive, vague and inaccurate and that they may prefer methods enabling them to be more specific about their experiences.

Comparing Standardised Questionnaires
and Qualitative Interviews

In the following section, the responses of participants to the questionnaires will be discussed. The participants had many critical remarks about the limitations of the questionnaires. Here are some examples:

Mrs. J.: "One week may include many ups and downs - this cannot be indicated when 'ticking a box' about 'the last week' is the only option."
Mrs. M.: "The questionnaires may not show it, however, music therapy has had the greatest impact on quality of life in the later part of my life!"
Mrs. L.: "What I find so difficult about these questionnaires is that the changes I have experienced cannot be attributed to any single influence. I know definitively that the apparent 'lack of change' in my scores [of which she was informed] was also influenced by my negative attitude towards them...Another thing is that I am sure I would have felt worse and might have scored lower on several items, had I not participated in this project... I have become more conscious about some of the more tiresome or difficult things in my life."

I consider the combination of self-report questionnaires and semi-structured interviews an important methodological advantage. Even if some of the six participants in the study had many reservations and critical remarks to the validity and reliability of the questionnaires they all did acknowledge their scores in the questionnaires as a valid source of information on aspects of their process and outcome. The interviews took place shortly after follow-up, that is, approximately 2 months after the last session/post-test and 7 months after the pre-test. This allowed me, the researcher, to calculate preliminary results of the quantitative investigation and include them in the interview. At that time, I did not regard this procedure as controversial, but later I realised that some researchers find it an inappropriate quantitative element in a qualitative method.

This procedure allowed me to explore aspects of the participants' experience in a very interesting way. At the time of the interview not all participants had a clear memory of how their state of anxiety etc. was more than half a year before. Some of them even questioned that it could be possible to see anything out of the questionnaires. However, I was able to document a positive development in several domains with all participants. When informed about this in the interviews the participants readily, if slightly surprised, accepted the effect/outcome and provided detailed descriptions of their therapeutic process, thus facilitating a richer interpretation of the quantitative data and adding important participant perspectives to the study.

It could be argued that the advantages of the use of multiple methods are best summarised as follows, 1) multiple methods (MMs) ensure that a voice is given to the participants, 2) questionnaires and interviews are a good combination in practice, 3) MMs enable a dialogue between research cultures and their representatives, 4) MMs contribute to the foundation of Evidence Based Practice (EBP)[4], 5) small scale MMs research may promote funding of large scale RCT, 6) MMs may lead to an adjustment of Cochrane criteria, including both MMs and qualitative studies, and 7) MMs may lead to the reference groups for (multiple) case studies.

However, consideration should also be given to potential disadvantages such as, 1) the use of questionnaires can be experienced as artificial or irrelevant by participants, 2) the use of interviews can be considered biased by some researchers, 3) standardised self-reports are always reductionist and may not always work meaningfully with qualitative interviews, and 4) small samples and no control group make less credible evidence that cannot always be compensated for by in-depth qualitative analyses.

Of course, the multiple methods applied in this study did not solve the problems of validity related to the small sample and the lack of a control group. The participants in the study may have had a special motivation influencing the results in a positively biased way, and this issue was not accounted for in the design. However, the quantitative data made it possible to compare results from this study with results from other studies

---

[4] And may also contribute to the support of music therapy positions in healthcare settings (Edwards 2002)

and relevant reference groups. I think this is a very important dimension of using multiple methods in studies of psychosocial interventions. The results of the quantitative investigations were presented to some of the oncologists I had consulted in the preliminary phase. They readily accepted the results as positive and sufficiently promising to recommend the funding of am RCT. The funding for a RCT of receptive music therapy with cancer patients in chemotherapy was provided and a protocol has been developed. This would not have been possible without the quantitative dimension of the study.

Critical Ontological and Epistemological issues

The apparent success of the multiple method study in a funding and professional perspective does not in itself solve the meta-theoretical problems of potentially conflicting paradigms and methodologies. I will address these problems through a clarification of my axioms, my paradigm, and my understanding of using multiple methods in one study. My starting point will be some of the critical questions posed by the evaluation committee of my dissertation:

How are the research questions 5-7 linked with the primary issue of causality?

What is meant by "evidence" in this study?

The author claims that idiographic and nomothetic perspectives are complementary and that triangulation of quantitative and qualitative analyses provide strong evidence of "both process and outcome" of BMGIM. The author needs to clarify this in terms of his central purpose, which is outcome, not process.

The author must respond to Bruscia on the mutual exclusivity of qualitative and quantitative paradigms, (for example claiming that the paradigms cannot be mixed, but rather the methods (Bruscia 1995, p. 73).

Many of the critical questions and comments above suggest that the main purpose of the present study was outcome (effect), and that it was based on causal thinking and thus in principle adheres to a positivist paradigm. This was and is not how I understand the study. For example, I stated that "I will look at how cancer patients in rehabilitation experienced BMGIM therapy and how it influenced the rehabilitation process" (Bonde 2005a, p. 119). I described the study as "a flexible research design study, including quantitative methods in order to a) cover a 'structural' aspect of the phenomenon (outcome), b) permit a certain degree of statistical generalisability, c) combine the micro-level of individual processes with the macro-level of norms and standards, d) enable a discussion on outcome with the participants, and with colleagues from other heath professions." (Bonde, 2005a, p. 123)

How can this – and the overall design of the study – be related to or identified with a positivist paradigm? It may be connected with certain properties of the dissertation, such as implications of the carefully differentiated reporting styles in chapters on the quantitative versus chapters on the qualitative investigation, as recommended by Robson (2002), and also with different interpretations of a central concept used in the basic research question. I will address the last option first.

The basic research question was "What is the influence of ten individual BMGIM sessions on mood and quality of life in cancer survivors?" Here "influence" is the key word. It has paradigmatic connotations, therefore I will have a closer look on the etymology of the word and then give my rationale for using it.

"Influence" is based on the Latin "influere/influens" which means that something is "flowing into" something else. A good example of its use is John Cassavetes' well-known film "A Woman Under the Influence" (1974) about a woman's attempt to find her own way in a world of spoken and unspoken expectations and prejudice. "Influence" is not the same as "effect", and it does not imply "causality" and linear thinking. In my understanding of the word (and its meaning) it is a metaphor, an ambiguous conceptualisation of a process where (in this case) music therapy "flows into" the bodies, minds and spirits of six cancer survivors. The "influence" concept was chosen deliberately with the intention of making the research question open and inclusive, in other words: it should not indicate any specific paradigm or research method.

The question was then broken up into the two main meaning components of the concept: a more positivist concerned with causes and effects, requiring a fixed methodology (sub-questions 1-3), and a more post-positivist concerned with processes and experiences, requiring a flexible, emerging methodology (sub-questions 4-7). Terms that are traditionally associated with quantitative research and positivism, such as "effect", "outcome", "causality", "evidence" and "significance" can be used within qualitative research, and post-positivist designs, but with different meaning. Such differences in meaning must however be made very clear and sturdy when using multiple methods.

The use of multiple methods reflects my understanding of the multi-paradigmatic nature and present situation of music therapy research, not a wish to mix paradigms or create an epistemologically naïve combination of methods. My basic philosophical stance is non-positivist[5]. As a human endeavour music, and the music experience, is a multi-layered phenomenon, not either a case of stimulus-response or an experiential paradigm. Thus, in my understanding, the research project was neither a study based on a positivist paradigm, nor split in two halves with separate paradigms, it utilised an eclectic approach. I use the word "eclectic" in the same way as Ferrara (1991) uses it when characterizing his method of music analysis: music is sound, structure and meaning[6]. This reflects the way in which each aspect or level of the research demands a specific methodological approach.

Paradigmatically and epistemologically I share Lakoff and Johnson's ideas about causality (Lakoff and Johnson, 1999). In this book the authors present many distinct conceptualisations of causation, each with a different logic. The – positivist – prototypical case: the manipulation of objects by force is only one of many cases of causality. Metaphorical concepts of causation may provide a much richer source of causal reasoning.

> "...the literal skeletal concept of causation: a cause is a determining factor for a situation, where by a "situation" we mean a state, change, process, or action. Inferentially, this is extremely weak. All it implies is that if the cause were absent and we knew nothing more, we could not conclude that the situation existed. This doesn't mean that it didn't; another cause might have done the job. ..." (Lakoff and Johnson, 1999, p. 177)

Robson (2002) has also discussed the issue of "causality" in comparing positivist and non-positivist paradigms. An axiom of positivism based on Hume's theory of causation is that "Cause is established through demonstrating such empirical regularities or constant conjunctions – in fact, this is all that causal relations are." (Robson, 2002, p. 20). This positivist, successionist view on causality is challenged by the realist, generative view, where qualitative analysis can be a powerful method for accessing causality, because "not only the explanatory structure of mechanisms, but also a knowledge of the particular set of circumstances" are provided (Robson, 2002, p. 475). Qualitative analysis can "identify

---

[5] I use "Non-positivism" as an umbrella term including all paradigms (or cultures) that do not acknowledge (most of) the basic axioms of positivism, including both classical humanistic traditions such as phenomenology, hermeneutics and critical theory, and more recent trends in qualitative research within the humanities and the social sciences.
[6] Helen Bonny, the founder of BMGIM, was also eclectic in her theoretical orientation (Bonny 1978 *Monograph #1*).

mechanisms, going beyond sheer association. It is unrelentingly local, and deals with the complex network of events and processes in a situation. It can sort out the temporal dimension, showing clearly what preceded what, either through direct observation or retrospection." (Robson, 2002, p. 475). In this quote, including several words normally associated with a positivist paradigm, I find several characteristics reflecting the properties and intentions of my own project, where the "influence" concept is meant to cover a broader understanding of "causality" than merely "empirical regularities" independent of circumstances. But what becomes of validity, and how can triangulation be used?

Multiple Methods, Validity and Triangulation: An Epilogue

Bruscia (1995) wrote about the music therapy researcher's "unavoidable dilemma" as follows:

> Notwithstanding the possibility of collecting both quantitative and qualitative data in the same study, and combining the different interests and methodologies, the two philosophical paradigms cannot be integrated or combined. They are mutually exclusive ways of thinking about the world" (Bruscia, 1995, p. 73)

Bruscia's standpoints have been very influential in the debate on paradigms and methodologies in music therapy research, and in the early 90'es there was a tendency in the music therapy research community to divide into two camps who were mutually exclusive – this was what Aldridge (1996, p. 278) called methodolatry[7]. In the last ten years a trend towards inclusivity and mutual tolerance and a more pragmatic than polarised paradigmatic understanding can be observed.[8] A standpoint close to Bruscia's can be found in a recent discussion of mixed methods in health care research (Sale, Lohfeld and Brazil, 2002).

The paradigms upon which the quantitative and qualitative methods are based have a different view of reality and therefore a different view of the phenomenon under study. As the two paradigms do not study the same phenomena, quantitative and qualitative methods cannot be combined for

---

[7] The term was coined by Mary Daly (1973)

[8] Examples are the development of the Nordic Journal of Music Therapy and, to a lesser degree, the Journal of Music Therapy from journals exclusively devoted to qualitative and quantitative research respectively to journals embracing all types of empirical research.

cross-validation or triangulation purposes. However, they can be combined for complementary purposes (Sale, Lohfield and Brazil, 2002). In this view, triangulation is only accepted within a paradigm (equated with methods). The in/exclusive paradigm discussion, or "war", goes on, and the result seems to be two separate research cultures. However, there are other options. Mason (1996) presents a different understanding of triangulation, closer to my own standpoint:

> At its best, I think the concept of triangulation - conceived as multiple methods - encourages the researcher to approach their research questions from different angles, and to explore their intellectual puzzles in a rounded and multi-faceted way. This does enhance validity, in the sense that it suggests that social phenomena are a little more than one dimensional, and that your study has accordingly managed to grasp more than one of those dimensions. (Mason 1996, p. 149)

Johnson and Onwuegbuzie (2004) go further and proclaim Mixed Methods Research as a (third) "Paradigm Whose Time Has Come". They call their philosophical standpoint pragmatism based on the classical theories of Peirce, James, and Dewey, and this is closely related to what I have called eclecticism above. In this philosophy, the linkage between paradigm and method is "neither sacrosanct nor necessary" (Johnson and Onwuegbuzie, 2004, p. 15), and an epistemological and paradigmatic ecumenicalism is considered within reach. Pragmatism judges the empirical and practical consequences of research ideas; it is a "needs-based or contingency approach to research method and concept selection" (p. 17). They consider pragmatism a "logical and practical alternative" to the paradigm war. I agree, recognizing that it is not possible to expand the discussion of this issue in the present context.

Also the question of validity and the possibility of triangulation between quantitative and qualitative investigations in one study needs further discussion, and there are no easy solutions (Johnson and Onwuegbuzie, 2004; Meetoo and Temple, 2002). Research is a social activity during which researchers and participants produce a context specific account, and social reality cannot be described unproblematic from one "correct" perspective. In a post-positivist (constructivist or interpretative) view of social reality, the context and conditions under which data have been produced are crucial, and adding together data collected from different methods is therefore problematic. However, comparing results from different methods is of value because social reality is multi-faceted and perspective is all-important. Thus, different methods may be used to verify each other – but they may also be complementary or contradictory.

Different methods use different processes to construct findings and these different processes are valuable in contextualising data generated in different ways. For example, one of the benefits of in-depth interviews are that they allow for dialogue and debate around what a concept means, whereas a questionnaire is often a de-contextualised choice of tick boxes. In social life we are often presented with both ways of choosing. Sometimes we have to choose between two fixed alternatives without being able to give the "ifs" and "buts" (Meetoo and Temple, 2002).

This was certainly the case in the present study, and I think the majority of participants in health care studies dislike a choice between fixed alternatives. As researchers we can provide a more flexible situation for the participants. We are studying their life world and have an obligation not to treat them as mere "informants". Such considerations must be included both in the formulation of research questions and in the design of the multiple method study; and when we report our questions and findings the rationale for our choices must be made clear:

Researchers should spell out their research process and their epistemological and social position within their research to enable the reader to actively engage with the arguments being put forward (Meetoo and Temple, 2002).

I would suggest it is also the participants who need to be considered. As I have demonstrated, the women who volunteered for this study were also engaged in the research methodology and reporting style. They readily gave me permission to use not only data from questionnaires and interviews but also transcripts of sessions, mandala drawings, poems and artwork. I have used this permission to include the dimension of art in every presentation of this project, and therefore I will close the article with a poem, written by one of the participants and based on her music therapy experiences.

Mrs. M's poem

On the beach / I watch the ocean / and the waves
I see a wave being born / roll along / roll over /die
Being reunited with the ocean
I see a new wave been born and I ask:
Wave, while you are wave - do you know
That you are also Sea?
I see the ocean / I see the waves
I see myself - a wave
And I know that I am also the sea!

References

Aldridge, D. (1996). *From out of the silence: Music therapy research and practice in medicine*. London: Jessica Kingsley.

Alvesson, M., and Sköldberg K. (2000). *Reflexive methodology: New vistas for qualitative research*. London: Sage.

Ansdell, G., and Pavlicevic, M. (2001). *Beginning research in the arts therapies. A practical guide*. London: Jessica Kingsley.

Antonovsky, A. (1987). *Unraveling the mystery of health. How people manage stress and stay well*. San Francisco: Jossey-Bass.

Bonde, L. O. (2007). Imagery, metaphor, and perceived outcome in six cancer survivor's BMGIM therapy. In A. Meadows (Ed.) *Qualitative research monograph series*. Gilsum: Barcelona.

—. (2006). Music as co-therapist. Investigations and reflections on the relationship between music and imagery in The Bonny Method of Guided Imagery and Music (BMGIM). In I. Frohne-Hagemann (Ed.) *Receptive music therapy: Theory and Practice* (pp. 111-139). Gilsum: Barcelona.

—. (2005a). The Bonny Method of Guided Imagery and Music (BMGIM) with cancer survivors. A psychosocial study with focus on the influence of BMGIM on mood and quality of life. Doctoral Dissertation, Aalborg University

—. (2005b). "Finding a new Place..." Metaphor and narrative in one cancer survivor's BMGIM Therapy. *Nordic Journal of Music Therapy*, 14, 137-154.

—. (2004). Musik als co-therapeutin. Gedanken zum verhältnis zwischen musik und inneren bildern. In I. Frohne-Hagemann (Ed.) *Rezeptive musiktherapie: Theorie und praxis I* (pp. 111-139). Wiesbaden: Reichert Verlag.

Bruscia, K. E. (1995). Differences between quantitative and qualitative research paradigms: Implications for music therapy research. In B. L. Wheeler (Ed.) *Music therapy research. Quantitative and qualitative perspectives* (65-78). Gilsum: Barcelona.

—. (1998). Standards of integrity for qualitative music therapy research. *Journal of Music Therapy*, 35, 176-200.

Burns, D. S. (1999). The Effect of the Bonny Method of Guided Imagery and Music on the quality of life and cortisol levels of cancer patients. Department of Music and Dance. Kansas, University of Kansas: 80.

—. (2001). The effect of the Bonny Method of Guided Imagery and Music on the mood and life quality of cancer patients. *Journal of Music Therapy*, 38, 51-65.

Daly, M. (1973). *Beyond God the father: Toward a philosophy of women's liberation*. Boston: Beacon.

Edwards, J. (2005). Developments and issues in music therapy research. In B. L. Wheeler (Ed.) *Music therapy research*, 2nd Edition (pp. 20-32). Gilsum: Barcelona.

—. (2002). Using the evidence based medicine framework to support music therapy posts in healthcare settings. *British Journal of Music Therapy*, 16, 29-34.

—. (1999). Considering the paradigmatic frame: Social science research approaches relevant to research in music therapy. *The Arts in Psychotherapy*, 26, 73-80.

Fayers, P., S. Weeden, et al. (1998). *EORTC QLQ-C30 reference values*. Brussels, EORTC Quality of Life Study Group.

Ferrara, L. (1991). *Philosophy and the analysis of music: Bridges to musical sound, form, and reference*. New York: Greenwood.

Johnson, R. B., and Onwuegbuzie, A. (2004). Mixed methods research: A research paradigm whose time has come. *Educational Researcher*, 33, 14-26.

Körlin, D., and Wrangsjö, B. (2001). Gender differences in outcome of Guided Imagery and Music (GIM) Therapy. *Nordic Journal of Music Therapy*, 10, 132-143.

—. (2002). Treatment effects of GIM therapy. *Nordic Journal of Music Therapy*, 11, 3-15.

Lakoff, G., and Johnson, M. (1999). *Philosophy in the flesh: The embodied mind and its challenge to western thought*. New York: Basic.

Mason, J. (1996). *Qualitative researching*. London: Sage.

Meetoo, D., and Temple, B. (2003). Issues in multi-method research: Constructing self-care. *International Journal of Qualitative Methods, 2*, Article 1. Retrieved March 15th, 2007 from http://www.ualberta.ca/~iiqm/backissues/2_3final/html/meetootemple.html.

McNair, D., Lorr, M., and Droppleman, L.F. (1971). *Profile of mood states*. San Diego, Educational and Industrial Testing Service.

Padilla, G., Grant, M., Ferrrell, B.R., and Presant, C.A. (1996). Quality of life - Cancer. In B. Spilker (Ed.) *Quality of life and pharmacoeconomics in clinical trials* (pp. 301-308). New York, Raven.

Ricoeur, P. (1978). *The rule of metaphor. Multi-disciplinary studies of the creation of meaning in language*. London: Routledge.

—. (1984). *Time and narrative: Threefold mimesis*. Time and Narrative Vol. 1, Chicago: University of Chicago.

Robson, C. (2002). *Real world research. A resource for social scientists and practitioner-researchers*. Oxford: Blackwell.

Ruud, E. (1998). *Music therapy: Improvisation, communication, and culture*. Gilsum: Barcelona.

Sale, J., Lohfeld, L., and Brazil, K. (2002). Revisiting the quantitative-qualitative debate: Implications for mixed methods. *Quality & Quantity*, 36, 43-53.

Smeijsters, H. (1997). *Multiple perspectives: A guide to qualitative research in music therapy*. Gilsum: Barcelona.

Snaith, R. P., and A. S. Zigmond (1994). *The Hospital Anxiety and Depression Scale (HADS) Manual*. NFER-NELSON.

Stige, B. (2002). *Culture-centered music therapy*. Gilsum: Barcelona.

Strauss, A., and Corbin, J. (1995). *Grounded theory in practice*. London: Sage.

Wheeler, B. L. (Ed.)(1995). *Music therapy research. Quantitative and qualitative perspectives*. Gilsum: Barcelona.

—. (Ed.)(2005). *Music therapy research*, 2nd Edition. Gilsum: Barcelona.

Wheeler, B., and Kenny, C. (2005). Principles of qualitative research. In B. L. Wheeler (Ed.) *Music therapy research*, 2nd Edition (pp. 59-71). Gilsum: Barcelona.

CHAPTER EIGHT

FOCUSING ON OUTCOMES: UNDERTAKING THE MUSIC THERAPY RESEARCH JOURNEY IN MEDICAL SETTINGS[1]

WENDY L. MAGEE, PHD

This chapter shares reflections upon my experience as a music therapy clinician who has embarked on the journey of research within a medical setting since 1992. The setting in which this has taken place is the Royal Hospital for Neuro-disability in London, an independent medical charity, which seeks, through research and the provision of specialist services, to meet the needs of people with complex neurological disabilities resulting from damage to the brain or other parts of the nervous system. The hospital provides assessment, treatment, and ongoing care to adults aged 18 and older who have profound disability as a result of neurological damage or disease. It has 260 beds for provision of long stay, short stay, rehabilitation, respite and day care.

There is an active research culture at the Royal Hospital, which seeks to advance the science of care for individuals with neuro-disabilities and improve treatment and long-term quality of life. People are admitted to the rehabilitation facility following sudden traumatic events such as head injuries and strokes, and to the continuing care facility for complex presentations of chronic neurological conditions such as Huntington's Disease and Multiple Sclerosis.

---

[1] Some of the material in this chapter was previously published as: Magee, W.L. (2000). Getting results: Planning to complete research successfully. In: Robarts, J.Z. (Ed.) *Music therapy research: Growing perspectives in theory and practice.* 1, 95-102. London: BSMT Publications. The author would like to thank the British Society for Music Therapy and Jackie Robarts for their kind permission to publish a revised version of this paper.

Between 1992 and 1998 I undertook doctoral research in addition to clinical and managerial duties. Although at that time music therapy was established as a clinical service at the Royal Hospital, it was not recognised as a research discipline, nor was any other allied health profession research. Indeed, music therapy research was not established within British health care or within even the profession in the UK at that time. Combining the role of clinician and researcher was also novel, although holding this dual role is now more typical practice. Completing the research was no easy feat on top of my existing workload. Since completing that project I have developed and undertaken research into a range of topics around music therapy and neuro-disability, including service delivery (Magee, 2005; Magee and Andrews, submitted for publication), the application of electronic music technology in music therapy (Magee and Burland, 2005; 2006), music therapy assessment measures (Daveson and Magee, 2005; Dixon, Turner-Stokes, Loveday and Magee, 2006) and evaluation of methods of music therapy for use in multidisciplinary treatment of people with complex neuro-disabilities (Magee, Brumfitt, Freeman and Davidson, in press; Hitchen and Magee, 2004).

This is a narrative account of the early part of my research process to point out some of the practicalities that need to be considered in order to complete research successfully within the hospital setting. This information is aimed primarily at the researcher who is embarking on doctoral or similar level research in the medical setting, highlighting points which are not discussed in textbooks. I will cover those aspects for which researchers don't necessarily plan at the start of research and which may present some problems along the way and prevent successful completion.

Starting in Research: My Early Steps

Research may be kindled by personal or professional experience, a thirst for greater knowledge, the pressure to prove clinical effectiveness, or a desire to validate a professional role with the client group. All of these are valid reasons for starting out on the road. My research initially developed from questions of culture and how this effected clinical practice. I trained in Australia before coming to Britain in 1989 and in 1990 I began working here as a music therapist. I found immediately that there were cultural differences both in clinical music therapy practice and also primary theoretical influences underpinning clinical practice.

Starting work in the UK, I found that therapists predominantly defined their work by the way they made music and which music was used in sessions. I found that descriptions of clinical work consistently emphasised the creation of live co-improvised music between client and therapist. Whilst the model in which I had trained involved the use of live music, improvisational models were not a particularly dominant feature, nor was thinking about the therapeutic relationship in dynamic terms. Particularly in my early work with brain-damaged clients in Australia, I was influenced by neurobehavioural models of treatment which emphasise the use of well-consolidated familiar material such as pre-composed music embedded in long term memory (O'Callaghan and Turnbull, 1987, 1988). Of course, other differences between the two cultures underpinned this observation, such as the primary models of music therapy which were practised in each culture. At that time, psychodynamic models of music therapy were the prevalent influence in British music therapy practice emphasising a process-oriented approach and a focus on the therapeutic relationship. Neurobehavioual models, on the other hand, are goal-oriented and aim to improve function. Such trends were notably absent in British music therapy practice.

At the outset of my research I became aware of the frustration felt by my music therapy colleagues here in Britain who worked with neurologically impaired clients, indicated by their questioning of using improvisational methods with this population. I frequently heard comments such as "It's not really music therapy, as he/she only wants to play/sing/listen to songs". For me, many questions arose about the cultural context of clinical practice, models of training and how well these fitted the needs of the particular client group with whom I worked. At that time, there had been no research comparing the different treatment modalities of improvised and pre-composed music.

The purpose of my initial research then was not to offer new models of music therapy. I intended to examine two different approaches within one population, and from research, to offer recommendations for clinical practice which could be generalised to similar populations. At that time, the term "evidence-based practice" was unknown to me however, essentially this is what stimulated my research: a desire to empirically explore the most effective music therapy approach with my client group. Ready to begin research, I then searched for an appropriate degree which could support the type of research I wished to do.

Registering for a Degree: Finding the Right Journey Companions

There are two important things to consider when enrolling to do research as part of a higher degree: your supervisors and the peer group with whom you will be able to share your research. When I registered my research in 1992, Masters and Doctoral programs specifically for music therapy did not exist within the UK. Finding a university at which to register was not difficult, as universities were keen to register potential doctoral students. I registered within a Psychology of Music MPhil with a view to upgrading to a PhD after the initial year.

I had two supervisors for my research: an academic supervisor from my own discipline at my university and a psychologist who was based at the hospital. Having two supervisors in this manner is usual for researchers in the health setting. An academic supervisor advises on the requirements to pass your degree, whilst the second supervisor can bring clinical expertise and familiarity with your clinical setting. I learnt quickly that I needed two things from a supervisor: availability and reliability. A supervisor should also be experienced in the methodology you are proposing to use. They may come from a different discipline, but they must be able to respect your discipline and demonstrate an understanding of the framework in which you work. Research is isolating and lonely, so your supervisor at times may be your only support. Having a supervisor from another discipline can be helpful as this can bring a different perspective to your work, introduce you to literature which you may not otherwise think to search, and offer an alternative critique of your research. Ultimately, this can improve the quality and standing of your research in the wider research community. Within my second year my academic supervisor changed to a music psychologist who brought a greater breadth and research experience to my work.

I was one of a tiny handful of music therapists registered for a Doctorate at that time who were all far flung around the UK and therefore isolated from each other. I never anticipated how isolation might affect my ability to complete my research and it was a real disadvantage for a variety of reasons. A research peer group provides not only emotional support, but also opportunities for peer review and sharing of research ideas. This can nurture your development as a researcher and your developing research ideas. It is important to think about whether to register on a music therapy program or a program with peers from other disciplines. A peer group of music therapists brings advantages in terms of understanding the foundations of the research topic, although philosophical and methodological differences can still be a barrier even within this supposed "homogenous" group! Peer groups formed from other disciplines can bring advantages such as widening the epistemologies from you which you will draw, and offering a wider range of methodological examples. It can also develop your skills in explaining music therapy concepts to those unfamiliar with the discipline, which can be invaluable on completion when you are required to communicate your doctoral findings in just a few sentences. I found psychology students where I worked a great support as all of them were researching Multiple Sclerosis (MS) and they had good working knowledge of current neuropsychological research into MS, sharing the literature they had. Since that time, the hospital has introduced research seminars at which researchers at all levels present their research at different stages, providing an informal multi-disciplinary peer review.

Finding the Right Design: Which Path to Take

My own journey progressed with a pilot study I conducted as part of my doctoral research. Knowing little about quantitative methodology and the underlying principles of statistical analysis, I followed the advice of a psychologist supervising my work. However, I was inexperienced as a researcher and inept at explaining what I wanted to examine. My supervisor was unfamiliar with music therapy as a clinical treatment or as a research discipline and my lack of confidence as a researcher meant that I was not assertive in maintaining the perspective I wanted in my research. This made me vulnerable. Trusting my supervisor's wealth of experience and wanting to come out with some "hard" facts about music therapy, I pursued a pilot study. I produced a research proposal to meet the requirements of an internal medical research advisory committee and an external regional ethics committee. At that time, I did not know of other music therapists who were required to fulfil this requirement however proposal development for research and ethics committees is now typically expected as part of the research process for hospital and university research and ethics boards.

Preparing the research proposal is one of the most helpful parts of planning, undertaking and reporting research. A proposal takes time to write well and is time well invested. The finished document helps to focus thoughts and plans and is invaluable in producing the final report and publications. The proposal is a research plan: why, what, with whom, how and by when. It is important to meet the specific proposal details required of the university and the hospital, particularly in issues around consent and ethics. Important considerations are the time plan and the financial resources required. Time in human and material resources is expensive. I failed to plan adequately for the human resources required in my project, believing that I could draw my research participants from my clinical caseload and conduct the research sessions as part of my clinical work. I did not realise that this would affect how I prioritised referrals, and also did not allow adequate time for interview transcription and analysis, nor the detailed analyses of the clinical sessions. I spent a lot of evenings and weekends doing this work. Although I had gained funding for my fees from a research foundation at my hospital, eventually I needed to find additional funding for my time. I also did not plan for the cost of others' time for tasks such as assisting with collecting the mood scales data at the start and end of sessions. This was a practicality for which I should have planned, costed and had prior agreement with the department concerned. Small practicalities such as this can be difficult to solve once research gets started.

Ethical approval from an external ethics committee is now required of nearly all research taking place in medical settings. In the UK this is gained through making an application to the Central Office for Research Ethics Committees or COREC (*http://www.corec.org.uk/*). The process for gaining ethics clearance has become increasingly complicated and laborious in recent years. Gaining advice and assistance from someone who is familiar with the process is essential, as approval may not be given, which can delay the start of your research.

In this pilot study I collected data using a measurement tool tested for validity and reliability which had been used in previous research with comparative client populations. Having a psychology supervisor was especially helpful for this aspect. I compared the effect of unfamiliar improvised music with the effect of familiar pre-composed music in clinical music therapy on self-reported mood states in 15 brain-damaged clients. The chosen measurement tool collected information about the research participants' mood states before and after music therapy intervention, and converted this information simply into numerical data. These data were then analysed statistically using Statistical Package for the Social Sciences software. The results were statistically significant, which was very exciting. My supervisor advised me on the analytical tests and software to use. However, I was dependent on someone else for carrying out the procedure of analysis. This was time consuming, and once more something I had not prepared for adequately in my planning of material or human resources. I was able to rely on the goodwill of my psychology supervisor to provide both, in addition to spending many unplanned hours of my own time in doing the analysis. This study has since been published and at the current time remains one of the few empirical studies examining mood with a neurological population (Magee and Davidson, 2002).

The design of my pilot study met the requirements of my examining body and also of the journal in which it was finally published. However, the design would have been vastly improved by including a control group. Whether or not this was something on which I was advised by a supervisor at the time, I cannot remember. If I was advised to include a control group, I was not able to find a way to do this which sat comfortably with my "clinician" self. I add this simple observation at this stage of hindsight given my own developed knowledge that including a control group helps to improve the rigour of research. This also exemplifies the type of conflict which can emerge when holding the contrasting roles of "clinician/researcher".

My chosen design also was not sensitive to two central aspects. These were individual differences, and the underlying processes of what was occurring. Although the results showed that differences in mood states after music therapy were higher than chance levels, I could not determine from the results why this had occurred. Furthermore, the measurement tool was not sensitive enough to reveal differences between the treatment conditions which was a central part of my research question. Drawing on anecdotal and behavioural data, however, it was quite clear that qualitative differences existed. My pilot study in fact reflected what had already been shown in the existing research into music therapy and neurology which drew on quantitative methodologies. This research has shown that music applied therapeutically results in changed behaviour. That is, the research provided measurable outcomes, but was not able to show why changes are occurring. The underlying processes that contribute to the change effect are neglected in this approach. It was at this point that my primary supervisor changed, bringing a greater understanding of the limitations of researching music therapy using this design, and helping me to review my approach. With hindsight, I can see that as a novice researcher I wanted both outcomes and an understanding of process without realising that the two often call for different epistemological frameworks: positivist and non-positivist.

I learnt from my pilot study that my design needed to be adapted to encourage data which included participants' own verbal or musical material as central to the analysis, in addition to observational data from the sessions. Single-case designs have been noted to be particularly useful for creative arts therapies research as they allow for analysis of the therapist-patient interaction and within-participant comparison rather than comparison to group norms (Aldridge, 1994). I also turned to research recommendations from the field of psychology of music. These recommended that when exploring emotional responses to music, designs should be open-ended, employing a strong element of natural history (Sloboda, 1991) and stressed that the interaction between music and the individual is highly complex and individualistic (Waterman, 1996). Adopting qualitative methodology also found a better fit with my skills and philosophical stance.

Revising the Design: Changing Paths

Hence from a clinical viewpoint, case study design was the most appropriate method to incorporate a combination of participant data, observational data, and empirical analysis, without losing the emphasis on the individual. Further to changes in the design, I needed to examine my own dual role as therapist and researcher, to which I had given inadequate thought. The research design chosen needed to enhance the therapeutic process rather than jeopardise it. This is a difficult issue, as when the therapist becomes the researcher, the focus of the therapeutic relationship and boundaries can change. When acting as a therapist, the central focus of the therapeutic contact is the client's needs. When acting as a researcher, the therapist has gains to be made from the alliance.

As Bruscia (1995) has elucidated "... the goals (between research and clinical practice) are different. Research is aimed at increasing or modifying the knowledge base in music therapy; in contrast, clinical practice is aimed at helping clients achieve health." (Bruscia, 1995, p. 22).

For the design I finally chose, there were benefits to having the researcher and therapist as one person. The trust and depth of the therapeutic relationship served to enhance the interview material I collected. Furthermore, acting in this dual role, it was possible to be sensitive to points brought up in the interview data that were relevant to or contrasted with previous therapeutic material. In this way, much greater complexity was revealed in each individual's processes.

Having reviewed my pilot design, I adopted a case-study design with six individual cases. The research participants recruited engaged in a prolonged course of music therapy, during which I collected data through focused interviews and session evaluations. A few thoughts should be added here about recruitment and timescales. The complications of research are always optimistically underestimated in terms of time. It is very rare to complete research on time for a host of reasons, the most common of these being successfully recruiting participants and keeping participants involved. Careful thought also should be given to the methods of recruitment. Although I recruited participants from a hospital which had dozens of people with MS, very few fitted the inclusion criteria of the project due to the complexity of their problems. Some of those who did fit the criteria did not wish to be involved in the research and then a further two of the participants dropped out of the research for various reasons. Problems with participant recruitment and retention have led some researchers to avoid using clients and instead opt for theoretical studies. For research which needs to fulfil the requirements of a higher degree, advice should be sought from academic supervisors as to the adequate number of participants in a study. For studies involving statistical analysis, advice should be sought from a statistician about the design, number of participants and resulting potential data sets. More participants than originally anticipated should be recruited for research to allow for attrition or missing data, particularly as consent always gives participants the right to withdraw at any time.

Research requires participants to give informed consent. Gaining ethical approval for research from independent governance bodies, such as COREC in the UK, is becoming increasingly complex due to the requirements concerning undertaking research with vulnerable people. The Department of Health (UK) website provides thorough guidance on good practice for gaining consent, including specific information on gaining consent from children, older people and from people with learning disabilities, (*http://www.dh.gov.uk/PolicyAndGuidance/HealthAndSocialCareTopics/C onsent/fs/en*). Consent forms are available from this website, including documentation in languages other than English. Thought should be given as to whether involvement of other staff such as psychologists might be necessary to assess the client's capacity to give consent.

Analysis of the Data: Tools for Ensuring Arrival at Your Destination

I used open coding procedures from grounded theory to reveal emerging concepts and themes from a group of participants' data (Strauss and Corbin, 1990). I then used axial coding procedures from grounded theory on a series of single case studies to gain greater depth from the data and explore individual differences. Data collection and analysis took place simultaneously, helping to engage me in the emerging themes which I could then follow up in future interviews. Although I worked from a neurobehavioural perspective, I took the musical and sessional material to a clinical supervisor who drew from psychodynamic frameworks. This was invaluable in picking up on points I had missed, and also in suggesting alternative explanations for events. This helped to thicken my analysis and assisted with triangulation, an important process to assist with making qualitative research more valid. I also triangulated clinical material with the multidisciplinary team members involved with the participants through peer debriefing. This was a natural part of the clinical evaluation process and once more helped to verify or contradict my interpretations of events by offering explanations from a differing perspective. It also helped to ensure confidentiality of clients' material was maintained and not shared outside of the immediate treatment team. In a similar manner, the interview analyses were triangulated with my academic supervisor. I had colleagues who were willing to be involved in the process of peer debriefing as I was able to convince them of the benefits this would bring to their clinical work. I was fortunate in having such colleagues, as I had not accounted for their time in my financial planning. Colleagues who have little experience of research may have little interest in it if it is not perceived to enhance clinical thinking. It is important to plan for others' collaboration in your project, particularly in terms of their time.

Checking through realms of data or analysis is time consuming and should be acknowledged in some way, such as joint authorship of publications. It is usual practice that supervisors are joint authors on any publications, although this seems to be something which is not well understood by students at the outset of their degree. My academic supervisor was closely involved in my analysis, being one source or triangulation, which has been acknowledged in joint authorship of all the publications from my PhD. However, I did not discuss this possibility with my clinical supervisor, whose insights made my research richer and who should have been acknowledged in my publications. Acknowledgement may have prompted a greater commitment on his part, which may have given the published material greater depth. I strongly recommend that discussion takes place at an early stage of the research with supervisors and others involved in some way so that all parties are clear of expectations and commitment to the project.

Completing the Research: Arrival at the Final Destination

Completing research successfully means two things. Firstly, completing the analysis, writing up and discussing the results in a final report. This might mean a dissertation or a report for the sponsors of the research. Planning is one of the key elements in completing research successfully, and the following section has a series of suggestions to help with this. The second indicator of successful completion includes disseminating the results in a variety of forums: conferences and publications in peer-reviewed journals, books and websites. Although my dissertation was about differences between pre-composed song and clinical improvisation, the novelty and significance of my research lay in a different focus about which I published. The people with whom I was working were living with chronic and complex forms of Multiple Sclerosis, a population about which little had been published in music therapy. The findings have therefore contributed to understanding about the experience of music therapy with this population. The group data which was treated with open coding provided a broader perspective of experience of music therapy (Magee and Davidson, 2004a), whereas axial coding of the single case studies revealed the individual differences which were not possible to reveal with the quantitative design of my pilot study (Magee, 2002; Magee and Davidson, 2004b).

Having finished the research I have reflected on all the things I learnt and recognised some exclusions which would have strengthened the research. For example, greater use of standardised scales to describe the functional abilities of the participants could have helped to communicate the findings and assisted with applicability to other populations. This would have been quite simple without jeopardising the integrity of the qualitative study. It is something which I intend to implement in a development of the study.

Moving on: Itchy Feet

I look back on the beginning of my own research process, and realise that although I enjoyed it at times, it also sometimes felt like a minefield. Starting out on the research journey presents many challenges which may result in the feeling of facing an uphill struggle. At the end of a project it is important to take time to reflect on all of the struggles in order to incorporate these as changes in follow on studies. Having now completed several research projects, I have come to understand that with adequate planning, obstacles can be overcome in order to complete research in the medical setting successfully.

References

Aldridge, D. (1994). Single-case research designs for the creative art therapist. *The Arts in Psychotherapy,* 21, 333-342.

Bruscia, K. (1995). The boundaries of music therapy research. In B.L. Wheeler, (Ed.) *Music therapy research. Quantitative and qualitative perspectives* (pp. 17-27). Gilsum: Barcelona.

Daveson, B., and Magee, W.L. (2005). Research proposal: A validation and reliability study of a musical assessment tool for low awareness states (MATLAS). London: Royal Hospital for Neuro-disability.

Dixon, M., Turner-Stokes, L., Loveday, C., and Magee, W.L. (2006). Research proposal: Development and validation of an assessment tool for music therapy in neurorehabilitation. London: Northwick Park Hospital.

Hitchen, H., and Magee, W.L. (2005). Research proposal: A comparison of the effects of verbal de-escalation techniques with music based de-escalation techniques on agitation levels in patients with neuro-behavioural disorders. London: Royal Hospital for Neuro-disability.

Magee, W.L. (2002). Identity in clinical music therapy: Shifting self-constructs through the therapeutic process. In R. MacDonald, D.J. Hargreaves, and D. Miell (Eds.) *Musical Identities,* (pp. 179-197). Oxford: OUP.

—. (2005). *Patterns of music therapy referrals in a neuro-rehabilitation service for complex disabilities.* Presentation at the British Society for Research in Medicine, Pan-London Annual Audit Meeting.

Magee, W.L., and Andrews, K. (2007). Multi-disciplinary perceptions of music therapy in complex neuro-rehabilitation. *International Journal of Therapy and Rehabilitation,* 14, 70-75.

Magee, W.L., Brumfitt, S.M., Freeman, M., and Davidson, J.W. (2006). The role of music therapy in an interdisciplinary approach to address functional communication in complex neuro-communication disorders: A case report. *Disability and Rehabilitation,* 28, 1221-1229.

Magee, W.L., and Burland, K. (2006). *Exploring the use of electronic music technologies in clinical music therapy: Establishing definitions and scope of practice. Final report.* London: Royal Hospital for Neuro-disability.

Magee, W.L., and Burland, K. (2006). Integrating electronic music technologies in music therapy practice: Preliminary findings of a research study. In *Programme and Abstracts, 'The Sound of Music Therapy', BSMT and APMT Annual Conference,* (pp. 9-10). London: BSMT Publications.

Magee, W. L., and Davidson, J. W. (2002a). The effect of music therapy on mood states in neurological patients: A pilot study. *Journal of Music Therapy, 39,* 20-29.

Magee, W. L., and Davidson, J. W. (2004b). Singing in therapy: Monitoring disease process in chronic degenerative illness. *British Journal of Music Therapy,* 18, 65-77.

Magee, W.L., and Davidson, J.W. (2004). Music therapy in Multiple Sclerosis: Results of a systematic qualitative analysis. *Music Therapy Perspectives,* 22, 39-51.

O'Callaghan, C., and Turnbull, G. (1987). The application of a neuropsychological knowledge base in the use of music therapy with severely brain damaged adynamic Multiple Sclerosis patients. *Proceedings of the 13th Conference AMTA.,* Melbourne, 92-100

O'Callaghan, C., and Turnbull, G. (1988). The application of a neuropsychological knowledge base in the use of music therapy with severely brain damaged disinhibited Multiple Sclerosis Patients. *Proceedings or the 14th Conference A.M.T.A.,* Adelaide, 84-89

Sloboda, J. (1991). Empirical studies of emotional response to music. In M.R. Jones and S. Holleran (Eds.) *Cognitive Bases of Musical Communication* (pp. 33-46). Washington: American Psychological Association.

Strauss, A., and Corbin, J. (1990). *Basics of qualitative research. grounded theory procedures and techniques.* Newbury Park: Sage.

Waterman, M. (1996). Emotional responses to music: Implicit and explicit effects in listeners and performers. *Psychology of Music,* 24, 53-67.

Acknowledgements

The author would like to acknowledge support from the Neuro-disability Research Trust in the preparation of this paper.

CHAPTER NINE

PARTICIPATION, MUTUALITY, RESISTANCE:
INTERCULTURAL MUSIC THERAPY
IN A POST-WAR REGION

SUSANNE METZNER
AND CONSTANZE BÜRGER

TRANSLATED BY ELEONORE HERTWECK

Layla, a thirteen-year-old living in a Muslim orphanage in Mostar, is a girl
with medium-length black hair and big, dark eyes, who is physically well
developed and appears very mature for her age. Following the end of the
music therapy hour in the library of the orphanage, the two co-therapists
from Germany and the Netherlands put away their instruments and
materials. Suddenly Layla and her girlfriend appear, neither of whom were
members of the music therapy session that just ended. Layla directly
approaches the German therapist and abruptly reaches out for the guitar,
the therapist is holding. The therapist keeps hold of the guitar. Layla talks
to her in Serbo-Croat without pausing, violently yanks on the guitar, stares
into the therapist's face with a demanding and defiant look in her eyes,
grabs her arms, and finally bangs with all her might on the instrument. This
scene, which the two other persons present watch in total bewilderment,
lasts only a minute. It is much too surprising and happens much too fast for
the therapist to react in any way other than in reflex. While on the outside
she tries to recover at least some composure and to de-escalate the
situation, on the inside she is overwhelmed by an almost indescribable
mixture of fear, helplessness, despairing fury, and shock. Finally, Layla
lets go of the guitar and runs out of the room as fast as she came in. The
therapist is left alone with her emotions, including feelings of shame for
having held on so hard to the guitar.

To live in a foreign post-war region for a certain amount of time and
conduct music therapy there with traumatised children and adolescents

poses a great challenge to music therapists (see Bürger, 2005), demanding much more than that what is compatible with an understanding of therapy as it has developed in western culture. The extension or modification of existing concepts of music therapy does not appear to be sufficient to unravel the strange, absurd, and puzzling phenomena in an intrapsychic and interpersonal crisis of this type. Yet, are there any chances, at least afterwards, to think about and understand a first encounter – not yet a relationship –as the one described, if it is not possible to stop it? Would it then be possible to overcome the mutual speechlessness and cultural alienation bit by bit, but in particular to end the experiencing of rampant violence? And is it all too presumptuous to want to calm down the war still raging in the hearts of these persons, to extinguish wild hatred, and to counteract the erosion of hope?

In the attempt to address these questions, we first put aside the extremely irritating and emotionally cathected material from the vignette, without forgetting it, and gather together information concerning its historic, socio-cultural, and music therapy context. This procedure allows us to examine and clearly define the social situatedness of client and therapist and rests on the basic assumption that the behaviour and experience of two persons in an interaction scene can only be understood if the social context is given consideration. Premature and one-sided interpretations, on the other hand, would lead to either considering the client pathological or criticizing the skilfulness of the therapist.

As made clear in the description above, we are not dealing with a therapeutic situation in the narrow sense of the term, but with an everyday situation. Here we hypothesise that two cultural communication patterns collide with each other. Therapeutic arrangements such as contract and role-distribution have not been made beforehand, which would have provided a framework and thus a sense of security. Everyday situations are more commonly sought and used in the area of community music therapy or in ethno-psychoanalytical field studies. For this reason we have chosen two terms stemming from these disciplines, namely "participation" from community music therapy and "social dying" from ethno-psychoanalysis, with which we intend to demonstrate the power of the unconscious phenomena of values, social norms and communication processes and discuss these in connection with the vignette. In the last step conclusions are drawn, which contribute to the further development of concepts of intercultural music therapy as well as open up new perspectives for already established areas of music therapy.

Our approach to operate with two terms stemming from two totally different fields of knowledge and application rests on the basic assumption that music therapy is the practice of co- created constructions of reality. That this is especially true in the case of intercultural music therapy will become increasingly clear in the course of this article. Obviously it cannot be expected that the description of such a complex professional field respectively its theoretical reflection be characterised by total unison. Rather, one must accept the existence of pluralistic concepts and diverse theoretical positions within the field of music therapy. By means of reciprocal references it will become possible to establish new relationships (make new connections), which will then be relevant for the concrete practice of music therapy. Our method differs from an eclectic approach insofar as single theorems are not pieced together in a patchwork style, but that we work outwards from central nodes. In a perpetual self-renewing network of referential relationships, these nodes result from two complementary processes, namely a) confirmation (repetition, recognition), and b) invention (modification, redesign) (cf. Metzner, 2004).

The Situation in Bosnia –The War, the History, and the Situation Today

In the following we give a (very) short overview of the historic and socio-cultural situation in the Balkan area, so that the reader can acquire a rough idea of what kind of an environment may be considered "normal" for a 13-year-old Muslim orphan girl living in post-war Bosnia. However, every attempt to do so is connected with the danger that in the attempt to understand one only reproduces one's own normality so that one misses the actual object of interest, namely the normality of the other, while one is not at all aware of this. Thus, it is important to be sensitive for mechanisms of perceptual defence.

Bosnia and Herzegovina is one of the successor countries of the former Republic of Yugoslavia and is one of the most complicated political constructions of modern times. The "Kingdom of Serbs, Croats and Slovenes", founded 1918 and renamed to Kingdom of Yugoslavia in 1929, was created from several regions which were very different in reference to culture, ethnicity, and economy. Despite efforts to create a national Yugoslavian identity, especially during the Tito era (1945-1980), nationalistic ideologies, religious strife, prejudices and animosities among the different ethnic groups have remained to the present day.

Following the end of the East-West conflict, Yugoslavia lost its special position between the capitalistic and socialist systems. In the first democratic elections in 1990, in almost all its republics people's parties or nationally-oriented parties gained access to the government. The planned Yugoslavian general elections never took place. The structure of society, which had always been instable and very difficult to maintain, dissolved completely. Due to the efforts of various republics to acquire more autonomy and the fact that the problems of the past had never been resolved, the conflict escalated, and war broke out. Driven by nationalistic forces on all sides and closely connected with international conflicts of interest as well, Serbs, Croats, and Muslims fought against each other in the middle of Europe at the end of the 20th century.

The war raged three and a half years – from 1992 to 1995 – in Bosnia and Herzegovina; in no other republic of former Yugoslavia did it take such a bloody course as there. It was an ethnical war, with massacres and expulsions, a war for territory, a religious war, a war of the country against the cities, in the end a war about gaining the best economic opportunities in view of the impending political reorganization of the Balkan region. But all were losers in the end: Over 200,000 deaths, more than 170,000 injured, thousands left disabled, these are the shocking statistics of the war. And whoever lives in the areas strewn with mines today is another potential victim increasing that sad number. As if this were not enough, there are still 35,000 missing persons, about 2 million displaced persons, refugees, and resettlers, ca. 40,000 raped women, of these 10,000 under 18 years of age.

Since the Dayton Peace Agreement about 10 years ago, the state of Bosnia and Herzegovina (with an area of 51,129 km^2 composed of two entities, namely the Muslim-Croat Federation and the Serbian Republic) has not been in a state of war anymore. However, everyday life in Bosnia and Herzegovina is still characterised by tensions among the three ethnical groups: the Muslim Bosnians (44%), Christian Serbs (31%), and Croats (17%). In all three groups, century-old hopes and fears still live on. Their religious affiliation is strong and deeply rooted; ethnic biases and prejudiced "bogeyman" images of the enemy continue to exist.

The economic situation of the country is desolate; Bosnia and Herzegovina is still occupied with reconstruction and is dependent on international development aid. Most of the inhabitants still live in conditions worse than those that existed before the war. In Mostar too, the former capital of Herzegovina, the aftermaths of the war are visible everywhere. Neither the reconstruction of the famous bridge nor the surrounding area, considered one of the most beautiful landscapes in Bosnia, can hide the fact that ruins of buildings destroyed by fire and bombs can still be found everywhere.

The Project: Music therapy with Traumatised Children and Adolescents in Bosnia-Herzegovina

In September 2004 the EAMTS ("European Association of Music Therapy Students") conducted a pilot project in Bosnia-Herzegovina, in which 8 students of music therapy from 4 different countries (Germany, the Netherlands, Denmark, and Slovenia) worked with war traumatised children and adolescents. In an orphanage and in a day centre for children with special needs these students held music therapy workshops, which aimed at both enhancing the sense of community and creativity and helping these individuals to cope with their experiences of war and their current situation. The term "music therapy workshop" is used here because the time period of the program was not long enough to achieve the depth, the quality, and the results of regular music therapeutic treatment.

Each workshop was held by two co-therapists, who had previously acquainted themselves with topics relevant to the project such as the history of Bosnia, Bosnian music, music therapy with traumatised children. In the orientation phase, these students also discussed their personal motivation for working in this project and, in particular, talked about their expectations and fears concerning the emotional burdens involved in this work.

The students lived in a house located on the premises of the orphanage in the eastern part of Mostar, enabling them to gain much information about these children's everyday life. The workshops were held in the library of the respective facility; musical instruments were provided by the music therapy department of the Pavarotti Centre, a music school which was reconstructed after the war. Altogether 12 groups were formed; each consisted of 6-8 children or adolescents of about the same age, and they met twice a week.

Communication with the children was accomplished with the help of mimics and gestures as well as a few Serbo-Croat words and sentences, but above everything else, by musical interactions. Furthermore, there were some children who had been refugees in Germany during the war and were able to speak and translate German very well.

The specific music therapy program for each group was geared to the needs of the children but was influenced to a much larger extent by therapists' prior knowledge of music therapy and previous practical experiences, but also by the country-specific conceptions of the field of music therapy. Here, concepts stemming from the so called community music therapy predominated.

An exception were the workshops held by the German student[1] of music therapy, which were strongly characterised by a psychotherapeutic-psychoanalytic approach, at least as far as the relationship and theoretical reflection were concerned. The main objective was to create a supportive, warm, and secure atmosphere by building a relationship of trust, which would enable the individual to playfully discover spaces for personal growth and to develop new ideas and translate them to action, as well as give him or her the opportunity to express distressing experiences (losses, loneliness, feelings of abandonment, destructive impulses). For this reason the groups were closed, and the course of the session was semi-structured. The work was client-oriented, and leadership behaviour was non-directive and partner-oriented. Great care was taken to deal responsibly with children's desires, needs, and problems emerging in the session – such as moments of great sadness or exaggerated gaiety – since the time to do any in-depth work was very limited.

The workshop sessions were accompanied by preparatory and follow-up discussions in the co-therapeutic teams. Moreover, a team meeting was held each day for mutual collegial supervision sessions and to clarify questions of organisation, as well as for the purpose of supervision by music therapists from the Pavarotti-Centre.

In order to ensure the continuity of the work they started with the children and adolescents, the students conducted several presentations and workshops in different psycho-social institutions in Mostar. Furthermore, in cooperation with music therapists working permanently in Bosnia, the First Sarajevo Music Therapy Symposium was held in a centre for children with special needs. Doctors, psychologists, teachers, speech therapists, and music teachers attended this event and received information about the methods and techniques of music therapy and the latest developments in theory and research. Through networking it was possible to ensure the further treatment of some children and teenagers and to start off the preparation for the next EAMTS-Project in the following year.

Community Music Therapy and the Concept of Participation

Community (cultural) music therapy has meanwhile become an umbrella term for very different applications of music for the promotion of health outside of a clinical setting. In our paper, we mainly follow the

---

[1] The therapist we mention here was in the final stage of training at the time the project was conducted.

work of Stige (2003, 2005) and take a put special interest in the concept of participation, which simultaneously is the definition of the objective as well as the methodical approach. This term receives its significance through the critique of the asymmetry of the therapist and client relationship in reference to equal opportunity, access to resources, and context-transforming power. Since it is based on the conditions prevailing in the post-modern western world, it is not possible to simply transfer it to the music therapy project presented here. In order to better explain our understanding of it, it is helpful to first give a lengthier overview of the history of music therapy in Germany. This survey also provides information on the historic and social context, within which the professional identity formation of the German therapist in our example took place. In so far, this excursus is to be seen as analogous to the description of the living environment of the Bosnian girl.

Excursus: Music Therapy in Germany during the Seventies

As Stige (2005) correctly points out, what is understood worldwide under the term community or cultural music therapy today, began in Germany (in both of the then divided Germanys, East and West) with a tradition, which had its golden age in the seventies of the past century. This tradition is connected with prominent and internationally known persons, such as (in alphabetical order): Hans-Helmut Decker-Voigt, Isabelle Frohne-Hagemann, Hartmut Kapteina, Christoph Schwabe, who took great personal risks in the former GDR, and Almut Seidel. Stimulated by the area of new music, open for experimentation, and borne by the "zeitgeist" of the times, which was to question existing social structures and to challenge commonly held ideas and dictions (key word: reform of psychiatry), these professionals strove for a differentiation between music therapy with a more psychotherapeutic orientation and one with a more social-therapeutic and pedagogical orientation but did not want this to result in a schism. For example, the works at that time of Decker-Voigt are acknowledged retrospectively as "a visionary attempt to see to it that socio-cultural activities with music on the one hand and music therapy on the other are placed in a common "space" as far as ideation, conception, and theoretical confirmation are concerned and retain the suspense particular to each area without putting one or the other aside too hastily (…)." (Seidel 2005, p. 32, translation by E. Hertweck). The same goes for the other persons mentioned above – interestingly all of them either born during the war or members of the post-war generation.

What was not explicitly mentioned in the publications was that the "zeitgeist" of the times above all had a strong political impetus. Set off by general social upheaval in many countries in the form of civil rights and student movements, the collective guilt about the Holocaust and the Second World War, which had been mainly suppressed until then, became an important topic in Germany in the late Sixties, at least in certain intellectual circles. Furthermore, successful attempts were made to uncover traces of the national-socialistic past reaching into the present day, be it in governmental agencies and institutions or in the sciences and the arts. However, this process of coming to terms with the past has not yet come to an end, because it is only now, after the second and third post-war generations have grown up – incidentally, both authors of this paper belong to this group - that the taboos which have been in effect for decades concerning family history are finally being lifted bit by bit and personal involvement with the Nazi regime reconstructed.

Actually, this topic should be discussed in more detail, in particular in reference to the respective East German and West German variants, but this is not possible in the scope of this article. Here, it should suffice to make the point that it does not seem unwarranted to assume that there is a connection between the development of the theory and concepts of music therapy of those times and the self-critical analysis of the history of one's own people as well as the (unconscious) desire to make retributions. Perhaps one can even go so far as to see in it the attempt to overcome the collective inability to mourn (Mitscherlich, 1998).

However, since the 1980's the idea of the integration of music (psycho)therapy and socio-cultural activities with music lost its influence especially in West Germany within an expanding group of professionals, who - concerned with the establishment of their professional field - were willing to bow to the pressure of the power structures of the social and health care systems (key word: Psychotherapy Act) and accordingly adapted the contents of most of the training programs to these requirements. However, in the meantime it is high time to realise that it is not conducive for the further development of the field to continue this strategy and that it is necessary to withstand the pressure to comply with these demands with more self-confidence.

The interest in and discussion of community or cultural music therapy, which has become very popular in many countries in the meantime, might prove to be quite useful in this connection; however, in Germany this topic is currently discussed with much restraint. In our opinion, this has much to do with the fact that the professional group has not managed to deal in a constructive manner with divergent concepts (psychotherapy vs. sociotherapy). To realise this, it would be intellectually satisfying and mutually rewarding to debate the matter, and everyone would profit from it in the end.

Now, back to the present: As Stige proposes, one of the three main characteristics of community music therapy is that it is "value-driven"

(Stige 2004)[2] Thus, if moral and ethical arguments are declared to be the
basic principles of a therapy concept, then it becomes necessary to define
the scope of application on the one side and the underlying motivation of
whoever defines the value on the other. This is suggested by experiences
made in intercultural music therapy, since in a world full of contradictions,
it is hardly possible to universally declare specific ideals and values (for
example, individuality, need satisfaction, self-actualisation, and harmony)
as ones which all cultures and social groups should follow. Furthermore,
only the self-critical examination of one's own motives could rule out the
possibility that collectively or individually unconscious contents are
projected onto values. Although perceptual bias due to projection does not
automatically preclude conscientious handling of the ethical matter, it is
better to curb unconscious tendencies to influence the client for other than
the declared goals.

   In our opinion and considering the experiences made with intercultural
music therapy, participation as a goal of therapy cannot simply be the
ability to participate in everything and with everyone, if the term is to have
any meaning for the client's state of well-being. If one wants to hold on to
it as a basic principle then it would have to be preceded by questions
concerning the self-ideal of the client, about his or her utopian conception
of a positive social space, and his or her personal ideas of how he or she
would like to be now or in the future. This must then be followed by the
question how the client uses the traditions and cultural patterns of his or
her society in order to do something about perceived injustices or to fulfil
subjective wishes, in other words, which possibilities for opposition and
moral autonomy are at his or her disposal. To find this out might be one
(sub)goal of music therapeutic work, which must include the possibility
for the client to bring in his or her resistance into music therapy and, for
example, also offer opposition to the music, the therapist, the procedure, or
the goals (such as participation).

   Analogous to the above exposition, if it is to have any meaning for
therapy, participation as a method cannot simply be an expression of a
low-threshold offering of music for needy clients in a non-clinical setting.
If one wants to hold on to it as a basic principle, then it would have to be
preceded by the question concerning the participation of the therapist in
the client's world. This means, in addition to the already mentioned
examination of own motives, questions must be asked about deeper
subjective, perhaps even ambivalent feelings of the therapist toward his or

---

[2] The other two characteristics are "ecological" and "music-centred". One could
also add "relational" (Stige 2005, p. 128).

her client, about his or her ability to tolerate irritations in reference to his
or her own role definition and self-ideal, and about his or her willingness
to undergo personal change or to allow himself or herself to be changed.
This requires courage and autonomy, the intellectual identification of
power structures and mechanisms of suppression (such as ethnocentrism,
androcentrism), and psychological knowledge of intrapsychic and
interpersonal processes. In the following section we look into a possible
source for this.

Psychoanalytic Music Therapy, Ethno-psychoanalysis, and the Concept of Social Dying

The basic assumption of psychoanalytic music therapy is the existence
and dynamics of an unconscious, which has an influence on interpersonal
and intrapsychic processes within and outside of the musical activity
(Metzner 1999). For this reason a distinctive feature of the therapeutic
relationship is that it is based on emotional participation, in other words,
the attentiveness of the music therapist to own reactions, feelings,
fantasies, and ideas, which are set off by messages of the patient. In the
following theory-guided reflection the therapist searches for the
underlying, unconscious meaning of both: message and reaction.

In therapy the dynamics of the relationship develop from the
dissimilarity of the two partners – therapist and patient – namely in
reference to their culture-specific psychodynamics and their cultural
milieu. Although this is true of every psychoanalytic therapy, it is
particularly obvious in intercultural therapy. Within the dynamics of the
relationship, which takes the form of resistance, transference, and counter-
transference, the manner in which the client as subject reacts to social and
institutional realities and how these affect his or her personal
consciousness and unconsciousness become visible. The subjectivity of
the individual can be seen as the individual embodiment of social
conditions (cf. the materialist theory of socialisation of A. Lorenzer,
1985).

Ethno-psychoanalyst Nadig, too, assumes the existence of a dialectic
relationship between individual and social structures: "The specific choice
made by an individual among different social possibilities is to be
explained by his or her life experiences, his or her specific position in the
social structure. Thus, the aim is not to draw a clear line between
subjectivity and social objectivity, but to see them in their special
relationship to one another" (Nadig, 1997, p. 34, translated by E.
Hertweck).

This now leads us into a special area of ethnological research, which is also relevant for the particularities of intercultural therapy (cf. Bürger 2005). This is so because in an intercultural encounter irritations and uncertainties arise, which the therapist would not expect in his or her own culture group. Here, we are dealing with behaviours, which result from the client's expectations of the therapist and his or her projections onto the therapist. These are blows against his or her self-definition. Reflexively, the therapist starts up self-protective mechanisms and defence strategies; these, however, distort his or her perception and interpretation of facts. Typical forms of defence in therapeutic settings include the declaration of strange behaviours as pathological on the one side, and the fascination with the exotic on the other, which also may appear together with feelings of melancholy. Underlying these are unconscious fantasies of omnipotence, being a great converter or a great healer which are supported and maintained through the chosen form of defence. A meticulous analysis of counter-transference by the therapist which focuses strongly on cultural aspects can, however, become an instrument to identify unconscious dimensions of one's own culture-specific and/or institutional influences and to gain unhindered access to the normality of the client.

Nadig (1997) describes the process to temporarily abandon firmly established role patterns in reference to class, culture and - to some extent - to gender together with the values connected with them as "social dying" – in our view, quite an extreme term. However, she points out which sources of information about the strange culture become accessible when the researcher (resp. the therapist) is able to accept the expectations and projections of others as a message within the (therapeutic) relationship. "Every projection of which one is consciously aware of is an aspect of the respective culture; the moment in and the circumstances under which it appears, the way it is used, and what leads it to disappear, all of this provides information about functional mechanisms and conflict structures of the respective group." (Nadig, 1997, p 45, translation by E. Hertweck).

However, the serviceability of "social dying" for therapeutic understanding in intercultural therapy should not obscure the fact that the personal risk undertaken by the therapist is too high without the security provided by in-depth training, a therapeutic framework, and accompanying supervision. Still, we believe that the sensibility for defence mechanisms which could follow irritations and uncertainties as well as the knowledge of how extremely unpleasant it can be to come in contact with one's own grandiose fantasies, can also be very helpful in therapy relationships with a less protective framework. Social behaviour does not simply follow a universal, genetically determined pattern. Rather, the preservation of culture-specific communication patterns, role prescriptions, and moral values are learned and practiced during childhood and adolescence in every society and in every social subgroup while needs are frustrated, so that objectively considered, it is difficult for anyone to acquire tolerance and understanding for the alien. In this connection, Alexander and Margarethe Mitscherlich (1998) state that a kind of dizziness easily overcomes us if we need to convince ourselves that one is able to lead one's life under another moral formula than the one that was instilled in us as children.

With this statement in mind, we take up the thread of the interaction scene between 13-year-old Layla and the German therapist with which this chapter opened.

The Vignette: Analysis and Interpretation

As described in the beginning of this paper, Layla approaches the therapist in a situation, in which she is occupied with an everyday task, namely tidying up, and is taken by surprise. The attack-like character of the following actions and the incomprehensible flood of words, which Layla must assume do not make any sense to the therapist, point to the possibility that Layla may be re-enacting a traumatic situation. Here, the same as in the warfare experienced by the civil population, it is a surprise attack on physical integrity, material possessions, and/or mental integrity. Following the classical psychoanalytic hypothesis, Layla communicates the feelings of the victim by displacing them onto the therapist. Fear, helplessness, despairing rage, and shock, which the therapist experiences, are understood as concordant counter-transference feelings. The actions of the therapist in the counter-transference – holding on and maintaining her composure – would be interpreted in this sense as unconscious identification with Layla's possible forms of defence, in other words, as a desperate attempt to keep control over her own body, possessions, and the situation. What is quite evident here is that Layla's bizarre (aggressive) way to establish contact also leads to subjective irritations in the therapist, which inevitably set off a conflict between her wish to approach in an empathetic-identificatory way and reflexive, boundary-setting withdrawal.

The witnesses of this scene and their inability to intervene most likely also play a role. However, it is totally unclear if we are dealing with a re-enactment of a triadic situation, in which Layla, for example, delegates being a witness of a scene of violence between third parties. (In this case the issue is not so much about what appears to be in the foreground of this scene, namely the interaction between Layla and the therapist.) On the

other side, it is also possible that simultaneously with the enactment of the
traumatic situation she externalises a trauma compensatory scheme (cf.
Fischer, Riedesser, 2003), for example the dissociation of perceiving,
feeling, and acting.

That this kind of interpretation does not suffice for our taste should be
clear from what has been said above in the theoretical exposition. Rather,
we see the danger of interpreting Layla's behaviours one-sidedly as
neurotic and individual - in this case traumatic - forms of defence; if not
both interactive (reciprocal) and culture-specific determinants are
considered as well.

Our discussion of the term participation indicates that the question of
the involvement and the motives of the therapist need to be addressed.
National aspects which are connected with the community of countries on
the European continent (geographic proximity of the war, moral-ethical
discussions concerning adequate foreign policy strategies, humanitarian
aid, etc.) should be considered the same as social developments, for
example the increasing interest in adventure-seeking and extreme
experiences in affluent Western society. However, we would like to focus
on another point, namely the fact that the young music therapists involved
in this project are the grandchildren of a generation which experienced the
Second World War and the post-war period in Europe as children and
adolescents. The experiences and survival strategies of those who were
children during the war in different countries of Europe as well as the
long-term effects of the war have increasingly become an important topic
in recent years. What has become clear is that these persons have blotted
out much from their perception and memory in order to continue living,
and there is much they have kept quiet about so as not to burden others
(their own parents or their children). But the inconsistencies in their
biographies and the parts left out in their tales have been conveyed to the
following generations, traumata and trauma compensatory schemata have
been passed on from one generation to the next, and await to be finally
dealt with, typically in the third generation. Thus, personal consternation
which must not be an individual consternation, on the one side and the
search for one's roots on the other side are most likely the strongest
motives for the young therapists to go to a post-war region and help war
traumatised children and adolescents there.

In reference to the German therapist, there is one more factor. By
having chosen a music-therapeutic approach with a clear psychoanalytical
orientation, she risks being identified with the perpetrator through the
transference-countertransference-relationship and therefore allows herself
psychologically to come in contact with hate, blame, and shame. Thus, she

exposes herself to a situation, which on the one hand is associated with Germany's past and on the other side with the deeply-rooted radical-nationalistic, ethnic "bogeyman" image of the enemy prevailing in the Balkan region and existing in all groups.

Personal motives of the therapist and transgenerationally relevant topics, which have an influence on perception and interaction forms, must –and this becomes clear here – be considered in the analysis of counter-transference; however, in our example – the same as for Layla – we are missing specific information, so that questions must remain unanswered. But this does not mean that our analysis of the vignette is already exhausted.

The girl Layla appears the first day of the project, however, not for the planned therapy session, but unscheduled. It can be expected that she, the same as other inhabitants of the Balkan area, does not see the therapist solely in a positive light as helper, but otherwise. Layla may possibly experience the therapist as a young woman, a Christian, who is free and able to determine her own life, who has an occupation and possesses valuables, could correspond to Layla's self ideal, which she admires and strives for, but also envies and wants to destroy, because it seems so out of reach for her and moreover belongs to a strange and hostile world. In refusing to participate in the therapy session and seeking contact to the therapist in a moment in which she is not protected by her role, Layla lets the therapist partake in her helplessness, despairing fury, and inner strife.

Furthermore, if we assume that with her opposition the client wants to present herself on a level that she does *not* break existing norms of her culture, not only the relation to her inner world but also to her environment become evident. In the eyes of the client, the therapist from a rich European country is somebody who has material goods to distribute, such as supplies of clothing, medicine, and other kinds of material. Layla does not know that the clothing are "Salvation Army clothes" for us or that donations are tax deductible. She has no idea that a music therapy student, whom she considers rich, is actually poor back at home. She does not know that the guitar is only borrowed, but believes the therapist owns the guitar and perceives that this young woman is willing to give something.

On the basis of their own subjectivity, Layla as well as the therapist interpret the events in their own particular outside world differently. The therapist sees herself as having come to Mostar in order to offer psychological help. Music and making music are her means of realising this, not the distribution of musical instruments. If the therapist would attempt to explain this to Layla, this would mean demanding of Layla the insight that she, the therapist, is right. She would also follow the impulse

to want to defend her shame. Shame about standing there with empty
hands, shame about the omnipotent fantasy of offering help - dissolved in
thin air within a second - and no longer able to be upheld, shame that she
herself instinctively acted in a culture-specific way by seeking first of all
to defend her own possessions.

At this point we would like to refer back to the thoughts about the
feeling of dizziness mentioned above, because when considering the
culture-specific tendencies in the interpretation, one recognises how
impossible it is to simultaneously grasp the various dimensions of a one-
minute interaction scene. In our specific example it was exactly the
subsequent shame which allowed the therapist to become aware of the
process of social dying and to accept it. Turning to one's own subjectivity
and giving up one's insistence upon it, made it possible for a moment to
see true "participation" in a strange living environment.

Is this a mutual thing? Unfortunately, it is not possible to answer this
question. But the fact that from that point onward Layla participated in the
music therapy group for girls of her age enabled the therapist to come one
step closer to Layla's reality, in which re-enactments of traumatic
experiences were also evident. To perceive these and to recognise these,
without being able to treat them in any depth or to work on them – this
was the special therapeutic challenge presented in this project. At the end
of this therapy there was an encounter between the two which could not
better express the intertwinements of personality and culture in the
therapeutic relationship. Shortly before the departure of the music
therapist, Layla came to say good-bye and handed her a plastic bag full of
presents: a teddy bear, a self-made bracelet, a Bosnian magazine for
teenagers, a stylish glitter shirt, a torn photo of her as a little girl, as well
as a long letter written in Serbo-Croat which contained her greatest wish,
namely not to be forgotten by the therapist.

Concluding Remarks

In view of the complexity of the material presented above, we would
like to make a few central statements. They can possibly serve as a
contribution for discussing concepts of intercultural music therapy. We
believe that they also can provide ideas for music therapeutic work in
other areas of practice as well.

Music therapists, who do intercultural work, must accept the fact that
the clash between two cultures - that of the therapist and that of the client
– is both an epistemological and methodical problem.

Focusing on everyday life on the one side (the approach of community music therapy) and on subjectivity in its conscious and unconscious dimensions on the other side (the approach of psychoanalytic music therapy) allows one to come - step-by-step - closer to reality and to the persons of the other culture. A clear line between subjectivity and social objectivity is not to be drawn; instead, one can only try to become aware of them in their particular relationship to one another.

The effectiveness of participation as a therapeutic method depends on the question if mutuality, irritation of one's image of oneself, and relativisation of culture-specific communication patterns and concepts of values are seen as constituting elements of the therapeutic relationship. The process of "social dying" sparked off by the participation of the therapist, must be accepted in order to prevent role fixations, which confine the perception of reality. In music therapy this also affects the understanding of music and the practice of making music, which however we have not discussed in the scope of this article.

Both client and therapist profit from an intercultural relationship. As otherwise only possible in music therapy training analysis, the specific experience and psychoanalytic reflection of intercultural therapy lead to a re-structuring of experience because in both cases the role systems, which support the own identity and guide perception, are shaken through the confrontation with that which is foreign.

The experiences of intercultural encounter and relationship heighten the awareness for the fact that – although it may seem trivial – even within one's own culture group, the other is truly an other. The particular choice which a client makes between different social possibilities is always to be explained with his or her life experiences and with his or her particular position in the social fabric. The formulation of the objective of therapy must always be preceded by questions concerning the self-ideal of the client, his or her utopian conception of a positive social space as well as the possibilities for resistance and moral autonomy he or she has at his or her disposition.

Epilogue

In this article we have addressed several questions. We first attempted to examine the possibility if and in which way a first encounter so strange as the one described can be understood in retrospect. In the above exposition - and borrowing from different fields of knowledge - we were able to show that this is basically possible and point out which extensive considerations are necessary.

However, if it would be possible to end the mutual speechlessness and cultural alienation, but in particular the experiencing of rampant violence – to this we cannot give a universal answer. In any case, we can expect this to be a long process, easily disruptable, with no guarantee for a positive outcome.

Finally there is the question if it is too presumptuous to want to calm down the war still raging in the hearts of these persons, to extinguish wild hatred, and to counteract the erosion of hope. We say yes, if the question is posed in this way, we believe it is too bold. But this would be no sufficient reason to not undertake this attempt, while applying all available powers, but in particular with an increasing sensibility for one's own individual and culture-specific perceptual distortions.

References

Bürger, C. (2005). *Fremde und Trauma. Ein Zugang zu musiktherapeutischer Arbeit mit traumatisierten Kindern und Jugendlichen in einem Nachkriegsgebiet.* Unveröffentlichte Diplomarbeit, Hochschule Magdeburg-Stendal (FH).

Decker-Voigt, H.-H., Mitzlaff, S., Strehlow, G. et al. (Hg)(2004). *Der Schrecken wird hörbar.* Eres Edition, Lilienthal/ Bremen.

Fischer, G., and Riedesser, P. (2003). *Lehrbuch der Psychotraumatologie.* Ernst Reinhardt Verlag, München Basel

Lang, L., and McInerney, Ú. (2002): Bosnia-Herzegovina: A music therapy service in a post-war environment. In: Sutton, J. (Ed.) *Music, music therapy and trauma* (pp. 153-174). London: Jessica Kingsley.

Lorenzer, A (1985). *Zur Begründung einer materialistischen Sozialisationstheorie.* Frankfurt a.M.: Suhrkamp.

Metzner, S. (1999): *Tabu und turbulenz.* Vandenhoeck and Ruprecht, Göttingen

—. (2004). Alterierte akkorde. Musiktherapie im wandel. *Musiktherapeutische Umschau*, 25, 291-299.

—. (Hg.)(2005): *Faszination musiktherapie: Hommage an Hans-Helmut Decker-Voigt.* Lilienthal/Bremen: Eres Edition.

Mitscherlich, A., und Mitscherlich, M. (1998): Die Unfähigkeit zu trauern. *Grundlagen kollektiven Verhaltens.* Piper, München 15. Auflage

Mitzlaff, S. (2002): Traumaverarbeitungsprozesse in der Gruppenmusiktherapie mit Kindern. *Musiktherapeutische Umschau*, 23, 219-231.

—. (2004): Trauma und Dissoziation. In: Decker-Voigt, H.-H. et a.l. (Hg.) *Der Schrecken wird hörbar.* Eres Edition, Lilienthal/ Bremen, S.103-112

Nadig, M. (1997): *Die verborgene Kultur der Frau.* Fischer TB, Frankfurt a.m.

Seidel, A. (2005): Anfänge oder: Die Schnittflächentheorie. In: Metzner, S. (Hg.): *Faszination Musiktherapie. Hommage an Hans-Helmut Decker-Voigt.* Eres Edition, Lilienthal/Bremen. S. 29-33

Stige, B. (2004). On defining community music therapy, Retrieved 29th November, 2005 from http://www.voices.no/discussions/discm4_05.html

—. (2005): Toward a Notion of Community Music Therapy. In *Jahrbuch des Berufsverbandes der Musiktherapeutinnen und Musiktherapeuten* (pp. 107-134). Wiesbaden: Reichert Verlag.

Sutton, J. (Ed.)(2002). *Music, music therapy and trauma.* London: Jessica Kingsley.

Chapter Ten

Music Therapy: Promoting Healthy Mother-Infant Relations in the Vulnerable Refugee and Asylum Seeker Community

Jane Edwards, Maeve Scahill and Helen Phelan

While music therapy is traditionally offered in clinical and health care settings, vulnerability in relation to mental health in parenting may not be easily detected or "treated" through current service provision in Ireland. This chapter reports a project, *Suantraí,* aimed at helping women with young children who had either successfully gained their refugee status or were currently in the asylum seeking process.

The *Suantraí* project was developed in 2004/2005 at *Doras Luimni* in association with the *Sanctuary* initiative, University of Limerick. Recognising the vulnerability of asylum seeker mothers and their infants and/or young children in the Limerick region, the music therapy program *Suantraí* was established to identify and address needs related to parenting during early childhood based on best practice as documented in the international literature. This paper provides, a. information about the asylum seeker framework within which the *Suantraí* program has been developed and operated, b. the role of music therapy in addressing these needs, and c. a series of case vignettes that describe how *Suantraí* has both identified and supported the needs of vulnerable mothers who have accessed sessions.

Immigration, Asylum and Citizenship in Ireland

The 1990's marked a new era in Irish migration. An unprecedented period of economic prosperity, popularly termed the "Celtic Tiger", coincided with a marked shift in emigration/immigration patterns. From the mid 19th century until the last quarter of the 20th century, emigration levels from Ireland were consistently higher than any other Western European country during this same period (Mac Éinrí, 2001). The Irish Diaspora subsequently spread throughout the English-speaking world, with emergent population cohorts in the UK, North America and Australia. Emigration levels dropped briefly at the point of Ireland's entrance into the European Union in 1973 however returned to previous levels with the economic depression of the 1980's.

Throughout this period, immigration into Ireland was relatively small and confined to a narrow demographic including a small number of returned emigrants from the Irish Diaspora; retirees, particularly from the UK, "counter-cultural" immigrants from other European Union (EU) countries such as Germany and Holland, and "non-permanent" immigrants working in the multi-national or university sector. Immigration from outside the EU or the Irish Diaspora was almost negligible.

The economic prosperity of the 1990's attracted a new wave of immigration, very different in profile to the demographic described above. The majority immigration wave included non-EU nationals offered employment under the work permit scheme or Irish nationals seeking employment in Ireland. A smaller but significant wave included asylum seekers, applying to Ireland for asylum under the Geneva Convention.[1]

While the number of people seeking asylum in Ireland is small in comparison to the wider European context, it has been characterised by a rise from an almost zero-base to a substantial number of applications in a very short period. In 1992, only 39 people had applied for asylum in Ireland, however by 2000 this number had increased to 10,938. Initially, most asylum seekers were accommodated in Dublin. As numbers continued to grow, so too did concerns regarding the ability of the centralised services of the Department of Justice, Equality and Law Reform to cope in a humane and efficient manner with the growth in numbers of applicants. In April 2000, the Irish government enacted a policy of dispersal, which allocated target numbers of asylum seekers to cities and towns around the country[2].

---

[1] See documentation compiled by the United Nations High Commission for Human Rights website, www.unhchr.ch
[2] For further information on the introduction of dispersal, see the website of the European Council on Refugees and Exiles, www.ecre.org

The Limerick Context[3]

The first asylum seekers arrived in Limerick in June 2000. Approximately 30 persons were housed in Barrington's Lodge, a facility which has since closed. As the numbers increased, new direct provision hostels opened. The hostels available locally at that time were primarily equipped to cater for single persons. As a result, most asylum seekers sent to Limerick city were single males, however a small number of women were also accommodated. Some asylum seekers, particularly persons with a disability, or women who had given birth to a child, were accommodated in the private rental sector until 2003.

Currently, there are three direct provision hostels in Limerick city, housing a total of 280 asylum seekers, the majority of whom are single males. The opening of the Knockalisheen accommodation centre in October 2001, realised the first custom-built accommodation centre, designed for family groups and children. Of the 266 asylum seekers currently at the centre, the majority of residents comprise one or two parent families. While this centre is located in County Clare, it is adjacent to Moyross in County Limerick and residents draw on many of the same Limerick city services as the residents in the three city centre hostels.

In November 2000, the first asylum seeker in Limerick City was granted refugee status. Since that time approximately 260 people have received refugee status. Some 3 people have received leave to remain status on humanitarian grounds and an additional 100 have received leave to remain (a parallel track to the asylum process) on the basis of an Irish born child. There have been approximately 40 family reunifications in the last four years.[4]

Mothers with Irish Born Children

Up until January 2003, mothers who gave birth to a child in the Republic of Ireland while in the asylum process were entitled to apply for leave to remain on the basis of having an Irish born child. Approximately

---

[3] The following narrative concerning the Limerick context is based on a field interview with Sr. Anne Scully Founder-Chair of DORAS Luimni, the Development Organisation for Refugees and Asylum Seekers in Limerick (January 31, 2005). Current figures for asylum seekers in Limerick are based on email correspondence with the Reception and Integration Agency (www.ria.gov.ie)
[4] The first major report surveying persons with refugee and leave to remain status in Limerick city was commissioned by the Reception and Integration Agency and authored by Helen Phelan and Nyiel Kuol (2005).

100 mothers were granted this status in Limerick city. This entitled them to establish a residence outside the direct provision system and to seek employment or education. Following a Supreme Court decision on January 23rd, 2003, the right to apply for leave to remain solely on the basis of an Irish born child was withdrawn. Therefore mothers with Irish born children were now required to remain in the asylum process, with decisions regarding leave to remain made on a case-by-case basis.

A further change to the rights and entitlements of mothers in the asylum process with Irish born children was brought about by the citizenship referendum of June 11th, 2004. The result of this referendum affirmed the inclusion of a new provision to the Constitution at Article 9:

> Notwithstanding any other provision of this Constitution, a person born in the island of Ireland, which includes its islands and seas, who does not have, at the time of his or her birth, at least one parent who is an Irish citizen or entitled to be an Irish citizen is not entitled to Irish citizenship or nationality, unless otherwise provided by law.[5]

As a result of this change in the constitution, mothers in the asylum process could no longer apply for leave to remain on the basis of an Irish born child, as this child no longer had the right to be considered an Irish citizen.

The full rigour of the legislation formulated to reflect this change came into effect on January 1st, 2005. Any child born of a parent who entered the asylum process before January 1st, 2005, was afforded a once-off, final opportunity to apply for citizenship before the end of March 2005.

Suantraí Music Therapy Project in the Context of Irish Immigration, Asylum and Citizenship

The *Suantraí* Music Therapy Project is a joint initiative between the Irish World Academy of Music and Dance, University of Limerick and *Doras Luimní*, the support group for refugees and asylum seekers in Limerick. It is funded through a Higher Education Authority initiative called *Sanctuary,* with a remit to building pedagogical bridges between the university and the refugee/asylum seeking community in Ireland. *Suantraí* commenced in November 2004 and employs a half-time music therapist.

---

[5] The full text of the Irish Nationality and Citizenship Bill, 2004, and additional documentation on the rights and entitlements of parents of Irish born children, is available in the documentation on 'Immigration, Asylum and Citizenship' at, www.justice.ie.

Music therapy is the planned use of music to develop and promote optimal functioning for people who face additional challenges to managing their day to day lives successfully. Working in a range of clinical and community contexts in Ireland, music therapists are allied health professionals providing group and individual programs following a process of referral and assessment. Music therapists' work with a person's presenting needs, interests and history, and music therapy approaches are adapted as needed to create meaningful relating through music. The past musical experiences of clients are of interest to the music therapist however the therapy does not require a client to have musical skills.

In identifying the needs of mothers and young children, *Suantraí* has engaged with women and children from all of the immigration categories described above, including mothers with leave to remain status attained prior to 2003 who were well established in the wider Limerick community, as well as mothers in the asylum process in the direct provision hostels, awaiting the results of their applications.

Although the *Suantraí* project has not been directly involved in assessing or treating mental health difficulties in the cohort of mothers identified as potentially benefiting from the support offered through the program, it is known that many asylum seekers in Ireland have mental health difficulties arising from their pre-migration experiences and their subsequent treatment on entry to the asylum seeker process.

A review of a two year period of psychiatric services offered to asylum seekers in a hospital in inner city Dublin, for example, showed that those presenting had a high exposure to pre-migratory trauma including torture, and the majority had been treated with pharmacological but not psychological treatments in Ireland (Kennedy, Gerrard-Dunne, Gill and Webb, 2002). The authors of the study proposed that their review indicated that more psychological support services should be made available to refugees in Ireland. As Kelly (2001) stated, "The mental health of refugees is intimately linked to their social and political situation in the host country. It is important to acknowledge the role of factors such as income and housing in their distress." (Kelly, 2001, p. 115).

The timing of the *Suantraí* project, beginning as it did after the referendum on the rights of the Irish born child but before the full implications of the referendum had been published in legislation, was a time of uncertainty and anxiety for most of the mothers accessing the music therapy groups. The "amnesty" announced at the beginning of 2005 for all children born before January 1st, 2005, created hope for some of the mothers, but also a period of new anxiety as they rushed to fulfil all legal requirements of application before the March deadline. It is against this backdrop that *Suantraí* must be understood and evaluated.

Parent-child Relationships: Importance of the Early Years

One of the most compelling and longest serving theoretical frameworks to support the importance of successful parent-infant bonding is *attachment theory*, proposed by Ainsworth (1963) and Bowlby (1969) (see also Bowlby and Ainsworth, 1965). Put simply, "...the primary caregiver of the securely attached infant affords emotional access to the child and responds appropriately and promptly to his or her positive and negative states." (Schore, 2001, p. 205).

Attachment theorists have undertaken hundreds of studies of infant behaviour, and have subsequently proposed four types of behaviour (labelled A, B, C, D) that the child could exhibit when either separated from the parent, or put under a similar stressful event. This manifest behaviour is considered indicative of the type of infant-parent attachment that has been formed. Under stress, the securely attached baby (type B) abandons exploratory behaviour and seeks the parent. The insecure-avoidant baby (type A) has an expectation that the parent will reject intense attachment behaviours so focuses on an object in the environment when under stress. The insecure-resistant/ambivalent baby (type C) is unsure how the parent might respond so will demonstrate intense behaviours that draw attention from the parent. The insecure-disorganised (type D) infant often "freezes" in a threatening situation because neither the fear eliciting environmental stimulus nor the parent offer a safe haven.

For some infants, type D behaviour is associated with their parent's loss of an attachment figure early in life (Ainsworth and Eichberg, 1991). It seems not to be the loss per se that is responsible for the infant behaviour, but the extent to which the loss has been resolved. In addition, this "freezing" behaviour under stress is also associated with frightened or frightening behaviour by the parent (Ainsworth and Eichberg, 1991). For children born of asylum seekers, either before migration or after the asylum process has been initiated, parental fear, anxiety and distress at least have been witnessed and experienced over a predominant period of their young life. It is therefore proposed this may be a cohort particularly vulnerable to attachment disorders, and so interventions to increase resilience in the mother-infant dyad offer an opportunity to decrease the potential risk of harmful consequences of the migration experience.

While attachment theory is firmly rooted in a psychological and psychoanalytic approach to work with parent-infant dyads at risk, Schore

(2001) undertook an interdisciplinary review of literature to find "…links between early relational trauma and a predisposition to postraumatic stress disorder, a neurobiological model of dissociation, the connections between traumatic attachment and enduring right hemisphere dysfunction, and implications for early intervention." (p. 204). He concluded that for parent-infant dyads at risk, "Early interventions…have life-long effects on the adaptive capacities of a developing self." (Schore, 2001, p. 246).

The *Suantraí* program is conceptualised as an early intervention to help offset the difficulties that may arise from the vulnerability experienced by the mother-infant dyads for whom the project is provided. By giving mothers and their children an opportunity for positive interaction through music, attuned to the child's development stage and needs, it is proposed that buffering against the potentially long term harmful effects of parental stress resulting from experiences prior to but also within the asylum process is offered.

Music in Parent-Child Relationships: Music Therapy Programs Enhance Skills

Music is intimately connected with parent-child interactions and bonding. Singing lullabies and rocking/moving to communicate with and soothe babies occurs across all cultural groups (Papoušek, 1996). Music is an inviting and engaging interaction that most children and infants enjoy, and most parents can use to relate effectively with their children (Abad and Edwards, 2004). Using music to facilitate interaction between a parent and child to help them develop a closer relationship is therefore a natural extension of regular social interaction within community life (Oldfield and Bunce, 2001).

It is well documented that when music therapy is provided to families within a group setting it can support participants to practice and refine skills that enhance parent-child relationships (Abad and Edwards, 2004; Oldfield and Bunce, 2001; Shoemark, 1996). Music has been demonstrated to be an effective way to involve the parent and child in a program that addresses the needs of both within a group setting (Abad and Edwards, 2004; Shoemark, 1996; Vlismas and Bowes, 1999).

Oldfield and Bunce (2003), based in the UK, have suggested that short-term music therapy work with mothers and young children is an unusual area of practice. One reason for this may be that music therapy has traditionally been offered as a treatment for identified disorders, rather than prevention, however music therapy work with parents and children in order to identify and prevent issues for which people who are at social disadvantage are particularly vulnerable is an area increasingly addressed by qualified music therapists, especially in Australia (see Abad and Edwards, 2004; Mackenzie and Hamlett, 2005; Shoemark, 1996; Williams and Abad, 2005).

Shoemark (1996) conducted a family-centred music therapy program within a playgroup setting with children diagnosed with conditions that may lead to developmental delay. The program aimed to nurture the creative expression and enjoyment of family members and to help build mothers' confidence in creating any kind of music in interaction with their children. Evaluation indicated that music was able to support families in developing skills to enhance their relationships. In formal and informal feedback, staff acknowledged the engaging quality of a music program when provided by a qualified music therapist.

Lyons (2000) described a family-centred social work group for women with children aged from birth to three years who were identified as belonging to marginalised social groups. This group program used music to help parents and children participate in a safe, developmentally stimulating group environment that fostered parent-child interaction and reduced isolation. Music provided a way to meet the different needs of the parents and children within the child-centred program. Participants reported that the group was the highlight of each week.

Oldfield and Bunce (2001) reported a mother and toddler group that was developed to help families who were experiencing difficulties affecting their parenting capacities. It was noted that many of the mothers involved had not experienced good parenting themselves. This music therapy program provided support for parents to interact with their children in positive and spontaneous ways.

Oldfield and Bunce (2003) conducted an investigation to study the impact of short-term music therapy programs with mothers and young children in two clinical settings and one control setting. The overall aim of the music therapy groups was to help mothers who were experiencing difficulties in the parenting of their young children by encouraging them to engage in playful musical interactions with their children. Through reflecting on this process after the sessions they aimed to help mothers gain new insights and more confidence in parenting abilities. Results showed that levels of engagement and interactions were high in nearly all of the sessions conducted. These results indicated that music therapy treatment was able to engage mothers and their children in positive interactions in play and music therapy sessions.

A study of depressed mothers found that music therapy was an effective short term intervention as reflected in changes to the mothers' right frontal EEG activation, a marker for depression (Field, 1998). It was suggested that the benefits available from music therapy are due to the way that this therapy is "mood altering" for the mothers and "arousal reducing" for the infants, allowing improved interaction in the dyad.

Sing & Grow is an Australian music therapy program that has offered weekly sessions to hundreds of vulnerable families in order "...to assist parents to extend their repertory of successful and nurturing parental behaviours in interaction with their young children" (Abad and Edwards, 2004, p. 15). Commencing in January 2002, Sing & Grow was originally offered in the Australian state of Queensland but now is a national initiative. The program has been evaluated by parents as successful in helping them feel closer to their children through using music in play and before bed (Abad and Edwards, 2004). In addition, the attendance figures for the program are impressive with 82% of parents referred to the program attending one or more sessions (Abad and Edwards, 2004). This Australian program has informed the development of Suantraí.

Suantraí

The Suantraí music therapy project currently facilitates weekly three groups for mothers and their young children. Two groups are run at direct provision accommodation centres for asylum seekers, and a group has been established at the administrative office of a support organisation for refugees and asylum seekers. There are no time limits on participation and, once assessed as having needs relevant to the group, mothers are encouraged to attend every week. Some 50 mothers, of many nationalities, and their young children have accessed the groups over the past seven months.

A regular weekly session is offered where mother and child engage in music, aimed at providing opportunities for increased positive interactions to promote the healthy development of the young child. Sessions are based on an open structure to facilitate the many cultural groups attending and to allow mothers to access the musical interactions in their own manner. Traditional Western nursery rhymes and children's songs are used, as well as rhymes and songs popular in the mothers' native countries. The session content varies from week to week and usually includes a number of sections, well known nursery songs, fine-motor action songs, interactive face-to-face play, songs promoting gross-motor actions, instrumental play, quiet time and individual song choice.

Observing the mothers and young children in the hostels at the commencement of this program, it became evident that experiencing closeness with their children and having positive experience in interactions were absent or infrequent. The aim of the program at the hostel therefore has been to facilitate and build upon any positive feelings exhibited between mother and child in order to set up the possibility for a sequence of interactions culminating in successful and responsive mother-child exchanges.

The *Suantraí* sessions have provided a special space for mothers and children in the asylum process through which they can experience a positive environment, and participate in a welcoming and encouraging group process. The following case vignette describes how an isolated, bereaved mother and her daughter found solace in being a part of the music therapy group and how they have changed their interaction style over a short period of time.

Sarah and her daughter Simone are living in private accommodation in the Limerick area. Two months prior to *Suantraí* sessions commencing, Sarah's husband was killed in an accident. Sarah has lived in Ireland for twenty-one months and it is reported that before his death, Sarah's husband had behaved in controlling ways, not allowing her to leave the house or make friends. The music therapist was introduced to Sarah when she was first bereaved. At that time Sarah was spending most days at the office of the support organisation; she did not eat or drink anything and mostly lay along the wooden benches in the waiting area. She often commented that she just wished to be among people at this time.

After a conversation with the music therapist Sarah reluctantly agreed to attend the sessions. Sarah then attended every week with her 9-month-old daughter. Simone presented as an infant with excellent gross motor skills and engaging eye contact, however her face was never animated, she rarely cried and was never observed to smile. From the first session Sarah participated actively, singing to her daughter as she lay in her arms. She quickly learnt lyrics to the songs and each week tried to engage Simone in musical play. By session nine Sarah stopped dressing in black and began to take care of her hair and general appearance. By this time a smile was becoming evident on Sarah's face and she showed positive responses when people gave her compliments.

Despite the complex emotions of gaining freedom from a hostile home situation and experiencing the loss of a spouse, Sarah took advantage of the opportunities presented in the music therapy sessions. As the sessions progressed Sarah, holding her daughter closely, demonstrated an eagerness to sing to her daughter and be involved in the action songs, using hand-over-hand facilitation to aid Simone's responses.

One week after Simone's first birthday (session 15) Sarah held Simone on her lap during the song "Rockin' to the music". As Simone lay on her back, Sarah began to rock her to and fro smiling at her as she sang. She asked her to show a smile, as she rubbed her tummy and Simone smiled and laughed. This was the first smile observed during a music therapy session. Sarah's joy was obvious and especially as it appeared that the smile was stimulated by her play actions and close facial interactions. Simone's smile was not repeated despite Sarah's constant efforts for the rest of the song. The other mothers present seemed to recognise the significance of the moment and reacted joyfully, commenting on her daughter's happy face.

The opportunities presented to mothers in *Suantraí* groups are beneficial to their development of play and interaction capacities through music and there is an optimistic expectation that the material used in the weekly sessions will transfer, in positive and spontaneous ways, into the daily lives and interactions of the participants. This extends the therapeutic process outside the group session as described in the following vignette:

Some of the children attending these sessions have been resident in accommodation centres since their birth.

After attending five sessions, a mother from north Asia described how her 2½-year-old daughter constantly talks about the music session during the week and asks her every day to sing songs from the group. This mother and daughter have attended sixteen of twenty-two sessions. She has commented that since the beginning of the sessions there has been a marked increase in the time she spends playing with her daughter and that much of this is initiated by her daughter asking her to sing songs offered during the program such as Four Hugs a Day[6] and The Wheels on the Bus.

The psychological stress for mothers living in direct provision units have, however, been reported to the music therapist time and time again. Many of the mothers have commented on difficulties encountered due to the loss of family and friends, the loss of freedom, plus having to conform to institutional schedules and rules, and some have reported the emergence

---

[6] Four Hugs a day, that's the minimum
Four Hugs a day, not the maximum (2x)
Step One, look them right in the eye
Step Two, nose to nose
Step Three, reach your arms
Step Four, you can't do any harm with...
©Robinson and Diamond, 1984

of depressive symptoms. Unfortunately, sometimes this has limited some mothers' access to the *Suantraí* program as the following vignette describes.

A mother in the hostel began bringing her baby to sessions when he was just ten days old. For seven weeks they attended on alternate weeks, participating in four sessions in total. During the sessions the mother was observed to be actively involved in singing to her newborn baby, initiating face-to-face play, surrounding the space above his body with percussive sounds and offering to sing a special song for her son in front of the group. For most of the sessions, she arrived in her nightclothes, commenting that they had been resting. In the weeks that followed, as was the norm, the mother was telephoned before each session and the response was always the same, "I was not feeling fine last week, but I am coming today" and yet she did not come. After five weeks of similar responses she entered the group at the end of a session and without her son, whom she said was sleeping. She joined in the singing and expressed her disappointment that she had not arrived earlier.

After the session she spoke of difficulty in leaving her room. She described her experiences of living in the accommodation centre and although she wished to be at the groups she said that for her the lifestyle was too depressing and stopped her from leaving the room she called "home". This mother demonstrated excellent capability to have playful interactions with her newborn however despite her expressed enjoyment of the session the feelings of depression were debilitating and prohibited her regular attendance at sessions. Sessions continue to be offered to this mother however it is concerning that she almost never leaves her room now.

For those who are able to attend Suantraí, it is possible for this program to offer mothers and children a way to feel closer to each other, to feel connected to a group, and to have ways to relate to each other that involve structure, fun and play.

On entering the accommodation centre at the 20th week of the program a petite 2-year-old girl, in a blue velvet party dress was noted circling the centre of the reception area dancing to the sound of her mum singing the *Suantraí* "Hello" song. As the music therapist opened the door, the little girl's face lit up with a smile and she started clapping and twirling around and around. Her mum was a little embarrassed at first but then just laughed and said; "This is her happy day".

Discussion

The case vignettes presented here show some of the ways in which the *Suantraí* groups have been able to identify the needs of some mothers and how the sessions have reached the targeted cohort. The common factor between the group members is their search for refuge in Ireland. However, alongside this common experience are individual traumas and many participants have a range of troubling personal issues leading to a complex needs set encountered in the group, some of which limits their capacity to access the program.

That which is commonly shared is not necessarily a source of support or connectedness for *Suantraí* group members. They all belong to a club which no-one, by choice, would join. Inherent in the process of *Suantraí* group participation are positive experiences provided through musical interaction such as instant engagement and interaction through accessible materials, enjoyment of the session, a growing desire to participate and engage their children, increased interaction, and positive development of their relationship. Spontaneous feedback from the mothers has demonstrated that accessing this sequence at any point has been effective in creating a difference in their day-to-day lives.

Mothers attending the groups have evidenced a number of areas of vulnerability including anxiety about their future, reporting depressive symptoms, occasionally displaying anger towards their children, and at times having difficulty in relating to their children in positive ways during sessions. This vulnerability is considered to have an effect on their children and thus the need for a program that can increase positive relating, in spite of some needs around the mothers' psychological vulnerability being beyond the remit of the project, was conceptualised as necessary and useful.

Conclusion

The introduction of *Suantraí* music therapy groups into the lives of many of the mothers and children in the asylum seeking process and those with refugee status locally has offered a positive addition to their lives, in the form of musical moments and significant and successive positive experiences in interaction with each other. It is proposed that participation in *Suantraí* can buffer the potentially negative effects of parenting a young child within the stressful context of the asylum seeking process in Ireland.

References

Abad, V., and Edwards, J. (2004). Strengthening families: A role for music therapy in contributing to family centred care. *Australian Journal of Music Therapy*, 15, 3-16.

Ainsworth, M. D. S. (1963). The development of infant-mother interaction among the Ganda. In B. M. Foss (Ed.) *Determinants of infant behavior* (pp. 67-104). New York: Wiley.

Ainsworth, M. D. S., and Eichberg, C. (1991). Effects of infant-mother attachment of mother's unresolved loss of an attachment figure, or other traumatic experience. In C. M. Parkes, J. Stevenson-Hinde, and P. Marris (Eds.) *Attachment across the life cycle* (pp. 160-186). London: Routledge.

Bowlby, J. (1969). *Attachment and loss: Attachment* (Vol. 1). New York: Basic.

Bowlby, J., and Ainsworth, M. D. S. (1965). *Child care and the growth of love* (2nd edition). London: Penguin.

Field T. (1998). Maternal depression effects on infants and early interventions. *Preventive Medicine*, 27, 200-203.

Kelly, B. (2001). Mental health and human rights: Challenges for a new millennium. *Irish Journal of Psychological Medicine,* 18, 114-115.

Kennedy, N., Jerrard-Dunne, P., Gill, M., and Webb, M. (2002). Characteristics and treatment of asylum seekers reviewed by psychiatrists in an Irish inner city area. *Irish Journal of Psychological Medicine,* 19, 4-7.

Lyons, S. (2000). "Make, make, make some music": Social group work with mothers and babies together. *Social Work with Groups,* 23, 37-54.

Mac Éinrí, P. (2001). Immigration policy in Ireland. In F. Farrell, and P. Watt (Eds.) *Responding to racism in Ireland.* Dublin: Veritas.

Mackenzie, J., and Hamlett, K. (2005). The *Music Together* program: Addressing the needs of "well" families with young children. *Australian Journal of Music Therapy,* 16, 43-59.

Oldfield, A. (1999). Listening, the first step towards communicating through music. In P. Milner and B. Carolin (Eds.) *Time to listen to children.* London: Routledge.

—. (1995). Communicating through music - The balance between following and initiating. In T. Wigram, R. West and B. Saperston (Eds.) *The art and science of music therapy: A handbook* (pp. 226-237). Amsterdam: Harwood.

Oldfield, A., and Bunce, L. (2003). An investigation into short-term music therapy with mothers and young children. *British Journal of Music Therapy*, 17, 26-45.

—. (2001). 'Mummy can play too...' short-term music therapy with mothers and young children. *British Journal of Music Therapy*, 15, 27-36.

Papoušek, M. (1996). Intuitive parenting: A hidden source of musical stimulation in infancy. In I. Deliège and J. Sloboda (Eds.) *Musical beginnings*. Oxford: OUP.

Schore, A. (2001). The effects of early relational trauma on right brain development, affect regulation, and infant mental health. *Infant Mental Health Journal*, 22, 201-269.

Shoemark, H. (1996). Family-centred early intervention: Music therapy in the playgroup program. *Australian Journal of Music Therapy*, 7, 3-15.

Vlismas, W., and Bowes, J. (1999). First-time mothers' use of music and movement with their young infants: The impact of a teaching program. *Early Child Development and Care*, 159, 43-51.

Williams, K., and Abad, V. (2005). Reflections on music therapy with indigenous families: Cultural learning put into practice. *Australian Journal of Music Therapy*, 16, 60-69.

CHAPTER ELEVEN

DEVELOPING COMMUNICATIVE RELATIONSHIPS IN MUSIC THERAPY WITH PEOPLE WHO HAVE MODERATE TO SEVERE DEMENTIA

ALISON LEDGER, MPHIL, RMT

Music therapy provides opportunities for people who have dementia to interact meaningfully through and within music with the support of a qualified therapist. This therapeutic approach emphasises developing communicative relationships with people who have limited opportunities for social and interpersonal contact due to severe losses in cognitive and communicative functioning. This chapter describes the work of a qualified music therapist in providing therapy programs to patients with dementia residing on a continuing care hospital ward. Music therapy is distinct from environmental uses of music in healthcare settings, as it involves the use of music to achieve health outcomes within the context of an ongoing therapeutic relationship. In music therapy, both music and relationships are "integral and interdependent parts of the intervention process" (Bruscia, 1998, p.127). It is not the music by itself that is considered to bring about therapeutic change, but the relating that occurs within the music and the developing relationship between the therapist and the client. A music therapist implements and reflects upon musical interactions based on their growing understanding of a patient's past, cultural background, and needs (Bruscia, 1998; Ridder, 2005). In Europe, music therapy is practised by qualified professionals, who have usually completed music therapy postgraduate training covering in-depth study of a range of topics such as music, psychology, physiology, social theory, and a range of models of therapeutic intervention. Qualified music therapists draw on this knowledge to develop individualised programs that identify and address patients' cognitive, physical, social, and emotional needs. In music therapy, patients are usually involved in live music-making, through singing, playing, composing, or improvising music. A music therapist's behaviour towards patients is bound by a strict code of professional ethics. Music therapy outcomes are evaluated and reported (Australian Music Therapy Association, 2005; Bruscia, 1998; Edwards, 2006).

The three case studies presented below highlight the importance of individualised programming of music therapy services for people who have dementia on continuing care wards, and emphasise the role of the therapeutic relationship in meeting patient's social, emotional, and stimulation needs.

The Continuing Care Ward Setting

The continuing care ward is different from other medical settings in that it provides ongoing hospital-based care to patients with dementia. The dementias are a family of disorders involving the development of multiple cognitive deficits, most notably memory impairment. Other problems include speech or comprehension difficulties, gait disturbances, mood and sleep disturbances, and behavioural difficulties (American Psychiatric Association, 2000). With increasing cognitive impairment, a person's abilities to socialise, to undertake functional tasks such as handling finances, preparing meals, travelling from place to place, and to carry out personal care responsibilities diminish. Twenty-four hour care is then required, which can place heavy psychological, physical, social, and financial strains on family carers (Access Economics, 2003).

Continuing care wards provide ongoing personal and medical care to people with dementia and can relieve some of the care burden experienced by family members. However, home-like attributes are often lacking in these environments (Reimer, Slaughter, Donaldson, Currie, and Eliasziw, 2004). Common features of ward environments include long corridors, lack of access to safe outdoor areas, busy nurses' stations, and large noisy dining areas. As patients with dementia typically experience communication, behavioural, and mobility deficits, they are often unable to independently initiate meaningful interaction and activity within these environments. Nurses have reported that they would like to offer more interpersonal contact to patients with dementia, but rarely have time to provide more than the basic physical care required (Morgan and Stewart, 1997). In Ireland, psychological and social therapies are only beginning to be recognised as a fundamental component of mental health services provision (Department of Health and Children, 2006). On many continuing care wards, social, emotional, and stimulation needs have been overlooked in the development and implementation of services for patients.

Music Therapy and Dementia

There is a growing body of research evidence to support the inclusion of music therapy as an effective intervention for addressing the unmet social, emotional, and stimulation needs of people with dementia. Although concerns have been raised about the methodological quality and reporting of some studies (Sherratt, Thornton and Hatton, 2004; Vink, Birks, Bruinsma and Scholten, 2003), music therapy has been shown to be successful in increasing levels of engagement, participation, and social behaviour among people with dementia (Ridder, 2005; Sherratt, Thornton and Hatton, 2004).

Despite other cognitive and communicative losses, people at all stages of dementia are capable of participating in music, whether through singing or humming (Clair, 2000; Prickett and Moore, 1991), movement or instrument playing (Ebberts, 1994; Pollack and Namazi, 1992), or listening to the therapist sing or play (Nugent, 2000). As people with dementia show preserved music skills, music is an ideal interaction to encourage social contact. Research studies have observed greater interaction, such as increased eye contact, touch, smiling/laughing, conversation, or walking with others, either during or after music therapy (Fitzgerald-Cloutier, 1993; Lesta and Petocz, in press; Olderog Millard and Smith, 1989; Pollack and Namazi, 1992; Rio, 2002).

Music therapy can also enable people with dementia to express feelings of fear, loss, loneliness, or frustration either through instrumental improvisation (Rio, 2002) or song (Short, 1995). A particular song may address unmet emotional needs by reminding people of their past activities and accomplishments, and affirming their identities. People with dementia have recalled pleasant memories or shown improved mood in response to familiar music (Ashida, 2000; Clark, Lipe and Bilbrey, 1998; Fitzgerald-Cloutier, 1993; Hanser and Clair, 1995; Lesta and Petocz, in press; Lipe, 1991), and particular music has evoked significant memories for people with dementia within music therapy sessions (Gaertner, 1993; Lipe, 1991; Tomaino, 2000). Familiar music may also serve to meet people's needs for stimulation through attracting and maintaining attention (Ridder, 2003).

Case Examples

The music therapy cases described here are from the author's clinical work undertaken as part of a research project conducted on a continuing care hospital ward for twenty-three people with dementia in Limerick, Ireland. Patients must display behavioural disturbances deemed difficult to manage in order to be admitted to the ward, and caring for these patients can be perceived as stressful by nursing and other care staff. A research project was carried out to investigate whether the introduction of music therapy and art therapy would result in positive changes in patients' behaviour, as well as changes in staff stress levels, morale, and responses to agitated behaviour (Edwards et al, 2005).

In the continuing care ward, most patients spend their days in one of two large day rooms. The first of these is beside one of the entrances to the ward, and staff, patients, and visitors use this room as a passageway to other areas in the hospital. The second day room is beside the kitchen, and sounds of staff taking meal breaks and cutlery and crockery clattering can be heard at intervals throughout the day. Before the introduction of therapies on the ward, it was observed that patients rarely interacted with each other. Those with reduced communication and mobility were observed to be limited in their abilities to initiate interactions, and those who were more mobile tended to wander up and down the long corridors of the ward. Nursing staff conversed with the patients whenever possible, but were often busily attending to patients' personal care and medical needs. Aside from daily visits from the hospital priest, no structured, routine activities were offered on the ward. Televisions were usually switched on in the day rooms, but patients rarely showed interest in the programs that were on. Patients appeared to have very little meaningful stimulation in their day to day lives.

As part of the research project, the author (from here on referred to as the therapist) assessed each patient's abilities, needs, background, and preferences, and implemented music therapy programs during the four days per week of music therapy services to the ward. As several patients were assessed as having social and stimulation needs, a regular music therapy group program was established three afternoons a week. The therapist usually invited up to ten patients to the groups, and these were held in the second day room described above. Sessions were approximately forty-five minutes in duration with a consistent structure, including greetings to each participant, an introduction medley, songs and discussion around a theme, and patients' song requests. Sessions ended with a parting song and farewells to each participant. Patients participated in various ways, depending on their levels of verbal, cognitive, and physical abilities. Some sang, requested songs, guessed song titles from lyric or melodic clues, and shared memories and opinions associated with the music. Others listened to music or answered simple, closed questions from the therapist. The following case description shows how one patient's social, emotional, and stimulation needs were met through attending this group.

Case Description 1 – Margaret

Margaret is a seventy-nine year old woman diagnosed with moderately severe dementia. She is a mother of two and a retired hairdresser. Friends recall that she was an outgoing person prior to her diagnosis of dementia, and especially enjoyed socialising at golf and at the races. However, Margaret did not display these characteristics in her interaction with others at the time of music therapy assessment. Instead, it was noted that she spent most of her time in front of the television in the sitting room, with her back to other patients. As Margaret required assistance from two staff to walk, she was not able to move from this position independently. She displayed difficulty in understanding conversation and directions from others, responding with incoherent speech or irrelevant answers to questions. Ward staff reported that Margaret was often aggressive during nursing interventions; she frequently screwed up her face, and grabbed and hit out at those attempting to assist her. These behaviours suggested that Margaret misinterpreted interventions as threatening and perhaps felt frustrated at her need for care.

The music therapy group program therefore aimed to offer Margaret a structured environment, in which she could understand and communicate successfully. Within the consistent structure of group sessions, Margaret was able to respond to greetings. She would shake hands, nod, and agree that she was "grand". She also gave meaningful answers to simple questions. She sat up straight in her chair and watched the therapist and other group members throughout sessions. As the sessions progressed, her former sociable personality became evident in her smiling, laughing, use of longer phrases such as "had a good time", and extending a hand out to others. These responses were evidence that feelings of confusion and frustration were lessened and that music therapy groups enabled Margaret to communicate and socialise to the best of her abilities.

While group music therapy may be effective in meeting the social, emotional, and stimulation needs of many patients on the continuing care ward, some patients gain more from individual music therapy. The following case example describes a progression from group to individual music therapy, to best meet the needs of a patient who displayed agitated behaviour.

Case Description 2 – Jimmy

Jimmy was a seventy-eight year old man, diagnosed with vascular dementia and recurrent health problems, including pneumonia. Nursing staff reported that Jimmy's behaviour was unpredictable, ranging from periods of drowsiness to episodes of crying, shouting, cursing, and physical aggression. When visiting, Jimmy's daughters shared memories of earlier, more jovial times, when Jimmy sang around the house and at family get-togethers. Jimmy was also known for his spirited singing on the ward and was therefore included in music therapy groups. However, within the group setting, Jimmy appeared to become overly excited. He tended to dominate sessions, singing and joking loudly and interrupting when other patients were making contributions to the group. Jimmy regularly continued singing after sessions and staff often encouraged him to do so, complimenting him and making requests. After two weeks of group therapy sessions, a clinical nurse manager approached the music therapist to report that sedative injections were being used to calm Jimmy down following sessions. While group sessions were successful in meeting Jimmy's needs for stimulation, social interaction, and maintenance of identity, it appeared that Jimmy remained in a state of high arousal after sessions had ended. In consultation with the clinical nurse manager, the music therapist then decided to alter Jimmy's therapy to individual sessions, to see whether this problem with equilibrium might be effectively addressed. Within individual sessions, Jimmy was still able to share his musical talent with another person. He continued to sing harmonies and instrumental fill-ins as the therapist sang, and he shared stories about singing in Irish pubs. In addition, the music therapist was able to play quieter and slower songs towards the ends of individual sessions, to encourage relaxation afterwards. Jimmy responded by closing his eyes, making positive comments about the music, and thanking the therapist. The use of sedative injections following music therapy then decreased. Individual sessions not only allowed Jimmy a time to succeed in music-making, but also assisted him to engage in more settled behaviour once his time to shine was over.

Individual music therapy may also be indicated with increasing progression of dementia, as lower-functioning patients require more assistance to participate in meaningful activities (Clair, 1996; Ebberts,

1994). While group programs are effective in facilitating social contact between patients who remain capable of interaction, patients with more limited communication abilities require individual attention and encouragement in order to facilitate their social responses. The following is an example of a patient who benefited from the additional one to one contact offered by individual music therapy sessions.

Case Description 3 – Mary

Mary is a ninety-one year old woman diagnosed with moderately severe dementia. She is a widow and a mother of six children. At the time of the research project, she communicated through facial expressions, responding to simple questions, and counting and reading visual stimuli in her environment. However, her opportunities to gain stimulation and initiate interactions were limited, as she was no longer able to walk and was always in either a bed or a chair. Upon music therapy assessment, it was discovered that Mary could sing ends of phrases in well-known Irish songs if gaps pauses were left for her to do so, and could sing complete lyrics to the songs Spancil Hill (Loesberg, 2003) and Daisy Bell (Dacre, 1892). Individual music therapy sessions were therefore recommended to maintain Mary's communication, social, and musical abilities. During sessions, Mary communicated verbally with the therapist through greetings, such as "hello" and "I'm good", and she gave clear yes/no responses to offers of music and simple questions about herself. She sang either complete songs or ends of phrases, and smiled and shook hands with the therapist when complimented. Mary also showed an interest in the musical materials within sessions, looking at the therapist's guitar and sheet music intently and counting their components such as the number of guitar strings and the staves on the sheet music. This participation in sessions not only assisted Mary to maintain her skills, but also seemed to increase Mary's levels of alertness and involvement with her environment. Rather than sitting slumped in the bed or chair, she sat upright, swinging her legs and watching happenings around her, even after sessions had ended.

Discussion

In the literature about music therapy interventions for people with dementia, the value of establishing and building upon communicative relationships through music has been emphasised (Odell-Miller, 1995; Ridder, 2005). Ridder (2005) stated that "only through social contact and communication is it possible to understand and validate psychosocial needs" (p. 64). In each of the three cases described above, musical interaction provided a means of communicating with patients, so that social, emotional, and stimulation needs could be addressed.

In order to establish communicative relationships with the three patients, the therapist used musical materials that were familiar and relevant to the patients' past experiences. Prior to commencing music therapy interventions, the therapist sought information about the patients' likes and dislikes, family, cultural, and working backgrounds from staff, family members, and medical charts. This enabled selection of music that was likely to hold meaning for the patients. For Margaret, songs commonly sung at social gatherings were played in group sessions. Irish pub songs and ballads were prepared for Jimmy and the therapist learned and played songs that Mary had reportedly sung all her life. The patients appeared to recognise these songs, smiling, nodding, or singing along when songs were introduced during the sessions. The live singing of these long-familiar songs also seemed to promote social contact and intimacy, as the patients responded to the therapist's singing through positive comments, facial expressions, and touch.

Through repeated contact with the patients, the therapist discovered communicative possibilities and developed relationships further. As the therapist came to know patients, she drew on techniques and approaches that would best suit each individual. It was discovered that Margaret could socialise with others once she became familiar with the repeated structure of music therapy group sessions. Mary could express herself if one to one encouragement was provided. It became evident that Jimmy benefited more from individual music therapy and his program was altered accordingly. As interventions were adapted according to patients' needs and abilities, each patient experienced successes in communicating and interacting. These successes may have encouraged further responses in later sessions.

The clinical work described above also emphasised the need for a music therapist to develop relationships with other ward staff. Before introducing music therapy to the continuing care ward, the therapist met with members of the team to draw on their knowledge of patients and to educate them about the aims of music therapy. This led to the therapist and other staff working together in order to best meet the patients' needs, as in the case example of Jimmy.

In each of these cases, music therapy enabled the patients to communicate and socialise to the best of their abilities. Patients displayed levels of alertness, interaction, and involvement that were not regularly observed outside of music therapy sessions. Patients expressed aspects of identity through musical interaction - Margaret shared her sociable personality, Jimmy performed his role as the pub larrikin, and Mary demonstrated her enjoyment of music. This degree of self-expression was rarely seen in the behaviour of these patients on the ward prior to the introduction of music therapy, and indicates that therapy sessions were stimulating, enjoyable, and meaningful.

Conclusions

Although continuing care wards meet patients' personal care and medical needs adequately, patients' social, emotional, and stimulation needs can be overlooked in these environments. Music therapy is one intervention that can meet this gap in service provision. Despite marked cognitive impairment, people with dementia are often capable of participating in music and through music. In music therapy, people with dementia can interact, express themselves, and have access to meaningful stimulation. Group music therapy can be effective for meeting social needs common to a number of patients living on a continuing care ward. Individual sessions may be more effective for people who display marked behavioural difficulties or for those in the severe stages of dementia. Through establishing and developing communicative relationships, music therapists can work alongside other continuing care ward staff to meet the multiple and varied needs of patients with dementia.

References

Access Economics. (2003). The dementia epidemic: Economic impact and positive solutions for Australia. *The University of Queensland Cybrary* [On-Line]. Retrieved September 21, 2003 from the World Wide Web: http://www.accesseconomics.com.au/reports/dementiafull.pdf

American Psychiatric Association. (2000). *Diagnostic and statistical manual of mental disorders* (4th ed., text revision). Washington: American Psychiatric Association.

Ashida, S. (2000). The effect of reminiscence music therapy sessions on changes in depressive symptoms in elderly persons with dementia. *Journal of Music Therapy, 37*, 170-182.

Australian Music Therapy Association. (2005). Frequently asked questions – and answers. *Australian Music Therapy Association Inc* [On-Line]. Retrieved May 4, 2006 from *http://www.austmta.org.au/*

Bruscia, K. E. (1998). *Defining music therapy*, 2nd edition. Gilsum: Barcelona.

Clair, A. A. (2000). The importance of singing with elderly patients. In D. Aldridge (Ed.) *Music therapy in dementia care: More new voices* (pp. 81-101). London: Jessica Kingsley.

—. (1996). The effect of singing on alert responses in persons with late stage dementia. *The Journal of Music Therapy, 33*, 234-247.

Clark, M., Lipe, A., and Bilbrey, M. (1998). Use of music to decrease aggressive behaviors in people with dementia. *Journal of Gerontological Nursing, 24*, 10-17.

Dacre, H. (1892). Daisy Bell (Bicycle built for two) [Recorded by Sean O'Neill Band]. On *Irish drinking songs* [Audio CD]. London: K-Tel. (1995)

Department of Health and Children. (2006). *A vision for change: Report of the Expert Group on Mental Health Policy*. Dublin, Ireland: Stationery Office.

Ebberts, A. G. (1994). *The effectiveness of three types of music therapy interventions with persons diagnosed with probable dementia of the Alzheimer's type who display agitated behaviors.* Unpublished master's thesis, University of Kansas, USA.

Edwards, J. (2006). MA in Music Therapy. *Irish World Academy of Music and Dance* [On-Line]. Retrieved May 4, 2006 from *http://www.ul.ie/~iwmc/programmes/mamt/index.html*

Edwards, J., Ledger, A., Bond, O., Loane, R., Newson McMahon, J., and Wale, S. (July, 2005). Music therapy and art therapy in the reduction of agitation in patients who have dementia. [Poster Presentation]. *11th world congress of music therapy*. Brisbane, Australia. World Federation of Music Therapy.

Fitzgerald-Cloutier, M. (1993). The use of music therapy to decrease wandering: An alternative to restraints. *Music Therapy Perspectives, 11*, 32-36.

Gaertner, M. (1993). The sound of music in the dimming, anguished world of Alzheimer's disease. In M. Heal and T. Wigram (Eds.) *Music therapy in health and education* (pp. 244-264). London: Jessica Kingsley.

Hanser, S. B., and Clair, A. A. (1995). Retrieving the losses of Alzheimer's disease for patients and care-givers with the aid of music. In T. Wigram, B. Saperston and R. West (Eds.) *The art and science of music therapy: A handbook* (pp. 342-360). Amsterdam: Harwood.

Lesta, B., and Petocz, P. (2006). Familiar group singing: Addressing mood and social behaviour of residents with dementia displaying sundowning. *Australian Journal of Music Therapy*,

Lipe, A. (1991). Using music therapy to enhance the quality of life in a client with Alzheimer's dementia: A case study. *Music Therapy Perspectives*, 9, 102-105.

Loesberg, J. (Arranger, 2003). Spancil Hill. In J. Loesberg (Ed.), *The Irish pub songbook* (p. 26). Cork, Ireland: Ossian.

Morgan, D. G., and Stewart, N. J. (1997). The importance of the social environment in dementia care. *Western Journal of Nursing Research*, 19, 740-762.

Nugent, N. (2000). *The effects of live versus taped preferred songs on individuals with dementia of the Alzheimer's type displaying agitated behaviours.* Unpublished master's thesis, University of Melbourne, Australia.

Odell-Miller, H. (1995). Approaches to music therapy in psychiatry with specific emphasis upon a research project with the elderly mentally ill. In T. Wigram, B. Saperston and R. West (Eds.) *The art and science of music therapy: A handbook* (pp. 83-111). Amsterdam: Harwood.

Olderog Millard, K. A., and Smith, J. M. (1989). The influence of group singing therapy on the behavior of Alzheimer's disease patients. *Journal of Music Therapy*, 26, 58-70.

Pollack, N. J., and Namazi, K. H. (1992). The effect of music participation on the social behavior of Alzheimer's disease patients. *Journal of Music Therapy*, 29, 54-67.

Prickett, C. A., and Moore, R. S. (1991). The use of music to aid memory of Alzheimer's patients. *Journal of Music Therapy*, 28, 101-110.

Reimer, M. A., Slaughter, S., Donaldson, C., Currie, G., and Eliasziw, M. (2004). Special care facility compared with traditional environments for dementia care: A longitudinal study of quality of life. *Journal of the American Geriatrics Society*, 52, 1085-1092.

Ridder, H. M. (2005). An overview of therapeutic initiatives when working with people suffering from dementia. In D. Aldridge (Ed.) *Music therapy and neurological rehabilitation: Performing health* (pp. 61–82). London: Jessica Kingsley.

——. (2003). *Singing dialogue: Music therapy with persons in advanced stages of dementia. A case study research design.* Unpublished doctoral thesis, Aalborg University, Denmark.

Rio. R. (2002). Improvisation with the elderly: moving from creative activities to process-oriented therapy. *The Arts in Psychotherapy, 29*, 191-201.

Sherratt, K., Thornton, A., and Hatton, C. (2004). Music interventions for people with dementia: A review of the literature. *Aging and Mental Health*, 8, 3-12.

Short, A. E. (1995). Insight-oriented music therapy with elderly residents. *The Australian Journal of Music Therapy*, 6, 4-17.

Tomaino, C.M. (2000). Working with images and recollection with elderly patients. In D. Aldridge (Ed.), *Music therapy in dementia care: More new voices* (pp. 195-211). London: Jessica Kingsley.

Vink, A. C., Birks, J. S., Bruinsma, M. S., and Scholten, R. J. S. (2003). Music therapy for people with dementia. *The Cochrane Database of Systematic Reviews, 4*, Article CD003477. Retrieved February 15, 2005 from

http://www.mrw.interscience.wiley.com.ezproxy.library.uq.edu.au/coc hrane/clsysrev/articles/CD003477/frame.html

CHAPTER TWELVE

ANTECEDENTS OF CONTEMPORARY USES FOR MUSIC IN HEALTHCARE CONTEXTS: THE 1890S TO THE 1940S

JANE EDWARDS, PHD

As regards the advisability of instituting a musical mission or guild for the treatment of illness…we must speak with some reserve…the function of this pleasing art is in most cases quite subsidiary, and its effects are merely temporary.
—*The Lancet*, July 4th, 1891, p. 44

Psychiatrists must learn more about the healing power of music and musicians must learn more about psychiatry before much can be accomplished to bridge the gap.
—Esther Goetz Gilliland, 1945, p.24

The primary purpose of the hospital has not changed, and the musical aide must never forget that medical care and rest come before all else
—Sidney Licht, M.D., 1946, p. 89

The use of music as an agent of health promotion or healing is not a new phenomenon, however examination of the uses and ubiquity of music in healing practices prior to the contemporary profession "music therapy" have only more recently received consideration from historical and anthropological perspectives (Gouk, 2000; Horden, 2000[1]). Given that one of the goals of this book has been to offer a contemporary snapshot of the ways music is actioned as healthful in contexts where people are receiving medical treatment or care, reference to past uses of music to attain healthcare goals can provide a backdrop to current practices. This chapter

---

[1] Both Ruud (2001) and Ansdell (2004) have provided music therapy commentary on these texts.

provides a brief review and discussion of some of the literature about music in health care published prior to the establishment of music therapy as an allied health discipline in the United Kingdom and the United States of America around the middle of the twentieth century. This brief survey reveals some of the negative reactions to proposed uses of music in hospital settings. It also indicates aspects of the contested nature of the term "music therapy" when it first appeared as a descriptor for practice.

Descriptions of the uses of music to assist hospital patients were sourced from music and medical journals in the UK and USA from the late 19th century up until the late 1940s in addition to published books and book reviews in English. The works of main interest for this chapter are those where the writer has described at least one case where they used music, or directly observed its use, as an agent of care or symptom modification for a person described as ill or hospitalised[2]. The reading of and response to these texts is from my perspective as a qualified music therapist practicing through the period of the late 20th and early 21st century[3] considering the aspects of psycho-musical and medical-musical discourses which have helped shape the development of current practices in music provision for hospitals.

The review of papers below is neither strictly chronological nor comprehensive. The main focus is on reports of the use of music with patients' hospitalised for treatment of medical conditions in general hospitals rather than mental disorders in psychiatric services[4], however the exception is for the texts which describe music practices to assist returned soldiers.

Music in London Hospitals 1891: "…its effects are merely temporary"

In 1891 a group of musicians led by Canon Frederick Kill Harford inaugurated the Guild of St Cecilia with a view to providing live music to hospital patients in London hospitals[5]. Letters to the editor written by Harford outlining the forward planning and subsequent execution of this

---

[2] As Davis and Gfeller (1999) have noted, there are many manuscripts from the 18th and 19th century that discuss the medicinal and therapeutic properties of music but few provide direct applications and observations of practice.
[3] see Edwards, 2005, 1999a, 1999b.
[4] For relevant additional reading see Mackinnon (2003; 2006).
[5] See also Bunt (1994), Davis (1988) and Tyler (2002) for other relevant research by music therapists about the Guild of St Cecilia.

proposal appeared in *The Lancet* (July 1891)[6] and in the *Magazine of Music* (August 1891). In September and October of that same year, further letters were published by Canon Harford in the *British Medical Journal*.

In these published letters, Harford described the activities of the Guild of St Cecelia and reported the outcomes of experiments with "soothing" and "exhilarating" music which were conducted in hospital visits. Patients were asked their opinion of the benefits of the music and these were recorded along with their comments. Physicians were also requested to send any observations of changes in patients and some did so, notably Dr Dunlop (described as the head physician at St Pancras) (Harford, *BMJ,* 1891).

In October that same year the editorial of *The Musical Times and Singing Class Circular* published an anonymous scathing riposte. Titled *Medicinal Music* it ridiculed Harford's proposal to have musicians available all hours to send out to hospitals. The response decried Harford's idea that hospitals should be able to call a central location where musicians could then play over the telephone into wards. At the end of the piece the author stated that the only merit in the proposal was its support from Florence Nightingale and the proposal is urged to seek the support of doctors in order to have validity. In general the tone is dismissive and derisory as the following excerpt demonstrates,

> Doubtless we shall come in time to have our electric call-boxes provided with a special signal for summonsing the medical musician, so that within a very few minutes of the first symptoms of influenza or mumps making their appearance we shall be able to nip the ravages of these maladies in the bud by the application of the proper musical remedies. There will be, we fear, a few ribald sceptics who will talk about the melody being worse than the disease...
> (1891, October, p. 587)

It is notable that Harford had not in fact proposed a "medical musician" treating conditions in the same way a physician might but rather had suggested that musical performances might assist very ill patients to be soothed to sleep, through the use of lullabies, and had reported the benefits of music listening in reducing fever. Sometimes in criticising a suggestion or phenomenon, it is necessary to turn it into something ridiculous so that it can be seen as bizarre and unnecessary.

---

[6] Two of Harford's letters in the *British Medical Journal* and one from the *Lancet* were recently reproduced in the *Nordic Journal of Music Therapy* with an introduction by Helen Patey Tyler (2002)

In November a further editorial in similar tone, possibly by the same author, cited a letter of complaint received about the previous attack. This missive repeated previous assertions attacking the poor quality of the musicianship, and snidely remarking of the performances to which the public and media were invited as witnesses "As medicine they may have been admirable but as music they were so inferior that out of very kindness the leading critics of the London press held their peace." (November 1891, p. 654).
In further defense of the original article the author wrote:

> Let it not be supposed for one moment that we intended to turn into mockery...accomplished artists... [who] employ their talents for the purpose of cheering hospital patients. It is the turning of the thing into a system that we loudly protest against. There is something terribly grotesque and American in the worst sense of the word in this notion of a central hall with telephone...
> (November 1891, p. 654).

It was concluded with the statement that the previous critical response cannot have been too offensively incorrect if only one reader protested its content (November, 1891).
As Tyler has observed, "Harford's own prediction of the enormous expense of his plan soon came to be an unpalatable reality" (Tyler, 2002, p. 40). Perhaps though there are additional twists to be found in the short tale of Harford's Guild of St Cecilia. On the one hand the "enthusiastic believer"[7] trialling experiments to examine the effects of music, and on the other hand a dual hegemony of musical and medical establishments knocking down the prospects for the development of such an idea.

Observing the Lancet's Piercing View of Music in a Medical Role

The current web site for *The Lancet* describes it as a journal unaffiliated with any medical or scientific institutions. Founded in 1823 by Thomas Wakley he described the choice of title as follows "A lancet can be an arched window to let in the light or it can be a sharp surgical instrument to cut out the dross and I intend to use it in both senses" (*The Lancet* web site, 2006). Medical lectures from the London teaching centres formed the basis of early papers in the journal and current commentary on political and social events was included. "Thomas Wakley and his

---

[7] Davison's (1899) description of Harford.

successors aimed to combine publication of the best medical science in the world with a zeal to counter the forces that undermine the values of medicine, be they political, social, or commercial." (*The Lancet* web site, 2006)

Since *The Lancet* seeks to uphold the "values of medicine" and provides research evidence for medical practices, it is interesting to examine some of the writings on music that have appeared in its pages at various times. Some tongue in cheek or humorous aspects of the discourse on music representation appears and is interesting in relation to the hospital contexts in which it was proposed to offer music.

In immediate response to Harford's letter published in *The Lancet* the editor added a comment on the detailed proposals:

> The fact that music is capable of acting as a sedative in certain nervous conditions and as a stimulant in others is generally admitted. Its soothing property would no doubt be appreciably enhanced by the use of muted instruments, and its total efficiency by the employment of skilled performers. As regards the advisability of instituting a musical mission or guild for the treatment of illness, however, we must speak with some reserve. It must be remembered that the function of this pleasing art is in most cases quite subsidiary, and its effects are merely temporary.
> (*The Lancet,* July 4th, 1891, p. 44)

Some years after Harford's attempts to develop a practice of systematic musical treatments for hospitalised patients, in June 1895, *The Lancet* published a short review commentary on an article that had appeared in the magazine *Punch.* The article was titled *notes from a patient's diary* and is a comic satire on the use of music for the treatment of ailments. For example, it describes how the doctor produces a stethoscope at bedside, the patient protests he has no deficiency in his lungs and it turns out the stethoscope is a cornet upon which the doctor, now treating all patients with music, commences playing. In the street outside the patient hears a poor family ask for five barrel organs to be played simultaneously so that their child with chickenpox may take the doctors prescription of "street music every three hours" (*The Lancet,* 1895).[8]

There was some serious reporting of the uses of music in addressing the needs of the sick, for example a report in *The Lancet* in 1892 of a paper presented by Dr J.G. Blackman at the Portsmouth Literary and

---

[8] This representation aligns with issues around street music and its irritations to men in London "who earn their living by the higher kinds of brain work" (September 1893) which was the subject of a number of papers at the time (for example, January, 1891).

Scientific Society. In this paper the findings of studies about physiological changes were cited and a patient's reduction in temperature was mentioned following a "dose" of melody. Twice the report referred to the use of music as an "elaborate" way to address patient needs, suggesting it is an unnecessary intervention in relation to the benefits gained. This short report concludes that any such treatment would take a "secondary place" to medical intervention (*The Lancet*, 1892).

In 1899 Davison, in a paper titled *Music in Medicine* cited Harford's work thus:

> During the last few years attention has again been called to the influence of music in disease. In London Canon Harford, an enthusiastic believer in this mode of treatment organised bands of musicians...who might visit hospitals where permission was accorded....The results obtained showed that in music a therapeutic element existed which was not to be despised and which...might prove of great utility to the sick.
> (Davison, 1899, p. 1160)

Musical Therapy, Musico-Therapy, Trained music therapeutists, and Recreational Music

Eva Vescelius is credited with founding the "National Therapeutic Society in New York City" in 1903. She titled the work of musicians caring for the ill through music "musico-therapy"[9] (Vescelius, 1918). She provided descriptions of her musical interventions undertaken alongside other musician colleagues and friends for sick patients in hospitals or ill visitors to her home. For example she described a friend suffering for some five months with chills and fever who received a complete cure through listening to a live performance by accomplished musicians in Ms Vescelius' home of various pieces including the Moonlight Sonata and The Pilgrim's Chorus (Vescelius, 1918). Her commentary suggests that there was some openness to the use of music beyond concerts and entertainment in medical establishments of the time. Although little information is given as to their backgrounds or where their work might be found, Vescelius cites the comments of a number of men titled Dr or Professor to support her view of the therapeutic work possible using

---

[9] The term "musicotherapy" was used to describe the course which commenced in 1919 at Columbia University taught by Margaret Anderton, a musician from England (Tyler, 2000) and Isa Maud Ilsen an early music therapy pioneer who was a qualified nurse credited with starting the National Association for Music in Hospitals in 1926 (Brooke, 2006).

music. In the same issue of *The Musical Quarterly* as her paper, a theoretical essay titled "Music as Medicine" was also published (Rogers, 1918) which outlines historical uses of music in healing and accounts of its benefits in historical documents.

Ilsen (1925) reported ward music provided from the New York Tuberculosis and Health Association, which was offered in 15 hospitals. Based on two decades of experience offering music in hospital ward environments, she concluded that "Music means so much – we cannot estimate how much – to sick folk, especially those who….are compelled to remain in hospital for long periods of time." (Ilsen, 1925, p. 982). She promoted the benefits of her work with support from testimonies of doctors as well as depictions of antecedents to her work such as corridor singing in St Thomas Hospital London[10] in the 1860s and a quote from Harford's letter in the Lancet, May 1891.

At around this same time in the US there was an active interest group, described as the "music reformers", part of a social movement of "progressivism" in the late nineteenth and early twentieth centuries (Campbell, 2000, p. 261). It is possible to see how the aims of musico-therapy teaching and activity were endorsed by the background of this middle class social action which constructed "good" music[11] as an agent for positive change within communities, laying the "cornerstone for not only for responsible personal conduct but for also for the parallel growth of individuals as citizens" (Campbell, 2000, p, 265)[12].

A later period in which a number of papers about music in hospitals appeared is the mid 1940s; the end of the Second World War. As Gouk has pointed out, it is no coincidence that the end of a period of trauma would be followed by musical attempts to "…restore harmony within the social body after the disruption of war." (Gouk, 2000, p. 173). Indeed Vescelius gives words to support this proposition in her conception of the role of music in 1918:

> After the present Great War is ended, a flood of humanity will doubtless pour in upon our shores – men and women fresh from scenes of horror, broken in fortune, broken in body, heartsick and homesick….music is a

---

[10] This was the hospital where Florence Nightingale founded a nurse training programme. Ilsen referred to Nightingale's support for music in wards in Crimean war hospitals.
[11] As Campbell has noted, this term "good music" was ubiquitous however no agreed definition existed
[12] A company which sold music books to schools used the slogan "Good Music Makes Good Citizens" in their ad campaign of 1923 (Campbell, 2000).

universal language, a harmonizer, comforter, educator. Cannot we
musicians devise some way of helping these, our brothers and sisters?
(Vescelius, 1918, p. 400)

The main practical reasons the pre-cursors to what we now know as the
profession music therapy prospered at the end of these modern wars was
the extent of the task of caring for the huge number of injured returned
soldiers and the large funds released to ensure this care was the best
possible. In the US the numbers of persons discharged from service for
"neuropsychiatric" conditions was estimated at 130,000, and in the state of
Illinois alone, for example, ten new hospitals were required to be
constructed for the care of returned servicemen (Gilliland, 1945).

Gilliland's paper describing the process as well as providing
documentary photographs[13] of music for the war wounded provides an
insight into some of the early ideas in the development of what we
recognise today as the profession of music therapy. Gilliland took care in
this paper to distinguish between *musical therapy* and *recreational music.*
No definition was provided for recreational music except to note that
extensive facilities were provided for recreation in most institutions and
the work of the personnel whether in voluntary or paid employ was to
"keep the patients in the right frame of mind" (Gilliland, 1945, p. 24). It
suggests that "recreational music" was in common use as a term within the
broad remit of recreational activities available to patients.

Gilliland defined "musical" therapy as the "...carefully prescribed
dosage of music, either by listening or participation, given under a
psychiatrist's supervision and closely watched and controlled." (Gilliland,
1945, p. 24) She made reference to the locked wards in the veterans'
hospitals and the importance of proper training before providing music to
the war traumatised within (Gilliland, 1945). Her papers particularly
exhorted music educators to provide music where they could to the newly
opened institutions (Gilliland, 1944, 1945).

The American *Music Educator's Journal* published a recommendation
that "definite steps be taken toward the promotion of a program for
licensing the persons who wish to teach or practice musical therapy"
(1945, p. 48). The same report also noted the receipt of a number of letters
to the journal on the topic of "therapeutic aspects of music" and one is
quoted in part there as follows:

---

[13] On the opening page of her article *Music for the war wounded* Gilliland provides
an unremarked photo of a nurse in uniform playing an upright piano beside a man
sitting up in bed in his pyjamas playing the mouth organ. The nurse has her back to
the patient and his eyes are fastened on her in a look of devotion.

Everybody writes about it, but nobody produces the techniques. We find
purposeful work in this field in only a few hospitals. What we need is a
thoroughly scientific approach to the problems, and not any more
enthusiastic sales talk – all of which is very fine but doesn't tell us how to
produce results
(1945, p. 48)

A letter in somewhat more acerbic tone from the office of the Clinical
Psychologist, Hoff General Hospital, Santa Barbara, California was
published in the same journal later that year.

To the music educators of America I would like to send this challenge:
Either produce something worthwhile in the way of musical therapy, or
admit that, to date, it is worthless and stop trying to force it upon us.
(Moore, 1945, p. 81)

Moore's desperation expressed in this letter in the face of the
psychological needs of the hospitalised men with whom he was dealing is
palpable. He described "I want, and need desperately, something that can
reach into a man's personality and draw out the horrors of war, the hell of
battle, and the repressed memories of his buddies' death rattles" (Moore,
1945, p. 81). In his letter, he accused music educators of feeding their egos
by producing papers on music(al) therapy, and of not being able to come
up with interventions that could do any more than soothe the war wounded
patients whom he was treating.

Antrim (1944) proposed that what was needed was research conducted
at "a music therapy clinic staffed by doctors in sympathy with the basic
idea and by trained music therapeutists" (p. 419). He then included a
footnote about the "the Institute of Musico-Therapy of New York, Frances
Paperte, Director". He stated that "some notable results are expected" (p.
419)[14].

Music in Medical Contexts

In Britain around the same time a paper titled the *Therapeutic qualities
of music* provided an historical overview of the way music had been used
medicinally in ancient times and suggested that modern heath care
practices could benefit from consideration of its inclusion (Gardner, 1944).
The paper referred to the writings of Canon Harford and presented
testimony from a senior house doctor at the Bolton Infirmary to confirm

---

[14] A paper based on the results of musical experiments at the Walter Reed hospital
which commenced in 1944 were published by Taylor and Paperte (1958)

that music was indeed soothing for patients. Gardner investigated the evidence for music as a treatment and concluded that "...it has been generally unsuccessful up to the present time for total cures." (p. 184)

In the next year, a letter to the editor criticised the lack of reference to Arab texts in Gardner's paper since, "So early as the ninth century the Arabs had noted the therapeutic value of music. In the tenth century it was being used in the hospitals." (Farmer, 1945, p. 59). This preoccupation with the link between historical uses of music and current possibilities was a prevailing theme in justifications for the contemporary applications of music for therapeutic purposes and a number of theoretical papers published at the time reviewed ancient documents' references to music as a justification for its current use[15]. It is beyond the scope of this chapter to extend a discussion of this phenomenon however it serves as a backdrop to the claims made for consideration of developing a systematic approach to the use of music for medical patients.

Gardner (1944) lamented that the Americans were ahead of the British in recognising the role of "music in therapeutics". The publication of this view coincides with the date of commencement of music therapy training at Michigan State University[16] in 1944 (American Music Therapy Association, 2006). Gilliland referred to two further trainings that were available in the US by 1945; i) a twelve week course by Arthur Flagler Fultz titled "Musical Guidance Plan" and accredited by the Boston School of Occupational Therapy and, ii) classes at New York University taught by Willem van de Wall (Gilliland, 1945).

In 1946 a Fellow of the New York Academy of Medicine Sidney Licht, M.D., observed "At present no accredited school of music or medicine offers a complete course of instruction leading to a degree in music in medical practice, or a major in that subject" (Licht, 1946, p. 122). Licht (1946) outlined a potential course of study in musical skills - recognisable as basic conservatoire training - and the medical subjects which would need to be covered, including among other topics; Psychology, Abnormal Psychology, Music in Medicine, and Kinesiology (p. 124). Reviewed by Gilliland in the *Music Educators Journal* that same year, it was received enthusiastically however Gilliland expressed her disappointment that Licht did not refer to his experience in army hospitals in this published lecture series. She wryly noted that the book's "...conservatism will satisfy even the most exacting of the medical

---

[15] See also Ruud (2001)

[16] Then known as Michigan State College; where Gilliland completed her music therapy training with the psychiatrist Dr Ira Altshuler. Esther Gilliland became the President of the newly formed National Association for Music Therapy in 1950.

profession." (Gilliland, 1946, p. 44). Her review of the book *Music in Hospitals* by Willem van de Wall (1946) appeared in the same issue. She described this text as a "practical handbook" (Gilliland, 1946, p 44) and noted the author's plea for greater availability of training for hospital musicians and the need for development of an appreciation for the role of music by other hospital staff.

Coming to America as a young man from his homeland Holland, Van de Wall was a harpist in the Metropolitan Opera Orchestra and the New York Symphony (Clair and Heller, 1989). His text describing music for hospitals was preceded by the book *Music in Institutions* (Van de Wall, 1936). In his 1946 book he described the hospital musician as the leader of all recreational music activities from patient and staff choirs to visiting musicians, as well as directing individual sessions. He noted the report of the National Music Council Inc. regarding a survey of music in mental hospitals. The survey asked for consideration of the qualifications music workers should possess. The findings reported that the "...desired qualifications fell into four categories: musical background, personality traits, attitude toward mental patients and hospital work, training and experience in mental hospital work." (Van de Wall, 1946, p. 81). Van de Wall suggested that these categories were also relevant to other hospital musicians.

Van de Wall was invited to summarise his 1946 book as a chapter in the text *Music and medicine* (Schullian and Schoen, 1948[17]). Sidney Licht is quoted on the back of this book as claiming it as "the best book of its kind". A contemporary review by Carroll C. Pratt[18] of *Music and medicine* appeared in 1948. The book is described as the "...kind of stuff to give musicians indigestion, and it ought to cause even the psychiatrist to long for the refreshing effects of David and his harp." (Pratt, 1948)[19] This dual criticism for the work of musicians offering services to hospitalised patients; reflecting a fear that it was neither sufficiently musical nor sufficiently medical is also reflected in the responses to Canon Harford's instigation of the Guild of St Cecilia in 1891.

---

[17] An extensive review and social contextualisation of this book appeared in a more recent book about music and healing within cultural contexts (Gouk, 2000).
[18] Carroll C. Pratt was a tutor at Harvard University in the philosophy department at the time of writing the review and an associate professor of psychology. He authored of a number of books including in 1931 *The meaning of music: A study in psychological aesthetics*.
[19] Pratt reviewed a book edited by Podolsky (1954) titled *Music therapy* which he described as "dreadful stuff" (1954, p. 227)

A review of Licht's book which appeared in *Notes* gives some idea of the surround to these "musical enough" concerns. The reviewer described how she

> ...witnessed a demonstration of "musical therapy" by a lady, an ex- or retired vocal teacher, with the title of "professor" who sang Lieder, in a manner calculated to bring back the infuriated ghost of Brahms, to a group of mentally ill veterans who deserved better of their country.
> (Lattman, 1946, p. 353)

Her review cautions against embracing too quickly the principles of therapeutic music since in her words such new ideas are often accompanied by charlatans and "witch-doctors" (Lattman, 1946, p. 353). This echoes a similar editorial comment in the journal *Notes* where the use of music as a therapy for returned servicemen was described as a "frequently abused topic" (Marriner, 1945, p. 161).

Without any claims of knowledge of either medicine or music, Leila McKay an army lieutenant provided an account of uses of music in a one year Music Therapy Project. This report of music as a "group therapeutic agent" for returned soldiers receiving medical care at Fort Logan AAF Convalescent Hospital[20] was published in the journal *Sociometry* (McKay, 1945)[21]. Her paper appears alongside that of Altshuler, a psychiatrist, credited as a pioneer of music therapy (Clair and Heller, 1989) whose theoretical paper is titled "The organism-as-a-whole and music therapy" (Altshuler, 1945).

McKay's report described how groups of men were taught how to make miniature pianos that could be played. They then underwent a course of instruction to learn how to reproduce popular tunes on the instruments. She described this as follows:

> It was not uncommon to have three men sitting at three pianos, with canes or crutches propped alongside, with their tongues pushing out one side of their mouth, plinking out "Don't Fence Me In". Within one week of their starting lessons they could play tunes that other patients could not only recognise but could stay and applaud.
> (McKay, 1945, p. 472)

---

[20] Described as one of ten convalescent centres for which Personnel Distribution Command were responsible.
[21] This issue of the journal contained over 30 full papers and a number of introductory and review notes which reported other creative methods in use including psychodrama, group therapy, puppetry therapy, motion picture therapy, and dance methods (see *Sociometry*, 1945, 8, 3-4).

McKay outlined a number of uses of music for these convalescent returned soldiers including music lessons, music instrument making, music listening at meal-times and teaching the use of public address systems and microphones. There was also a Fort Logan Band at the disposal of the convalescents and some 6,000 records which were on loan to phonographs used in the day rooms and some wards (McKay, 1945).

While McKay described these interventions as therapeutic, there is not much of what she has outlined that would fit with methods in what is now the professional practice of music therapy. There is something intriguing however about both the scale and scope of the music activities offered to these recuperating returned soldiers in practical and matter-of-fact ways; both soliciting the needs and preferences of the patients and recording their subsequent involvement.

Similarly Guy Marriner[22] (1945) described how music began to be used over a two year period as part of the "reconditioning"[23] program for returned servicemen with physical or mental injuries after he had been commission by the Surgeon General to undertake a survey of the ways music was used in hospitals. He reported five ways that he had found music to be helpful to the range of patients treated in these hospitals; 1. as physical reconditioning (through playing instruments), 2. in post-operative exercises, 3. for educational benefits, 4. for resocialization, which he defined as "a self-realization of one's relationship to other people" (p. 161), 5. in neuro-psychiatric treatments (Marriner, 1945). While he did not refer to this work as therapy he did make a note of the term as follows:

> Many people assume that the emotional reactions to music are evidences of the therapeutic value of music. Until doctors, psychiatrists, psychologists and musicians have made scientific clinical tests over a period of several years and have proven music to have definite curative powers, the medical profession will not accept the term "Musical Therapy".
> (Marriner, 1945, p. 162)

It is beyond the scope of this chapter to investigate what exactly was happening to the development of "music" and/or "musical" therapy at this time but in the same year as Marriner's report, and Moore's exasperated letter, the *Music Educators Journal* published a recommendation in the column "Do you have the answers?" that "Perhaps the best course would

---

[22] Head of the Hospital Section, Music Branch, Special Services Division
[23] Described as a programme designed to "send the soldier-patient back to duty in the best possible physical condition in the shortest possible time" (Rusk and Taylor, 1945, p. 53).

be for music educators to eliminate from their vocabularies for the time being the word "therapy" in any connection with musical activities in or out of hospitals." (1945, p. 84). Licht (1946) had proposed that until proper training was completed the person providing music in a hospital context should be called a "musical aide". Van de Wall mentioned psychoanalysis and group therapy however in the main wrote about the "hospital musician" as distinct category of arts and health worker.

Just a few short years later, the "institutionalization of affective music" was described as taking place in the field of "music therapy" (Drinker, 1948, p. 290). This account described twenty Gray Ladies[24] selected to visit the wards of several hospitals in the US where "Working separately or together each one modifies beautiful, simple melodies into music of therapeutic value adapted to the emotional state of the different patients" (Drinker, 1948, p. 290). This recognition of the benefits of music for hospital patients was conceptualised by Sophie Drinker as having the potential to create "...a new class of official women musicians" (1948, p. 290); a view in keeping with her feminist ideals. That same year in the UK, the Council for Music in Hospitals was officially formed (see Trythall, 2006).

Antecedents and Consequents: What can we Learn From Those who Went Before?

Some support for the uses of music to assist hospital patients is evident in the published documentation sourced here. The negative commentaries reveal some possible reasons that music is not currently as widely used in medical care contexts by comparison with its uses and applications as a therapeutic and social medium in special education and mental health services. Perhaps too there are some ways of using this source material to begin to understand why music therapy is more widely available in acute hospitals in the USA in comparison to the UK. This historical review also provides a context for possible reasons music therapy education began in the mid 1940s in the USA but only in the late 1950s in the UK; a topic ripe for further discussion.

Suggestions about musical possibilities in health and healing were in some cases responded to derisively in the materials sourced here; first by overstating the claims made by those suggesting the benefits of music, and

---

[24] A type of hospital volunteer "The Gray Lady runs errands, directs visitors, arranges and waters flowers, delivers mail to patients, fills in headings on charts, and gives many other services" (Wetzel, 1945, p. 443).

next by invoking the "values of medicine" as incompatible with the practice of music as an adjunct in healthcare services. The values of medicine by comparison are somewhat more immune to this procedure of scrutiny through retorts that over-state the claims made and then engage in derision of these claims. For example, it would be accurate to describe paracetamol as having effects that are "only temporary" as in the example about the effects of music above, however this is never the description given to this ubiquitous source of pain relief.

Roy Porter gives us a way to consider these issues in his discussion of the absence of patient experiences from the historical record of medicine. He stated that medicine,

> ...has tended to produce histories of itself essentially cast in the mold of its own current image, stories of successive breakthroughs in medical science, heroic pioneers of surgical techniques, of the supersession of ignorant folkloric remedies and barefaced charlatanry through the rise of medicine as a liberal, ethical, corporate profession.
> (Porter, 1985, p. 175)

He further suggested that even historians and sociologists taking a critical view of medical history discourses find themselves nonetheless conforming to the view that "the history of healing is par excellence the history of doctors" (Porter, 1985, p. 175). Perhaps the commentary above reveals that there might have been something quite threatening about the idea of adding music to the repertory of responses to pain, fever and anxiety in medical work[25]. The conceptualisation of music as an intrusion into quiet places of rest and attentive care, possibly gave a perfect target by which to demonstrate medicine's capacity for "cutting through the dross" and suppressing "charlatanry".

The action for the musician framing their work in hospitals as helpful, therapeutic or even "medical" in its orientation is jeopardised by a multi-faceted threat. The desire to make the complexity of music outcomes directed, specific and predictable fails in the testing. The desire to stand aside from medical hegemony and claim a different space for music experience, as part of a health seeking psychological and social fabric woven around the patient's everyday experience of their health with reference to illness and disorder falters; partly because the order and structure of the hospital system precludes interactions that are not

---

[25] At the same time I am aware that since I worked as a music therapist in hospital for many years (and undertook my PhD in a Faculty of Medicine), I may be particularly drawn to the beestings rather than the bouquets of the historical record; highly sensitised to the "not medical enough" claims.

systematised, predictable and quiet, and partly because of the emphasis on interventions which act directly to ameliorate the disorder, rather than addressing secondary symptoms or experiences, such as anxiety, fatigue, and depersonalisation.

Constructing music participation as inherently healthful rather than a "treatment" potentially subverts the values of the dominant, hierarchical system of the hospital, built to support the edifice of medical treatment and medical care of "illness". Suggesting the necessity for music in hospital contexts proposes the replacement of medical authority with the independence and identity appraisal that music with its sounding of instruments and the voicing of individual needs and affect allows. Instead of a recognition in the historical accounts above that music experiences are not offered to supplant medical treatment but rather as healthful actions within an overly illness-focused context, many of the responses over-state the claims for musical offerings and then deride them; or alternatively suggest that music is not particularly useful in medicine because it cannot effect "total cures" (Gardner, 1944, p. 84). This can also be seen in Marriner's (1945) account of music not being therapeutic because its "curative powers" had not been scientifically established, and also in the view that music could only ever be ancillary in the treatment of illness (*The Lancet*, 1891).

At the same time it must be acknowledged that these accounts occurred within a different era than the other chapters appearing in this book. The reports sourced and cited here from the end of the second World War are from the time when up to 8,000 factories in England had "industrial music" programs broadcast from the BBC over the newly installed public address (PA) systems[26] (Beckett and Fairley, 1944)[27]. One report found 95 articles, books and pamphlets on the topic of industrial music, 73 of which had been published since 1940 showing that the sudden interest in music to help workers via music was part of the war effort (Beckett and Fairley, 1944).

Both Licht (1946) and Ilsen (1925) referred to patients' sensitivity to noise. While the US army convalescent hospitals seemed to embrace any opportunity to give men access to music of their interests (see McKay, 1945; Marriner, 1945) the widespread use of music in work settings was possibly adopted inappropriately by hospitals leading ultimately in some cases to a total rejection of the value of music for patients. Van de Wall for

---

[26] These were installed as a warning system for air raids however were soon put to other uses such as recreational music listening (Beckett and Fairley, 1944)

[27] Antrim (1944) also described this as "applied music" and cast music therapy as a type

example wrote about the urgent need for regulation of radio, phonograph and other publicly broadcast music in hospitals as follows:

> There is no reason why all patients should be exposed to the raucous noises of radios and phonographs merely because it suits the whim of someone. Neither is there a valid excuse for the continuous flooding of halls and corridors with the metallic screeches of public address systems used for broadcasting phonograph recordings.
> (Van de Wall, 1946, p. 61)

At the earlier time of Harford's attempts to make music part of hospital care, London had spent the nineteenth century becoming the largest metropolis in Europe housing a population of 4.5 million people (Horall, 2001) with street music[28] on every corner. The music hall was seen by many in the middle class as the ruin of its lower class patrons and poor children (Horall, 2001). While it is pure speculation to suggest that there is a link, something in the quickly negative view of the musical and medical establishments to the proposals for music live or via telephone into wards suggests that perhaps a larger issue of music everywhere for everyone was not a shared utopian vision.

On a further point of difference between current times and the readings reviewed here, it is notable that Altshuler (1948) credits a solo violinist playing live music with the calming of agitated patients during their hydrotherapy treatments. Up until the introduction of anti-psychotics in the 1950s hydrotherapy was a commonly used, at the time scientifically proven, therapy in which patients with severe mental illness were treated with continuous baths or with wet packs (Braslow, 1999). While some of the techniques within these methods involved restraint so that the patient could receive the treatment, it was not considered a type of physical restraint; an unpopular intervention in the first half of the 20th century (Braslow, 1999). Altshuler (1948) noted that in spite of the best precautions, patients often developed the idea that "hydrotherapy is used as a punitive measure and not as a definite treatment" (p. 275). His rationale was that if the "turbulent" patient could be calmed with music, they would be able to benefit from the proven effects of hydrotherapy.

The ways in which music might act upon illness and the means by which it would be allowed to become part of ward life bear some reflection. Marriner's hierarchy of those who should undertake the

---

[28] In the 1891 census of the 10,000 Italians in London, 1,440 listed their occupation as musician, including organ grinders (Hooker, 1894). One estimate put the number of Italian born organ grinders working in London city in 1891 at 920 (September, 1893).

scientific testing of the idea of music as therapy, "doctors, psychiatrists, psychologists and musicians" (1945, p. 162) is perhaps not so different than the steps of approval the music therapy profession still seeks today. Marriner's certainty that "therapy" was not the word he was looking for to describe his use of music in the rehabilitation of war veterans is possibly an antecedent for the contemporary hospital arts community music movements. One can't help think of Marriner as a loss to the early developments of music therapy with his ability to conceptualise a broad role for music across the different areas of need for the returned serviceman. How might the profession have been different if it had not called itself "music therapy" before meeting his proposed criteria?

Conclusion

While Tyler (2002) has suggested that the warning to music therapists not to try to find a continuous historical link between the descriptions of music and healing in the past and current practices (Horden, 2000) is usefully heeded, nonetheless within the historical commentary reported here there is potential for further exploration. It would be interesting to further research the responses to some of these criticisms and to reflect on the polarisation of the not medical enough and/or not musical enough challenge to music in healthcare practices.

Aspects of this historical survey have revealed issues aligned with the current pressures of promoting the work of music therapists and other music and arts workers in medical and healthcare contexts discussed elsewhere in this book, such as looking for approval from the medical establishment, and being recognised as "accomplished artists". The requirement to generate observable clinical change through patients' responses to music is still present, as well as the tension of the implicit expectation that music will keep patients in "the right frame of mind" (Gilliland, 1945, p.24). This can at times be at odds with the patients' to have opportunities for self-expression. This survey also contributes to a debate about the ways in which the actions of music and the musician threaten a corruption to the "values of medicine". Further consideration of the value of the arts in offering healthful experience in medical settings is warranted.

With thanks for Barbara Wheeler and Michele Forinash for their comments and
feedback on early drafts of this chapter.

References

(1891, January). Noises, necessary and unnecessary. *The Musical Times
and Singing Class Circular, 32,* 14-16

(1891, October). Medicinal music. *The Musical Times and Singing Class
Circular, 32,* 587-588.

(1891, November). Occasional notes. *The Musical Times and Singing
Class Circular, 32,* 654-656

(1892, December). Music as a remedy. *The Lancet,* 140, 1282 587-588

(1893, September). London street music and the county council. *The
Musical Times and Singing Class Circular,* 34, 529-530.

(1945, May). Functional aspects of music. *Music Educators Journal,* 31,
48

(1945, Sept-Oct). Do you have the answers? *Music Educators Journal,* 32,
83-84

Altshuler, I.M. (1945). The organism as a whole and music therapy.
Sociometry, 8(3-4), 227-232

—. (1948). A psychiatrists' experiences with music as a therapeutic agent.
In D. Schullian and M. Schoen (Eds.) *Music and medicine.* New York:
Henry Schuman.

American Music Therapy Association, retrieved November 11th, 2006
from http://www.musictherapy.org/faqs.html

Ansdell, G. (2004). Review P. Horden (Ed.) Music as medicine: The
history of music therapy since antiquity. *Psychology of Music, 32,* 440-
445.

Antrim, D. (1944). Music therapy. *Musical Quarterly,* 30, 409-420

Beckett, W., and Fairley, L. (1944). Music in industry: A bibliography.
Notes, 2nd ser. 1, 14-20

Braslow, J. (1999). History and evidence-based medicine: Lessons from
the history of somatic treatments from the 1900s to the 1950s. *Mental
Health Services Research,* 1, 231-240

Brooke, S. (2006). *Creative arts therapies manual.* New York: Charles C.
Thomas

Bunt, L. (1994). *Music therapy: An art beyond words.* London: Routledge

Campbell, G. (2000). "A higher mission than to merely please the ear":
Music and social reform in America, 1900-1925. *The Musical
Quarterly,* 84, 259-86.

Clair, A., and Heller, G. (1989). Willem van de Wall: Organizer and innovator in music education and music therapy. *Journal of Research in Music Education*, 37, 165-178.

Corder, F. (1885). The music of the people. *The Musical Times and Singing Class Circular*, 26, 456-459.

Davis, W.B. (1987). Music therapy in 19th century America. *Journal of Music Therapy*, 24, 76-87.

—. (1988). Music therapy in Victorian England. *Journal of British Music Therapy*, 2, 10-17.

Davison, J. (1899). Music in medicine. *The Lancet*, 154, 1159-1162.

Drinker, S. (1948). *Music and women: The story of women in their relation to music*. Washington: Zinger.

Edwards, J. (2005). The role of the music therapist in working with hospitalized children: A reflection on the development of a music therapy program in a children's hospital. *Music Therapy Perspectives*, 23, 36-44.

—. (1999a). Music therapy with children hospitalised for severe injury or illness. *British Journal of Music Therapy*, 13, 21-27

—. (1999b). Music therapy in medical settings. *Annual Journal of the New Zealand Society for Music Therapy*, 6, 7-30.

Gardner, B. (1944). Therapeutic qualities of music, *Music & Letters*, 25, 181-186

Gilliland, E. (1944). The healing power of music, a challenge to educators. *Music Educators Journal*, 31, 18-21.

—. (1945). Music for the war wounded. *Music Educators Journal*, 31, 24-25, 51.

Gouk, P. (2000)(Ed.) *Musical healing in cultural contexts*. London: Ashgate.

—. (2000). Sister disciplines?: "Music and medicine" in historical perspective. In P. Gouk (Ed.) *Musical healing in cultural contexts* (pp. 171-196). London: Ashgate.

Harford, F. (1891). Music in illness. *The Lancet*, 139, 43

—. (1891). The Guild of St Cecilia. *British Medical Journal*, (n.v) p. 714

—. (1891). Is exhilarating or soft music best for invalids? *British Medical Journal*, (n.v) p. 770

Hooker, R. (1894). The census of 1891. *The Economic Journal*, 4, 175-181.

Horall, A. (2001). *Popular culture in London c. 1890-1918: The transformation of entertainment*. Manchester: MUP.

Horden, P. (2000). *Music as medicine: The history of music therapy since antiquity*. London: Ashgate

Ilsen, I. (1925). Music's new vocation. *The American Journal of Nursing,* 25, 981-985

The Lancet http://www.thelancet.com/about retrieved 1 November, 2006.

Lattman, I. (1946). Review: Music in medicine by Sidney Licht. *Notes,* 3, 352-353.

Mackinnon, A.D. (2006). Music, madness and the body: Symptom and cure. *History of Psychiatry,* 17, 9-21.

—. (2003). 'Jolly and fond of singing': The gendered nature of musical entertainment in Queensland mental institutions c1870-c1937. In C. Coleborne and D. MacKinnon (Eds.) *Madness' in Australia: Histories, heritage, and the asylum* (pp. 157-168). Queensland: University of Queensland.

McKay, L. (1945). Music as a group therapeutic agent in the treatment of convalescents. *Sociometry,* 8, 233-237

Marriner, G. (1945). Music in reconditioning in army service hospitals. *Notes,* 2, 161-163.

Moore, J. (1945). A letter. *Music Educators Journal,* 31, 81.

Porter, R. (1985). The patient's view: Doing medical history from below. *Theory and Society,* 14, 175-198.

Pratt, C. (1948). Review of *Music and medicine* Schullian and Schoen (Eds.)(1948). *Notes,* 2nd ser. 5, 237-8.

—. (1954). Review of *Music therapy* Podolsky (Ed.)(1954). *Notes,* 12, 226-227.

—. (1931). *The meaning of music: A study in psychological aesthetics.* New York: McGraw-Hill Book Company.

Rogers, J. (1918). Music as medicine. *The Musical Quarterly,* 4, 365-375.

Rusk, H., and Taylor, E. (1945). Army air forces convalescent training program. *Annals of the American Academy of Political and Social Science,* 239, 53-59.

Ruud, E. (2001). Music therapy - history and cultural contexts: Two major new texts on music therapy. *Voices: A World Forum for Music Therapy.* Retrieved December 1, 2006, from http://www.voices.no/mainissues/Voices1(3)Ruud.html

Taylor, I., and Paperte, F. (1958). Current theory and research in the effects of music on human behavior. *The Journal of Aesthetics and Art Criticism,* 17, 251-258.

Trythall. S. (2006). Live music in hospitals: A new 'alternative' therapy. *The Journal of the Royal Society for the Promotion of Health,* 126, 113-114.

Tyler, H. Patey (2002). Frederick Kill Harford – Dilettante dabbler or man of our time? *Nordic Journal of Music Therapy,* 11, 39-42.

Van de Wall, W. (1946). *Music in hospitals*. Philadephia: Russell Sage Foundation

Vescelius, E. (1918). Music and health. *The Musical Quarterly,* 4, 376-401

Wetzel, S. (1945). Wartime nursing procedures. *The American Journal of Nursing,* 45, 443-444.

CONTRIBUTORS

Betty Bailey, PhD, MA attained her graduate degrees in Psychology of Music at the University of Sheffield, UK. She has published in a number of international peer reviewed journals including *Musicae Scientiae, The Nordic Journal of Music Therapy* and *Psychology of Music*. Presently, she is the Executive Director of the PEI Health Sector Council, Prince Edward Island, Canada.

Kari Bjerke Batt-Rawden is Associate Professor, Department of Nursing, Akershus University College, and PhD student at the University of Exeter, England. She is a sociologist with a salutogenic approach to health and illness issues.

Constanze Bürger works as a music therapist at a clinic for psychosomatic medicine in Hannover, Germany. She gained music therapy experiences in Bosnia-Herzegovina. She has worked mainly in music therapy and trauma and she is intensely engaged as a musician.

Lars Ole Bonde, PhD is associate professor in Music Therapy at the Department of Communication and Psychology at Aalborg University (DK). He is former head of music therapy studies and former head of the music department. He is a BMGIM therapist (FAMI) and is currently involved in music therapy cancer care research projects. He has published several books and book chapters and many articles on BMGIM, cancer care, music analysis and research methodology.

Jane Davidson, PhD, MA, MMus, BA, Dip Ed, Cert Couns. holds the Callaway Tunly Chair of Music at University of Western Australia and is Professor of Music Performance Studies at University of Sheffield. She has published more than 100 academic articles on social psychology, therapy and education relating to music. She is also an opera singer and stage director

Norma Daykin, PhD is Professor in Health, Community and Policy Studies at the University of the West of England, UK. Her training is in Sociology, Health Policy and Music. She has specialised in evaluation of health care interventions and has published extensively on a number of topics including working conditions and health, health promotion, user involvement in health care services, and music therapy.

Tia DeNora, PhD is Professor of Sociology of Music and Head of the Department of Sociology and Philosophy at Exeter University. Trained in Sociology and Music, she is author of Beethoven and the *Construction of Genius* (California 1995; Fayard1998), *Music in Everyday Life* (Cambridge 2000) and *After Adorno: Rethinking Music Sociology* (Cambridge 2003). Her current research is concerned with interrelations between cultures of music performance and science and with lay-musical-expertise and the care of self.

Jane Edwards, PhD is a qualified music therapist and associate professor at the Irish World Academy of Music and Dance, University of Limerick, Ireland. She directs the MA in Music Therapy and provides consultancy to a range of community and hospital based music therapy programs in Ireland.

Alison Ledger, MPhil is a PhD student at the Irish World Academy of Music and Dance, and manages a music therapy program for parents and young children at the Blue Box Creative Learning Centre, in Limerick. Previously, she worked as a music therapy practitioner and researcher in nursing home and hospital settings.

Joanne V. Loewy, DA is the Director of the Louis Armstrong Center for Music and Medicine at Beth Israel Medical Center, NYC. Dr. Loewy conducts ongoing research in the areas of chanting and sedation, winds and asthma, and pain. She has edited the books; *Music Therapy in the NICU*, and *Music Therapy in Pediatric Pain,* and also edited the book *Music Therapy at the End of Life* with Cheryl Dileo.

Wendy L. Magee, PhD holds a post-doctoral fellowship at the Institute of Neuropalliative Rehabilitation and an Honorary Senior Research Fellowship at Kings College London. She has been a music therapy clinician, manager, and researcher since 1988 in the field of adult neurology publishing in international forums on research and practice.

Susanne Metzner, Prof. Dr. sc.mus., directs the Music Therapy Training Course at the University of Applied Sciences at Magdeburg, Germany. She has published in many journals and books, particularly about the

psychoanalytic frame for music therapy, about improvisation and aesthetics, about her clinical work with psychiatric patients as well as music therapy pain treatment.

Hilary Moss, MBA, SRAT (Mus) is Arts Officer at the Adelaide and Meath Hospital, Dublin. She is a State Registered Music Therapist (UK) and has an MBA in Health Service Management. Her current role involves managing a large acute hospital arts program, as well as carrying out research for the Arts Council.

Clare O'Callaghan, PhD is a Clinical Associate Professor, Department of Medicine, St Vincent's Hospital, and Honorary Fellow, Faculty of Music, University of Melbourne, Australia. A Music Therapist at Peter MacCallum Cancer Centre and Caritas Christi Hospice, St Vincent's Health, Clare has published widely in palliative care, oncology and interpretive research methodology.

Helen Phelan, PhD is Director of the MA Chant and Ritual Song, Irish World Academy of Music and Dance. She is Director of *Sanctuary*, coordinating cultural projects with the refugee and asylum seeking community. Her research publications are primarily in the area of music, ritual and new cultural communities in Ireland.

Maeve Scahill, MA graduated from the MA Music Therapy at the Irish World Academy of Music and Dance in 2004. Maeve has worked as a music therapist for a project involving offering group work programs to mothers and babies/young children in the asylum seeker and refugee community as part of Doras in Limerick city. She is a traditional concertina player.

Susan Trythall is a PhD student at the University of Exeter researching music, well being and health promotion.

INDEX